SURRENDERED

The Rise, Fall and Revelation of

KWAME KILPATRICK

Library of Congress Control Number: 2011932233

ISBN: 978-0-9824730-2-3

Design by Ron Dorfman
Front Cover Design by W.G. Cookman
with Ilustration by Frankie Fultz
Published by Creative Publishing
Signature Book Printing / www.sbpbooks.com

PRINTED IN THE U.S.A.

SURRENDERED

The Rise, Fall and Revelation of

KWAME KILPATRICK

Kwame Kilpatrick

with Khary Kimani Turner

CREATIVE PUBLISHING

Carlita, Jalil, Jonas, and Jelani.

dedication

I DEDICATE this project to the enduring love of my wife, Carlita, and my sons Jelani, Jalil and Jonas.

The greatest moments and times of my life have been spent with all of you. Whether having our hilarious discussions at the dinner table, piling into Mom's and my bedroom for family movie night, turning all the house lights off and playing the scary movie game, or even Carlita and I beating the boys in basketball (and *tackle* football in the yard), my most treasured thoughts are of you four. We are family! But I have taken you all for granted, ignored and even abused the abundant blessings of our family relationship far too many times. I have let you down, and caused all of you a great amount of pain, confusion and despair.

I sincerely ask for your forgiveness.

I know that the process of forgetting seems nearly impossible, because of the sustained, aggressive assaults in our lives. But I would hope that you all will remember and look for the fruit or the results that accompany my true repentance. It takes time to grow, but I believe that all of you can see the positive transformation taking place within me. Our renewed relationship with God and each other has already taken root and sprouted.

Carlita, Jelani, Jalil, and Jonas, thank you so much for being *my crew!* Your support, encouragement and godly love has provided the blessed hope of new beginnings. I love you all so very much.

Daddy's Home!

in gratitude

MY TWO Grandfathers, James B. Kilpatrick and Marvell Cheeks Jr., instilled in me a tremendous respect and appreciation for history. They both firmly believed that going back to the beginning of something is the best way to find original facts; therefore, you find the truth. Thank you, Granddads!

In that regard, I thank my Creator, the One who makes all things possible, the Author of truth. This book is named Surrendered, and so many times while writing it, I experienced inspiration, an idea here or a memory there, that was vital to the work. Each time, it happened not by my power or might, but by His spirit. I surrendered. To God be the Glory.

I am thankful to many for this process. This book, as mentioned earlier, is not casually dedicated to my wife and children, but explicitly. They are truly the wind beneath my wings. Jelani's funny and sarcastic comments, Jalil 'pretty boy swag' moments, Carlita's goober/nerdy expressions, or the awesome spirit-lifting sound of Jonas' voice; it all nourishes my soul. Thank you so much, Kilpatrick crew.

I am eternally grateful to my Mom and Dad. Mom, you are one of the most remarkable public servants of our time. Thank you so much for your guidance, support and love, and for never missing a parent/teacher conference, or allowing me to miss homework assignments. You did it all. Dad, thank you for always being authentically you. You told me, when I was ten years old, that you would always be there for me. Through every football or basketball game, election, child birth, triumph or disaster, you were there. Thank you so much for keeping your word. You are still The Man!

To my sister, Ayanna, I thank you immensely. You took this project under your wing and moved it forward, often doing the heavy lifting alone. You organized meetings, conference calls, follow-up strategy, marketing opportunities, etc. You are the bomb! When we were kids, folks called us "Kwameyanna", as if we were one person. But I want to tell you, that you have grown into a strong and loving individual, sister and Mom. It was your passion, work ethic, tenacity and organizational skills that got this done. Thank you, Bone!

To my sister, Diarra, who I affectionately call the smartest Kilpatrick of all, thank you, as well. Your encouragement, uncanny wit, comedic talent and love has been a buoy for me. An e-mail, phone call or visit from you would force me to reach beyond the thoughts I bought into at times, and inspire within me a greater awareness of the spiritual light at the center of my being.

I also want to honor my other parents, Carlton and Pamela Poles. Thank you so much for your unyielding love, support and encouragement. You have given Carlita and me an amazingly powerful example of what being united in marriage truly means. I love you both.

To all the descendents of Marvell and Bessie Cheeks (MBC), the greatest family on planet Earth, I thank you all so much for always having my back, front and sides. Also to my Kilpatrick and Simmons extended families, I thank you for your support and encouragement.

No matter how many copies this book sells, it has already been a successful endeavor. I asked Khary Turner, nearly three years ago, to help me do this. He is an outstanding writer, poet and storyteller. I soon became very impressed with his keen thinking skills and infectious positive energy. We developed a rhythm and vibe with one another that transcended our basic notion of writing a book, to a higher calling of spreading knowledge, wisdom and understanding. It was my considerable pleasure to work with Khary on this project.

I'm also thankful to Catherine Van Harren, who did an outstanding job editing the project, and went out of her way to consider and understand my story. Thank you, Catherine, for your expertise and insight.

To my 14 line brothers, the ones who "crossed the burning sands" and joined Alpha Phi Alpha Fraternity Inc., on the evening of March 14, 1990, in Tallahassee, Florida. Nubians, I can never say thank you enough. You looked out for my wife, my children and even kept me from falling so many times. I've lost a lot of so-called brothers over the past few years, but you all have consistently held up the light of brotherhood. You further cemented, in my spirit, that your commitment was not for that day, but for all of our lives.

In no way do I intend to devalue or disregard the magnitude of the crisis faced, particularly by communities of color, as a result of ongoing mass incarceration, or give any notion of positive credit to what author Michelle Alexander calls "America's new caste system." However, I must say, that I am so much better because of the prison experience. My fall has enabled my life, and my remaining life's work, to rise. I have met several men, while held behind prison walls, who played a major role in helping to rebuild my character and my life. I am grateful for brothers like; Charles "Fish" Fisher, Nate Cox, Akil Powell, Corey Nelson, Karl "KG" Graves, Terry "T" Tyler, Demetrius "Knowledge" Wilson, Andy "Shoop" George, Mark X, Joseph "Chip" Stines, Marcel "Cell" Asbell, Jajuan "Weezy" Gardener, Jerry Oday, Terrence "TC" Coles, Tony "TP" Powell, Larry Adams, DeAndre "YB" Shaw, Larry "WB" Richards, DeWan "Wan" Smith, Brian Green, Derrick Shirley, and so many more. Thank you, Brothers! You will NEVER be forgotten.

To my Pastors, Bishops J. Drew Sheard and T.D. Jakes. I remain exceedingly grateful to both of you, for answering your call. God, in His infinite wisdom, caused my life to intersect with yours, at precisely the perfect moments. Your encouragement, honesty, and love provided much needed direction and hope for a new day, for me and my family. I also want to thank the great congregations that you both lead, my Greater Emmanuel Church family in Detroit, and also my Potter's House Church family in

Dallas. You have been an amazing gift to my family. Your love never fails!

During my time of incarceration, I've read more books than I've read in my entire life. Many of these authors have become my invisible counselors. Their ideas stoked my intellectual curiosity. Their prose entangled me in webs of suspense, fear, excitement, and joy. Most of all, their personal testimonies enabled me to gain valuable insight, mentorship, guidance and the soul-stirring unction to rebuild Kwame Kilpatrick, mentally, physically and spiritually. Nelson Mandela, Johnnie Cochran, Charles Colson, C.S. Lewis, James Weldon Johnson, Joyce Meyer, The Honorable Elijah Mohammed, Max Lucado, Napoleon Hill, Michelle Alexander, Paulo Coelho, Jemal Gibson, Andy Andrews, Ekhardt Tolle, Carter G. Woodson, Muhammad Bashir, Esq., Jim Collins, John Maxwell, James Patterson, Renita Walker, Sydney Sheldon, Pearl Cleage, Dan Brown, Walter Mosely, and so many more. Thank you all for sharing your gift with me.

Finally, I want to thank the people of Dallas, Texas, and of Detroit, Michigan. Over the past couple years more than 250,000 people have moved from places all over the United States and beyond, and now call the Dallas/Fort Worth Metroplex home. On behalf of my family, who were a part of that number, we thank you for welcoming us to your community with open arms. Quite simply, you all loved us in a way that we didn't know was possible for a community the size of the DFW area. You turned the lights on for us, and I thank you.

To the people of Detroit, you played a major role in my life. From my teachers, coaches and childhood mentors, to my classmates, neighbors and friends. I can never thank you enough for all that you have done for me. The moments are few and far between that Detroit's unique, authentic and revolutionary spirit was not present in my ideas, thoughts, emotions and actions. That cutting edge, innovative, sometimes radical flavor is the real Detroit.

Detroit moved the world by putting it on wheels, birthed the Motown sound, even gave a platform to a young southern preacher named Martin Luther King, Jr., who delivered his "I

Have a Dream" speech months before he captured time on the steps of the Lincoln Memorial. That Detroit birthed men and women who dare to be different, to be bold, to be free. And its those Detroiters, and their unmistakable Motown swagger, who raised me. To them, and their children, I owe a tremendous amount of gratitude. I hope and pray that they are empowered by this book. By learning the truth, you are free to speak with courage, conviction, passion and, most of all, love. As it says in the Gospel of John, "Then you will know the truth, and the truth will set you free." Go and get your freedom! Its always been about Detroit Love!

prologue

We're not always a forgiving nation.
We do intolerance and rigidity when
it fits our purpose.

~TIM KEOWN, *ESPN columnist*

KWAME MALIK KILPATRICK, the former mayor of the City of Detroit who is currently serving a one-and-a-half to five-year prison sentence for violating terms of his probation, is a brilliant man. That's no understatement. He is one of the most intelligent individuals I have ever known.

I should qualify that statement. U.S. President Bill Clinton was known for remembering the names of people he'd shake hands with in even the most obscure places, such was his gift of recall. Kwame also has that ability. His retention skills sometimes seem photographic. He's a natural conversationalist and possesses that rare, innate talent that makes just about everyone feel at ease in nearly any social setting.

He's also clear on his abilities, which makes him very confident. His decisions tend to come quickly and resolutely. If he says, "Let me think about that," he doesn't waste a lot of time. He returns with a decision, and an argument to support it. But even in disagreement, he remains affable and open to other perspectives. He is one of those individuals who balances a firm strength of conviction with a fair-minded quality of temperance. Needless to say, it's a disarming quality for adversaries, but fortunately, Kwame rarely meets an enemy. He is a humanist who sees the natural good in people. That might have hurt him early in his career, but more on that later.

I've communicated with Kwame several times a week for the past two and a half years, and we've disagreed on things, but we have never argued or debated. We shared points and counterpoints, and arrived at amicable decisions befitting successful writing partners.

All of the aforementioned observations amount to good leadership skills. But Kwame's most impressive quality, his sense of compassion for people in need, probably clashed with his most glaring fault, professional immaturity, and created a perfect storm of controversy and conspiracy that ruined his career. He went from a rising star to one of the most scandalized political leaders in American history. This book explores it all.

Among the many details in that "perfect storm," Mayor Kilpatrick had a vision for Detroit, and the chops to make it reality. Perhaps his willingness to enforce checks and balances threatened the wrong peoples' bottom lines. Striking an imposing figure at 6'4", and being black and assertive in a city with a long history of racial discord didn't help, either.

The other element of that storm was the personal strain the Kilpatrick household endured, due to the pressures of his job. This is where Kwame's maturity failed him. His actions and reactions regarding his personal life and his underestimation of the dangerous political atmosphere around him led to his downfall.

If a perfect storm is a convergence of critical events that aggravates a situation, then Kwame Kilpatrick's story qualifies as a hurricane. My fear, even as we go to press, is that the storm continues to rage, and that this book could either balance public perspective or further upset it, leading to his federal trial. I'm afraid that some of Kwame's enemies wouldn't mind seeing him dead, not just imprisoned. In a society that is fiercely individualistic and too singular of thought to concern itself with, be outraged over, or suspicious of the kind of conspiracies that claimed the lives of icons during the Civil Rights era, it's not far-fetched to think it could happen to him.

Kwame wrote me from prison about two weeks before I composed this prologue and asked me to be brutally honest in my process—specifically, about my opinion of him. I initially thought it odd to ask a supporter to lend a public critique, but he truly wanted me to disclose my true feelings about him and his situation, even after working so closely together for such an extended time. I've been a proverbial fly on the wall of his life for more than two years. But after some thought, I understood and respected his rationale.

I've felt the same fear as Kwame's one-time supporters, who have distanced themselves from him, either out of fear of career suicide or frustration. On the latter point, Kwame is loyal, possibly to a fault, and some believe that individuals in his administration created enemies for him, even as he made allies. He may offer a different opinion on that assertion, but the conversation certainly made rounds in Detroit political circles. How much loyalty it cost him is anyone's guess, but I can understand why he would want to know what his remaining allies think of his situation. It's akin to the question Jesus asked the Disciples—"Who do you say I am?"—just days before His crucifixion. The Disciples tried to dodge the question at first, describing what *others* said about him, but when Jesus pressed, only one, Peter, spoke up. The others masked their doubt with silence.

At times, I have doubted Kwame during this process. It's hard not to when newspapers run salacious headlines almost weekly. The political atmosphere in Detroit became overwhelmingly negative, and the city became emotionally depressed. To Kwame's credit, however, he never ducked. I took my doubts to him in the form of questions, and he responded, apolitically. I also paid close attention to the feelings of people in the streets. Neighborhoods are great sources of intuition. So-called everyday folk often sense what they don't see. And those on the streets overwhelmingly sensed that something was not right in the media's portrayal of Kilpatrick.

I soon became convinced that the media had as much of an agenda in his saga as anyone.

I also became convinced, after much interaction, that if Kwame were mayor of Detroit today, he'd not only be in his third term, but would be considered by many as one of Detroit's most progressive mayors. Beyond his faults, he truly believed he owed the people of Detroit his service. His eye on community development and his empowerment of his staff to fulfill that vision with a certain degree of autonomy would have, ten years on, triggered an educational resurgence that by now would have resulted in a sharper sense of professionalism among Detroiters, most of whom are African-American. That would have triggered pride, which would have encouraged neighborhood care, cleanliness, concern, and heightened safety. In short, people would be happier and hopeful. I'm not saying things would be perfect, but I believe they would be better.

Detroit would still be in the national conversation as a city that matters, instead of being described as a town whose time has come. I think Kwame, as he'll describe by finally telling his story in this book, had the ability to lead such a charge.

I have other opinions on the former mayor. To me, his youth was both a blessing and a curse. To voters, it's sexy to be young, smart and talented. It's also dangerous if you are not attuned to the dangers of image, and the depth of the ever-present political cesspool. Kwame knew these dangers existed, but I truly believe he thought he could build bridges over them by embracing them, when he should have protected himself more carefully. His vision clashed with the city's wealthy and elite, and damn how much they liked him, he wasn't good for their bottom line. Those kinds of people are usually eliminated, by removal from position, or even death.

My problem with Kwame—my friend, brother and cousin (full disclosure: we are related by marriage, but I am also very close to some of the people who, at times, disagreed with him – Detroit is "towny" that way)—is his rose-colored perspective that keeps him from protecting himself. He gives people too much credit. Other than that, the only thing I believe he actually *did* wrong, without outside influence, was cheat on his wife, and then lie about it under oath. That's a misdemeanor and, in a just world, he would have gotten no more than 90 days in jail for being a first-time, non-violent offender, and his future would be left to the druthers of the voters in the next election. But in this scenario, he wouldn't have resigned, and he wouldn't be in prison today.

I wanted to help Kwame write this book because innocence is not nearly as much of a question in his case as is fairness. He is not a villain, as the local media and the Wayne County prosecutor have characterized him. And the *only* way anyone will come to understand that is by reading his story—uninterrupted and unreported.

I also wanted to help him because Kwame Kilpatrick is too valuable not to become a contributor to someone's community, if not Detroit's. Talent like his is uncommon, and he was once blessed and unfortunate to be given control of a major city before he had firm control of his own life. A mature Kwame Kilpatrick, however, would be like a mature Malcolm, a mature Tupac Shakur. Today, he is ferociously visionary, and consistently representative of the people. For once, we need to preserve those of this ilk, place their imperfections in perspective, and protect them from those for whom money and power are all that matter.

The last reason I wanted to help him is that, even as this book goes to press, the Detroit media has firmly established itself as the sole biographer of Kwame's professional history. That's just flat-out dangerous. I am a journalist, as well, but I'll be the first to say that newspapers and Op/Ed columns should *never* be treated, nor act, as historians.

Famed journalist A.J. Liebling describes newspapers as well as anyone. The role of newspapers, he said, is to inform the people, but their *functions* are to make money. History will reflect that the Detroit newspapers were fighting for survival, as were near-failed entities like *The Boston Globe* and *The New York Times*, when the Kilpatrick story landed on the desk of a reporter via illegally obtained text messages from Kilpatrick's two-way pager. The Internet gave newspapers a tough run for their money, and sales plummeted. But running the Kilpatrick story into the ground (they're still printing stories) and making the headlines as bold and exciting as possible was great for business. Even Ron Dzwonkowski, the *Detroit Free Press'* executive editor, estimated during a group interview I conducted with him in March 2008 that newsstand sales leapt from seven to twelve percent after January 24, 2008, every day that Kwame's name or likeness appeared on the front page.

How ironic is it that, even in his darkest hour, the mayor fulfilled his own vision, generating enough revenue to save the city's most storied news rag?

Television and radio are no less neutral, because many of their storylines took their cues from the newspapers.

This is why history should not be the responsibility of reporters. We don't fight the battles. Instead, we count the bodies. Proper history should involve the subject's perspective, and Kwame's was omitted. The truth is, his administration was leading Detroit through revolutionary changes when his scandal surfaced. That progress has not been reported or mentioned with any significance since 2007, and the City of Detroit is still benefiting from the strides he made.

Kwame is a subject of what psychologist Irving Janice called "groupthink," which occurs when a group or population makes a faulty collective decision about a topic through deteriorated mental efficiency and judgment, due to group pressure. One-sided press coverage in a city that takes its news as gospel can do that. It's the kind of phenomena that once caused people to believe that the world was flat.

An old saying suggests that history is written by the winners. Thanks to the increased independence that technology has created, that is now a false statement. History, today, is written by many voices.

That is why I am helping Kwame Kilpatrick tell his story. He did enough for the City of Detroit that he deserves to tell you about it. Had he been properly punished for the crime he committed, he'd have been charged with the aforementioned misdemeanor, possibly given a short jail sentence (ninety days or fewer), and then left to the mercy of the voters. The man should not be in prison.

Likewise, if he does tell his story, it must be transparent. I believe Kwame has no room for anything but blunt honesty. Not to say who is right and who is wrong, but simply to tell you *what he saw.*

Kwame and I had a conversation just weeks before his first jail sentence (yes, there were two) in October 2008 regarding how he felt about working on this book.

"I don't know," Kwame said, "but I'm ready to talk. I'm ready to talk about everything. Carlita (his wife). Christine (his friend and the woman with whom he had a publicized affair). Detroit. The job. Everything, brother. People think they know me, and they don't. They think they know what happened with the job and the City, but they have no idea."

I then asked him how he felt about the prospect, knowing that a 300-page spin job would be heavily discredited.

"Brother, I'm terrified," he said. "Carlita and I are still healing, and I don't know how this process will affect us. But I'm no good to anybody if I don't heal. And this is critical to that process. So let's do it."

This process, two years later, has helped the Kilpatrick family heal and move forward. I'm personally thankful to former First Lady Carlita Kilpatrick, an excellent writer herself, for her contributions. I found it heroic, and courageous. I thank the Cheeks-Kilpatrick family for trusting me with the responsibility of accurately representing this story. My remaining hopes are for Kwame's freedom, Detroit's resurgence, and the world's understanding of an American epic.

~KHARY KIMANI TURNER

Out of the night that covers me,
black as a pit from pole to pole,
I thank [God]
for my unconquerable soul.

In the fell clutch of circumstance
I have not whinced nor cried aloud.
Under the bludgeonings of chance,
my head is bloody, but unbowed.

Beyond this place of wrath and tears,
looms but the horror of the shade.
And yet the menace of the years
finds, and shall find me unafraid.

It matters not how strait the gate,
how charged with punishments the scroll.
I am the master of my fate:
I am the captain of my soul.

~"INVICTUS," WILLIAM ERNEST HENLEY

chapter 1
Happy Birthday, Inmate #702408

I T WAS the most unforgettable day of my entire life. The day the twins were born, my wedding day, and the night of my re-election as mayor of the City of Detroit in November 2005 were all wonderfully memorable occasions, and I'll never forget them. But this day was extraordinary because it plunged my spirit to a new low, while simultaneously forcing me to lean on every ounce of faith I had.

Why the depression? Simple. I was on my way to a Michigan maximum-security prison, just two years after resigning my post as mayor. It was also my birthday, June 8, 2010, and I was forty years old.

The guard woke me up, startling me a little. Breakfast at the Michigan Department of Corrections Reception and Guidance Center, in Jackson, always came with a 6 a.m. wake-up call. Corrections officer Sam Allen, a cordial enough guy, entered the room with my usual helping of prison oatmeal, two slices of toast and a plastic carton of orange juice.

"Good morning, Officer Allen," I said.

"Good morning, Mr. Kilpatrick," he responded. "Here is your fine cuisine for the morning."

"Thank you, Officer. Always a treat."

He left the room and I began to eat. I was quarantined in a unit that was painted stark white. It was a self-contained space with a shower, bed, sink, toilet and a small storage locker. I thought it was horrible, but I'd soon think of my room at Jackson with fond memories.

My routine went like this: I was locked up for twenty-three hours each day, with a one-hour "recreation period" in a small 20-by-20-foot fenced yard with razor-sharp barbed wire circling around it. I was thankful to another prison official, Officer Mark Bradshaw, for making sure that I got at least *some* fresh air during my time there.

After breakfast, I got up to wash my face. I then knelt to start my morning prayer when I was interrupted, even more abruptly than the wake-up call. Officer Allen, who seemed to work day and night and must have racked up a decent amount of overtime, turned his key, which had a familiar sound, in the door. I thought he may have forgotten to tell or give me something, maybe a magazine or a book. Maybe the keys to let myself out? I wished. Instead, he entered with another C.O. I didn't know this guy. He was cagey, and he looked at me authoritatively.

"Pack all your personal items in this bag. You're leaving now." He heaved a large duffel bag my way. It was a large green bag with "MDOC" printed on it, along with my inmate number, 702408.

"When you say 'leaving now,'" I asked, "what do you mean?

"Immediately!" he snapped.

I then asked, cautiously, sitting on the bed, "Where am I going?" Both men, in unison, replied that they could not tell me where I was going, and that officers would arrive in fifteen minutes to pick me up. Sam, however, looked like he wanted to tell me what I was in for. I could tell he felt sympathetic.

I stood and threw all of my personal things in the bag—deodorant, comb, toothbrush, T-shirt, pen, paper, many letters of encouragement I had received (mostly strangers) and a couple of pictures of Carlita and the boys. I moved quickly, and the officers stood and watched me the entire time.

"Is that all?" they asked. It was. I had only been there fourteen days. My true "personal items" were in Texas, the place I'd come to regard as home.

They closed the bag and told me to put on my State prisoner outfit. It was blue, with orange patches on the shoulders and legs. I started to get dressed as they left, and a strange silence settled in the room. A boding despair began to settle over me. I can't say the feeling was alien. I'd spent the past two years pleading with God, wrestling with my own sense of self, my own dignity, to make sense of my life. How could I have gone from making history as the youngest elected mayor in a city's history, to a publicly lambasted pariah whom many misunderstood, and seemingly wanted dead? I didn't deserve this, and I began to wonder if I'd steeled myself enough to handle it.

The sun hadn't fully risen. It was a cloudy morning, but beautiful. Sunrays poked through the clouds, creating a picturesque scene outside my small window. I sat there and tried to think about where I could be going. I started to ask myself a ton of questions. Was I headed out of state? How far would I be from Detroit? Would they force me to remain in protective custody? Was I going to a boot camp?

My thoughts disturbed my peace, and the room became noisy with them. I began to feel crowded, and a little anxious. So I began to pray. I thanked God for that moment in my life. I thanked Him for allowing me to see another birthday. And I asked Him to give me the grace to accept and overcome whatever was about to happen. I asked for a calm and relaxed spirit.

A moment later, the noise in my head settled, and I opened my eyes and looked toward the window. I tend to pray decisively, meaning I make my petition to God, and then I go about doing my part. The work. In that moment, I decided that the noise in my mind would decrease, just for that moment. No matter what, I would have to trust and believe Him, and know that He is able. That was the work—acceptance. Calm returned, and none too soon.

Sitting on the edge of my bed, I waited. Soon, the officer's key clanked against the door. This time, two much larger Corrections officers entered the room. Sam was with them. They wasted no time. One of them told me to take off my clothes for a strip search. I knew that this was not the time for questions. Immediately, I disrobed, and they made me go through the whole battery of movements. If you've ever seen the movie American Me, it's all real. And I had to endure it.

Open your mouth. Lift your tongue. Lift your nutsack. Turn around. Bend over and spread your ass cheeks. Cough. Turn back around and lift your arms. I stayed calm as they searched me, and then searched my clothes. I told one guard, in jest, that I left my cell phone and contraband in the car. He didn't find that funny and continued his work.

I put my clothes back on, and the other officer pulled what looked like dozens of chains, padlocks and handcuffs from his waistband.

"What's all this?" I asked. He told me that I was being transferred under the classification of a Level 4 Prisoner. Maximum security.

"Officer," I said, as calmly as possible. "I'm a Level 1 inmate. I know that, as a Level 1, I'm deemed non-threatening. Most Level 1 prisoners are transferred in handcuffs. Some are allowed to walk with their hands free."

My official classification is the lowest security level in the Michigan Department of Corrections. Their treatment was appropriate for a violent offender. A very thorough process establishes each inmate's classification level: background, nature of offense, mental health, and so forth. It involves several days of physical, psychological and background evaluation. You might imagine, then, that I had a slight problem seeing the C.O. come at me with enough chains to subdue King Kong.

"I know," he said, "but this is how it's going to be." That meant I was being outfitted with the Department's full Level 4 regalia. Ankle cuffs. Belly chains. Handcuffs with waist chains. Padlocks. I couldn't move my arms more than four inches from my body. I had to take short, wide steps to keep from falling as I was promptly marched out of the facility.

"Sam," I said as they chained me, *"where am I going?"* Sam looked down and breathed deeply.

"You're going to a prison up north," he said. The two big

guards shot him a look, and he didn't say anything else.

"Well, will I be able to call and let my family know where I am?" I asked.

I got no answer on that one. It would be a few days before I was able to contact anyone.

We began walking past all the other inmates and employees. I could only shuffle my feet, moving in a hopping walk. My hands were bound to my waist. For every journalist who editorialized me during my time of scandal, it was a missed photo op for the ages. Kwame Kilpatrick, former Mayor of Detroit, in body chains. I needed every bit of peace God gave me, because my mind was tripping.

An empty prison van sat waiting in a garage as we exited the facility. I was put into the van and driven about ninety minutes to a stop in St. Louis, Michigan. I wondered if this was my destination, but the C.O. told me it wasn't. I was headed to "The Oaks" in Manistee, Michigan, on the State's northwest coast. This was just a stop to transfer me to another bus. As he spoke, I saw something that will haunt me for the rest of my life.

There was a very large horseshoe-shaped drive in front of the prison. As we drove through the barbed wire gates, I saw what looked like twenty other buses pulling into the facility. Some resembled Greyhound buses. Some were smaller, and some were vans, like the one I was in.

The haunting sight was the cargo—scores of inmates, dressed in their "State blues," pouring from each vehicle like black chattel. I had a perfect vantage point. Dozens—I do mean dozens—of young men, mostly African-American, all in belly chains, ankle cuffs, hand restraints and padlocks like mine, stepped from these buses and formed lines. Corrections officers, most of whom were white, ordered them, ordered them again, and they shuffled to other buses.

I thought about Jamestown, Virginia. It looked like a slave trading post, the marketplace where slaves were bought and sold. Strong, able-bodied black men were moved from plantation to plantation, from one person's control to another. These young men's transgressions made them State property. And these were just the ones being transferred. How many more were holed up in the state's penal system? It was shocking, and daunting.

Is this where all the black men are? How many of these men have children? What are they in for?

This public trading went on for more than an hour. After all the lines had been formed, it was time to reload. The entire time, I managed to completely distance myself from the scenario, as if I were watching a documentary. I forgot that I was actually a part of it. In fact, my opening scene was about to commence. The hour had passed, and I was told to get off and get ready to be loaded on the bus headed to "The Oaks."

I stepped out of the van and was spotted immediately by brothers who began shouting.

"What's up, Kwame!"

"Keep your head up, Kwame!"

"Stay strong, Kwame!"

Guys were throwing up their fists (as much as their restraints allowed) and holding up peace signs. I gave them many head nods and fist salutes on the way to my bus. As soon as I stepped into the bus, the brothers seated let out a collective, "Ooooh…!" Every seat was filled, except one that they held for me, near the back. I said, "What's up" and threw more head nods all the way back to my seat. I was in the midst of brotherhood, and I had always been comfortable in that spirit.

The bus was divided into three sections, separated by locked gates. I could only speak to the folks in the rows in my section. I was prepared for a quiet ride, but who was I fooling? That ain't me, and it damn sure wasn't the brothers on board.

Just after pulling off, one of the guys remarked that we had all missed lunch, and that he knew it should have been provided. The C.O. yelled back, after several attempts to reason with him, that we were dropping one inmate off at a prison around the corner, and we'd eat right after that. It was during this exchange that I learned we'd make several stops before arriving at Oaks Correctional Facility.

Lunch was served after the first stop. They gave us peanut butter and jelly sandwiches, an orange and some red juice. We then made the two-hour trek to our second stop, near Baldwin, Michigan. I had some incredible conversations about everything, from State, federal and local politics, to sports and the inmates' favorite subject, the MDOC and the criminal justice system. The brothers gave me invaluable advice about the prison community and how to function there. They were very helpful and knowledgeable.

Not one person in my section had less than eight years' experience in the penitentiary. Three of them had more than twenty-five years. One brother was twenty-seven years old, and had been in for ten years. All of these guys were smart, conversational, engaging and knowledgeable about current events. They kept telling me that the fourteen months I had to serve "ain't shit." It seemed like forever to me.

"Knock that shit out, Kwame!" one shouted. They were experts. Most were from Detroit or surrounding areas, and they were very familiar with my case. They gave me the best orientation on prison and prison life that I could have ever imagined. It was thorough and detailed, and I received it well. After we dropped the last set of guys off and headed for The Oaks, the guys began telling me more about that particular institution. Oaks is one of two prisons in the state with segregated units exclusively for high-profile inmates. White Boy Rick, an infamous Detroit drug dealer sentenced to life in the 1980s, was housed in the same unit I'd be in. He and I would have opportunities to occasionally greet each other.

I learned about the staff, guards, food, rules and everything else pertaining to Oaks. I also got a comparative analysis of Oaks to several other places throughout the state, with specific instructions on how I could transfer if I didn't like it. The main difference between Oaks and Bellamy Creek, the other prison with a segregation unit, was that Oaks' staff was all white, and Ionia, a penitentiary closer to my hometown Detroit, employed far more African-American guards. I wondered if I had been sent to Oaks to make sure I had no sympathizers among the black guards.

More than ten hours after my morning wake-up call at the Guidance Center in Jackson, I arrived at Oaks Correctional Facility in Manistee, Michigan. It was around 4:40 p.m., and we were escorted, still in chains, into the prison intake room where each of us were checked in. I was told to go last. After a quick verbal questionnaire by someone called the "healthcare lady," our chains were removed, one at a time. Again, I was last. We were taken into another room and strip-searched again, given our brink numbers, and sent out to the yard to find our new homes.

"Stay up!" everyone told each other as they dispersed. I was held back by one of the officers and told that the Warden wanted to speak to me. Warden Cindi Curtin and Deputy Warden Tim Ball took me into a conference room for a brief conversation. Curtin's been with the Department of Corrections for more than twenty-six years. She was very calm, sincere and knowledgeable, and told me that I was being placed in protective custody because they were "very concerned about my safety."

"Why are you concerned?" I asked.

She explained to me that over the previous twenty-four hours, she had been out and about asking inmates about me, and had heard a mixed bag of opinions. Some guys hated me. Some loved me.

"So, guys actually threatened me?" I asked. She said she received no actual threat by an inmate or staff member, but Warden Curtin asked me to be very careful, and to watch my back. I told her that I was fine. I had been around these guys my entire life, and that I didn't expect to have any problems. I also explained that I wanted to move to a Level 1 facility as soon as possible. Protective Custody means that you're locked up for twenty-three hours a day. At Level 1, you're free to move from 7 a.m. until 11 p.m. daily. The one hour per day that you have out in Protective Custody is with all the other people on your block. It's also the only time that you have to use the phone and call loved ones or exercise. The conditions led me to believe that P.C. was a bad deal for me, but she politely listened and shut me down with a cool, firm "No." The Department was locking me in to "keep me safe."

The Warden gave me an opportunity to use the phone later that night around 8:45 p.m. I called home to talk to Carlita, and Jonas, the youngest of my three sons, answered the phone.

"Hi, Daddy!" he shouted with all the enthusiasm of a brilliant and talented eight-year-old. It was so good to hear his sweet and innocent voice. I missed him so much! I asked how he was doing and where his mother was. I had to hurry, because I was only allowed ten minutes to talk. He told me that she had just taken his brothers, Jelani and Jalil, to basketball practice. Because I only had a few minutes, I told Jonas that I was going to try Mama on her cell phone and would call him tomorrow.

"Wait, Daddy," he said. "Happy Birthday! I love you very much." He then said, "Hey, Daddy, if you could have anything in the world for your birthday, what would it be?" I told him, "I wish that I could hug you and your brothers so badly." That was it. That's all I wanted. He told me that he really missed me, and I told him I also missed him, and that I loved him very much. I hung up and called Carlita on her cell phone. She answered and started crying as soon as I said hello, which, of course, got me going. I was already on the edge after talking to Jonas.

The Michigan Department of Corrections wasn't trying to keep me safe; they were keeping me under control. Prisons run smoothly when the routine of daily prison operations is uninterrupted. Prison administrations want the same things to happen every day. No surprises, uprisings, questions, or scrutiny. And certainly no transparency, especially from the media or the public.

I was a media hot potato for the entire department. The MDOC, as well as the Oaks Facility, were inundated with hundreds of calls from press outlets about me, my care, treatment, whereabouts, attitude and more. So, the best plan of action was to lock me up all day and all night. Doing this took away a great deal of administrative concern, because they also knew that I would be very popular in the prison community. They also wanted to isolate me as much as possible from other inmates. The thought of prisoners organizing, thinking, studying and listening is negative to prison administrators in all fifty states. That's why many prison study groups have been broken up, particularly if they were non-Christian. Also, access to educational programs, legal materials and educational pursuits (beyond G.E.D. preparation) have been all but eliminated in Michigan prisons. The systematic elimination of any access to positive programs has not only fostered ignorance, but has given greater control—typically mental control—to prison officials and employees.

I thanked Warden Curtin for her honesty and forthrightness, and I was escorted out of the building and over to my cell block, 1 Block, a few moments later. This is a fairly large unit, housing 175 men. It didn't take long before everyone knew I'd arrived, and the inmates greeted me with a display of smiles, frowns, fist salutes and other hand gestures that required fewer fingers. The haters, who were very few in number, kept their distance. I got it all in my first two minutes on the block.

They quickly escorted me to cell 104, and Master Control shut the door behind me. It was a 6 x 9-foot, dark, humid room. Two stacked cement slabs lay across the far wall for beds, with a mattress on top that was just as hard. A small, stainless steel sink with an attached toilet sat close to the bed in the small cell. The cement floor was covered in chipped, gray industrial paint. The cinderblock walls were painted the same color. BOOM! went the door behind me.

Prison was my reality now. No reading materials or television, the only noise came from the loud conversations between other inmates on the cell block. Shouting. Guys would call out daily bets on sporting events to the cell block bookie, who happened to be located in the cell next to me. The process was organized. Inmates quieted their conversations during placement time for bets. The bookie would call out a name, and inmates took turns calling their wagers. New gamblers waited until the veterans were on the books. And then, guys talked. Politics. Women. They talked trash during chess matches. We got out of our cells for an hour a day, but we socialized on "the rock," or in our cells, on lockdown. A few altercations between inmates involving weapons occurred. In one incident, an inmate was stabbed during a fight with another. The prison alarms sounded throughout the compound, and we were hurried to our cells, locked down for the rest of the day while officers searched for the weapon, fed through a slot in the cell's steel door while locked down. The guards found the weapon, and determined that it was fashioned from the metal prongs inside one of the toasters. So, from that day forward, we had no more toast. Stabbings were normal, but having no toast pissed people off! Insane as it was, I sat through it, stoic in my cell, silently coming to grips with my world.

It wasn't my first time being locked up. I'd done four months in the Wayne County Jail the year before, after pleading guilty to charges of perjury and obstruction of justice. But now I am here. And as God would have it, the solitude, privacy and harsh reality of this situation has given way to deep and focused reflection, reflection that, driven so deeply, resulted in sincere repentance. And repentance inspired my revelation.

Mine was a monumental time in Detroit's history, an international story that cast an incredibly bright light on an incredibly painful time. It was a surreal, revelatory period for Detroit citizens, for me, and for my family. It was also a time of hidden political agendas, opportunism and savage advantage.

My story is *wrought* with public misunderstanding. As mayor, I made history, did some great things, and made some egregious errors. I made many people's lives better, and pissed some people off. Like any political saga of epic proportions, there are no simple explanations for the direction in which my career went. But there are two sides to the story, and probably three. The world has heard the press' side for almost ten years, and it's caused a tidal wave of sentiment against me.

Now, it's my turn, because I never got a chance to tell my story without editing or interruption. I'm not going to tell you that I'm right and others are wrong. I'm telling this story because what you think you know about Kwame Kilpatrick is largely inaccurate. I'm not a thug. I'm not arrogant. But I am flawed and passionate. I did make mistakes that deserve to be aired out. But I'll be damned if I deserve to be here, in a Level 4 maximum security prison.

And with that, I thank you for reading. It's the equivalent of lending an ear, but also lifting up truth. For we know that the truth shall make us free.

Let's go!

chapter 2

Offensive Lines

I'VE ALWAYS been good at relating to people and motivating them, but I began to truly nurture these qualities at Florida A&M University, in Tallahassee.

FAMU. "FAM." It was an interesting place—hot, humid and brimming with that slow, Southern vibe. It was quite different from Detroit, and took some adjustment on my part. I arrived there in 1988 and immediately noticed that many black people seemed to have a designated, submissive place in Floridian society. Subservience was foreign to me. It was synonymous with subsistence, and black people in Detroit didn't do subsistence, especially in my family and community. So I had to contend with that right away, consciously drawing on things that I'd taken for granted back home.

But draw, I did. I pulled from my awareness. My appreciation for the city increased when I compared the collective mindset of some Southern blacks to that of Detroiters. In Detroit, black people saw themselves as the majority, the empowered ones, the decision-makers.

I drew on what we called "Detroit Love," the unspoken kinship that coursed through the streets like arteries. It linked people, neighborhoods, and entire sides of town. West Side. East side. Southwest. North end.

Detroit Love flowed through the Considine Recreation Center on the North End, and the Joseph Walker Williams

Center, on the West Side. We played basketball there as children, safeguarded from the streets, never feeling as if the D was the national murder capital statistics purported it to be in the 1980s. We danced and fellowshipped at backyard barbecues, where anyone who showed up could partake of whatever was on the grill. We gave "pounds" in the streets, those handshakes-to-hugs that brothers gave when meeting. It all acknowledged an unspoken understanding that we were the defiant antithesis of black stereotypes.

I also drew from my family legacy. My maternal grandfather, Marvell "Rub" Cheeks, Jr., our patriarch, taught the entire clan how to live as one. He taught us so well that I felt like I knew *his* parents, and all of his descendants, although they'd passed long before I was born in Detroit.

I drew from our church, the Shrine of the Black Madonna, and its ethos, which was steeped in liberation theology. It stood in the heart of the city, on Linwood Boulevard, just a few miles from the cradle of the 1967 rebellion. The community was the church's pulse, and the love and support I received from it sustained me. We filled those pews and worshipped as a united people. As a child, I'd soak up the elders' refrains and reinforcements—*Say a poem for us, Kwame! You can be whatever you want to be! That boy smart! That boy gon' be somebody!*—like a sponge. I buried those memories in my spirit, and referenced them when I got to FAM.

I drew from my parents' support. It never waned, not once during my youth, not even when they divorced. They kept me and my sister Ayanna going, and growing. They remained team players. I lived with both of them at different times – with Dad while attending Pelham Middle and Cass Technical High School with Ayanna, and with Mom in Lansing when she served as a Michigan State Representative. My youngest sister, Diarra, attended Country Day on the other side of town. She's the actress in our family, an NYU graduate who has honed her brilliant craft working in Los Angeles.

Bernard Kilpatrick and Carolyn Cheeks-Kilpatrick, the doting father and the loving, disciplined mother, drove me, literally and figuratively, to higher heights.

I'd chosen FAMU after my father and I visited two other schools, Central Michigan and Bowling Green State Universities. I was an All-City football player at Cass Tech, and I knew I'd be receiving a scholarship to go somewhere. But it had to be the right place. Central and Bowling Green were too extreme for me. For example, there were fewer than 500 black students at Central, among a student body of 16,000. To say that I experienced culture shock when touring the campus is an understatement. The white kids partied and socialized in ways that were just foreign to me. Also, it was common for football players to be hosted by other players when visiting campuses. They'd show you the academic and social side of campus life. So I went to a party at Central. The kids were drinking, pouring beer on each other, flashing their breasts, screaming "Wooooo!" It wasn't me. Bowling Green offered more of the same.

Like many people, I believed that historically black colleges and universities were all poor and run-down. My only experience at a black college had taken place just a year earlier, when I participated in the Detroit Branch of the NAACP's Black College tour. I had a great time, but I didn't remember much about any parts of the actual tour, or the colleges. We traveled to really small schools like Livingstone, Fisk and Virginia State. We did go to the Atlanta University Complex, where Morehouse, Spelman and Clark are located. But we spent more time talking to girls and trying to get some play than paying attention to the institutions. Our chaperones meant well, but there were only two of them on a busload of teenagers with raging hormones. They made an effort to keep us focused, but lost that battle before they even got started!

However, I do remember not wanting to attend those schools. No one made any prepared presentations, and everything seemed to be very unorganized. This furthered the belief by many of us that black colleges were inferior to their white counterparts.

That stereotype changed in January 1988. Not only had Spike Lee's movie *School Daze* made black college life hot again, but one of my father's best friends, Josh Giles, who coached the FAMU basketball team, asked me to send him one of my high school films.

I admired Josh a great deal. He was born and raised in Detroit, and graduated from Northern High School. He took a lot of kids off the street through basketball. At Shaw College, he became a coach, and then he went down to Florida. He gave my film to coach Alonzo Highsmith, the defensive coordinator at FAMU, who called me. "Man, we wanna give you a scholarship," I remember him saying. The next thing I knew, they'd flown me to Florida.

The greatest thing I did was schedule FAMU as my third visit. My father and I got off the plane and went straight to a basketball game. As soon as we arrived, they escorted us inside, just as the band stood. It was during a time out when I heard the horns.

Dn-dn-dn-dnnnn-dnnnn-dnnnn-d-d-dnt! They were playing Doug E. Fresh's "The Show." The girls started dancing, and the crowd went crazy. I thought, "What the hell is this? I'm goin' *here!*"

My father, seemingly reading my mind, looked at me and said, "You probably should come here."

I had never seen or heard anything like that. Mind you, I was fresh off the plane. I hadn't seen anything about the football program, and I didn't know what the campus looked like. We didn't even know anything about the educational programs. But after going around campus that weekend and meeting everyone, we decided we liked the situation.

I'd never have been there if it weren't for Josh Giles. He passed away a few years ago, and I give him a lot of credit and gratitude.

After all this build-up, you'd think I would have had a great first year. Well, I hated it. It was 100 degrees every day, and most of the student body didn't like Northerners. Back at Cass, I didn't feel like I belonged either, at least not until my sophomore year, because I'd come from a middle school in Lansing, where I was living with my mom. Cass just wasn't my neighborhood school, so I was a kid without a clique. Freshman year at FAMU was the same way.

On my first day, I arrived on campus with my mother and sister. I was very nervous and excited. We were told to report to the football building. Mom dropped me off and went to the hotel to relax for a while, and I reported to the locker room, just in time for dorm room and roommate assignments.

The only people who were not assigned a room were me and a 6'1", 300-pound guy named Tim Green. Tim was from Bainbridge, Georgia. I remembered him from the recruit visit back in January. He didn't say a word to anyone, and he barely even spoke when someone addressed him. He was just a big, quiet guy.

I walked over to him after we were given our room assignments, and he still didn't say anything to me. He just gave me a look, grabbed his bags and started walking towards the dorm. *This is a crazy-ass mother…!* We were in the room for a few days before he started talking. I still remember those days fondly, though, because once Tim got started, he didn't shut up until five years later, when we left school! Tim was my brother! God brought us together on that campus, and we learned so *much* from each other. It turns out Tim also was crazy, but equally hilarious.

One night, freshman year, the upperclassmen decided to shave the heads of every freshman player. They went through the hallways kicking in doors, dragging people out of their rooms, and shaving their heads. Some of the guys even got their eyebrows shaved. They came to our room last. Why, I still don't know, but that was a mistake. They'd given Tim time to get a huge knife out of his duffel bag. The upperclassmen rushed through the door, and Tim lunged at them, screaming, "I will kill all of you motherfuckas!" He then lunged harder, barely missing a couple of guys. They closed our door and returned later, knocking diplomatically and asking if they could negotiate a haircut! Tim replied that he and I would cut our hair ourselves, and that they should go to hell.

That was my brother. He wasn't a politician at all, but he

knew the value of a good negotiation. And just like back home on Linwood, a knife can be a valuable tool sometimes. It provides leverage when wagering.

Tim and I were roommates our entire time at FAMU, with the exception of one semester. Due to a clerical error, we were assigned new roommates in the second semester of our third year, but our rooms were right next to each other. My roommate for that term was a guy named Hampton, from Mobile, Alabama.

Hampton was a small offensive guard, but he had very good blocking skills. He knew football, but when it came to life, he just couldn't get it right! Seriously, he had trouble figuring out some key functions. For instance, on one of our usual nights of immense alcoholic consumption, he stumbled back to the room and passed out. I returned a few hours later and was met, upon entry, by the incredibly pungent, malodorous smell of shit. It hung in the air like a swamp. I turned on the light and found Hampton lying in a pile of the real thing. It was all over the wall near his bed, on his sheets, hands and clothes.

This had to be one of the biggest dumps he'd ever taken, and he was too inebriated to make it past his own bed. I went to get every ball player I could find to help wake his ass up. I used a stick, and started jabbing and yelling at him. He finally awakened, and stumbled to the shower to clean himself. The odor was stubborn. It overpowered the scent of soap. In fact, it never went away. I had to do something, so I went to the school's Housing Director and negotiated a room change. Tim Green once again became my roomie. Hampton left school after that semester, and I never heard from him again. Every now and then, however, I still can smell him.

Those were just two crazy experiences at FAMU. The campus culture bore no shortage of shocking occurrences. I still remember some of the comments thrown at me, early on, when I encountered Southerners on campus. They'd cuss at us, and repeat themselves. But they'd change the attributions.

"You one of them Northerners."

"You one of them Up-North dudes."

"Y'all think y'all better than us. Forget y'all!" They were really aggressive. I'd never been in a situation like that. Plus, I thought I was a big guy until I got there.

"Dang, man!" I would say. "I don't even know you, man!"

Of all the people on the football team, there were only four guys from the North—one from New Jersey, one from New York, another from Chicago, and me. It was a heck of a learning experience, but I always managed to get along with everyone, and it always worked out. That's been a gift of mine all my life. I'm affable, and I look for the good in people. It's always helped me diffuse aggressive situations, no matter who I'm talking to, or where they're from.

Still, FAM wasn't for the faint-hearted. Although many Southern African-Americans had more docile attitudes than those of typical revolutionary Detroiters, the proud, strong, aggressive and diligent nature of "FAMUans" always made me feel at home. Those currently enrolled were complemented by the tremendous number of graduates who had returned to work at the university or who held elected offices on the state and federal level. They routinely spoke to our classes, or to the football team. They emanated a kind of strength, perseverance and tenacity that was only matched by the spirit of Detroit, and that really drew me in. The men and women of FAMU truly believed that they had a responsibility to their community, and that they were born to serve. Those people, and that place shaped me, and made me who I am today. But it started with the discomfort of the dreaded first semester. I'd begun the journey to adulthood, away from my incredibly nurturing family and community, which gave me a firm foundation.

Detroit.

Man… Detroit had everything I wanted. There seemed to be nothing else at first, and the prospect of adjusting to another community during my freshman year only made me more homesick. Matter of fact, I left. I decided I'd had it and up and bolted FAM, driving home with a guy from Detroit. We were eating in the cafeteria and said, "Man, we hate this place. Let's get outta here."

It was a Tuesday at 6 p.m., and we literally left and drove home.

Non-stop. Sixteen hours.

We pulled into Detroit Wednesday morning. When I got to the door, my mother was worried sick because my coaches had called, telling her I'd disappeared. This was before cell phones. You couldn't catch a man if he wasn't sitting by a line. So when I got to her house on LaSalle Boulevard, she was worried. And she was mad.

"Oh my gosh! What happened?" she said. "What are you doing here!"

I said, "Ma, I don't wanna go there anymore. That's it. I can't take it. Them some crazy folks down there, and it's too hot!"

Mom was like, "Oooh…" She launched into me. Called me "sorry." Asked me if I was a punk. That was the first time she'd done that. It really messed me up.

"You're just going to *quit?*" she said, raising her voice. "What, you a punk?"

"Punk? I ain't no punk!" I said, jumping to my own defense.

My coach, Conway Hayman, was the one who had been talking to my mother. "We got a ticket for him," he told her. "Don't even worry about it. Go on down there and put him on that bus." I boarded a Greyhound at 10:00 that night, and rode twenty-seven hours straight back to FAM. Upon my arrival, Coach Hayman made me run to the airport every morning, for two weeks. The airport was almost eight miles away. And then I had to bear-crawl the whole football field, walking on my elbows.

Coach Conway Hayman was what I call certifiable. They should've locked his ass up a long time ago. He was an offensive guard with the Houston Oilers. He blocked for Earl Campbell. And he was our coach. A good coach, but he was crazy.

It would be 104 degrees, and Coach Hayman would say, "Oh, my God! What a great day for football! You know what I'm a do today? I'm a kill each and every one of you! I'm a kill ya! I want somebody to die, right out here on the field! So we're gonna just run until somebody dies!"

What do you do? In that experience, you either grow up or die. It was just something that you had to contend with—we had to practice, running around with all that equipment on, and it just happened to be 96 degrees with 100 percent humidity. Guys were passing out. It was crazy, but it was either that or never get in any practice. I learned to overcome it because I had no choice. I learned then that in life you can't run from anything.

By my sophomore year, Tallahassee felt like home. With the exception of trips to Detroit during Christmas holidays and the Summer, I stayed in Florida. The football team always had a game on Thanksgiving weekend, the Florida Classic, against Bethune-Cookman. That's a big game that happens every year.

A large contingent of students from Detroit attended the school. They weren't on the football team, which was in essence its own community. That was a problem for me. I've never been able to function in just one population. I can't do it—I need interaction outside of my own group, now and then. I needed to do different things. I wanted to act, go to plays, sing. I grew up playing the drums in church. I can't be a black nationalist on the basketball court. I wanted to always be in several different communities.

That was the great thing about my parents. I believe I got these qualities from them. Although they subscribed to, and were very much a part of the Black Power Movement, they always believed that you had to have a wide range of opportunities and experiences. So I couldn't just be a football guy. All they liked to do was hang with each other. And then, there were football women. All this insulation made me miss entire sects of campus life.

chapter 3

Interceptions

GIRLS LIKE Carlita Ebony Poles didn't date football players. They thought we were crazy. I give myself credit—and other guys I played with will do the same—for pulling many of the football players out of that football-only mentality. I was the low man on the totem pole as a freshman, so I really couldn't say anything, but I felt trapped in that football culture. Once I became a vet, my stance changed. "Nah, man" became my standard response to a lot of football-related activities..

My eclecticism probably drove people nuts, but there was a whole campus out there. There were the other parties to go to, and I had other interests other than football. There were also other girls, the ones who weren't attracted to football. There was the occasional Epicurean Modeling Night, a talent show in which I *sang* (and don't get it twisted; I definitely did my thing).

I give my teammates some credit, but they bought in when I started to do different things. They wanted to shed the football mentality as much as I did. I was just one of the first to step out there.

I had also chosen Political Science/Public Administration, with a teacher's certification, as my major because I knew I'd eventually enter public service. A professor, however, advised that a teaching certification would position me to find a job immediately following graduation.

I pledged Alpha Phi Alpha as a sophomore, another thing

football players didn't do. They normally joined the Omega Psi Phi fraternity. Alpha Phi Alpha, Inc., was the first of all African-American fraternities. It's history attracted me—not stepping, not colors. African-American fraternities, for the uninitiated, are known for "stepping," a form of dance derived from African boot dances. It's driven by aggressive, hard-stomping, syncopated routines. And the art form is legendary.

Now, I don't mean to brag, but the Brothers of the Beta Nu Chapter of Alpha Phi Alpha could step! We were too damn cold! Smooth, aggressive, well-rehearsed and united! We won state and national competitions. But as enthralled as I was by step, I was drawn by the lore.

Cory Brown, an Alpha from Chicago, stayed in our dorm during my first year when he pledged. He gave me the fraternity's history book and said, "Man, read up on this. You're a deep brother. You know about black men. Here, read *this*." I did, and I was impressed.

History tells the story of seven black men who had a meeting on Cornell University's campus in 1906. They decided to form a fraternity. Theirs was a unifying cause, centered around scholarship, empowerment and confidence, all of which were critical to any black student's success, especially in an Ivy League school. They started the fraternity with the support of a woman, Annie Singleton, who allowed them to meet in her house. They convened secretly because, at that time, blacks weren't allowed to engage in this kind of activity.

All of that background appealed to me. Psychologically, it brought the plantations to mind, to slaves who would steal away and learn to read and to the brothers who met in the lodge and committed to becoming Prince Hall Masons. Men, on the sly, started building institutions to protect their wives, their women and their children. That sense of history really appealed to me.

The fraternity they started has hundreds of thousands of members today, and it spurred the growth of other fraternities. I just thought that was exceptional, along with the symbols of the fraternity, its history, and the Conversations about the Ethiopian

Brotherhood. All of this made me want to be a part of it.

Those seven black men, in 1906, graduated from an Ivy League school and would go on to become doctors, teachers and engineers. As a matter of fact, one of the "jewels," Charles Henry Chapman, left Cornell and taught at Florida A&M University. So, FAMU had what was called a "jewel" chapter because of Chapman's influence.

I was happier when I felt I'd carved my own identity, one that wasn't defined solely by football. I may have been a little provident, as well, because these decisions ultimately directed my path to Carlita.

I'd first noticed Carlita when I was a freshman, and met her as a sophomore. Life at FAMU was very clique-y. Everyone "belonged" to some crew on campus. When we met, I was pledging Alpha (pledges were said to be "on line"), and she had friends of her own. And a boyfriend. He was older, and lived off campus. I suppose this worked for her, because she behaved and carried herself far beyond her years. She was responsible, didn't go to a lot of parties, and studied hard. This made her a minority as an undergrad. I wasn't ready to go there yet—at least not as a sophomore. I was still hanging out, doing what college students do—playing ball, hollering at women. But I always thought she was cute.

One day she saw me walking through Tucker Hall, one of the political science buildings, when the fatigue of life on line had gotten to me. For the uninitiated, being on line is intense. It means that pledges get a beat-down in many ways, and on a regular basis. We had to be outside at 4:30 every morning for physical training, and dragged ourselves to class afterward. Then, I had football practice in the afternoon. But it didn't stop there, because you met with the "bruhs" again, the frat members who'd crossed and were pledging you, that evening.

It was grueling. There was no time to eat, so I'd lost about thirty-five pounds. I guess I looked tired and pekid when I ran into Carlita, because she gave me a Snickers bar.

"Hey, thanks, Carlita," I said. I thought that was nice of her.

I took it and walked away. It was just a brief exchange, but I appreciated it.

I saw her weeks later, though, after I'd crossed and been accepted as a member of Alpha Phi Alpha. I thanked her for the Snickers bar, and asked if she still had that "old-ass boyfriend." She said yes.

"Oh, well," I said. "Nice talking to you." She gave me her phone number, though and said to call. Again, it was a friendly gesture, and I took it that way.

I was in my room with Mahlon Clift, my friend from Chicago, a few days later, and he was flipping through my little book of phone numbers. I kept them all in one place and, while browsing, he saw Carlita's number.

"Man, you ain't called this girl yet?" he said. "Man, call her!"

Like I said, I wasn't trying to be with a good girl. I was out having fun, so it began to feel like denying the inevitable when, days later, Mahlon and I ended up at a Burger King drive-through where Carlita worked. We ordered a couple of meal deals, but she gave us a whole bunch of Whoppers. Again, Mahlon started pushing me to call her. I finally made the call in my junior year.

We had a class together, American National Government, in the fall of 1990. The professor, who we called Attorney Williams, was famous at FAMU. He passed a few years ago, but when he lived, you couldn't get a degree at the school without taking his class. I don't care if you were a biology major, you had to take American National Government. For some reason, it was the class where all the majors met, a forum course comprised of about seventy students when I took it.

Atty. Williams was also crazy, by the way. He spoke with a high, shrieking voice that always carried a distressed tone, almost like the comedian Gilbert Godfrey. Carlita sat behind me one day, and I finally decided to talk to her. I turned to face her.

"Hey, we should go to a movie or something," I said. Why did I do that?

"*Mister* Kilpatrick!" Atty. Williams shrieked. He called my name a couple of times. "Stand up! Stand up now!"

I sat there, like, "Oh, shit." And this is what he did to embarrass me.

"Mister Kilpatrick, why are you talking to that girl in my class? She doesn't like you! Get your bad breath out of her face and tell me what policy is!"

"Well, it's, uh-"

"What? Policy *is!* Policy *is!* I ask you a question, you start with 'Policy *is!*'"

"Policy is, um-"

"It's not 'Um'! You're a dummy! Go to the library and learn what policy is! Get out of my class!"

True to his word, he threw me out. Several other football players were in the class, and they cracked up. I had to pack my bag and walk out of class, but not before he added a directive.

"Before this class is over, I want you to come back with the working definition of what policy is."

I did it. At the end of the class, I returned and handed it to him, upon which he balled it up and threw it in the trash.

After class, Carlita said she felt a little sorry for me. She found it funny, but she felt bad. She said she'd go to the movies, but that first we had to go to library. Our first date took place there. Carlita was highly organized—a bookworm, really. She was a journalism major, was on her way to graduating magna cum laude, and the library was where she studied. I'd gotten more serious about studies, but the library was not my workspace. I invited two of my partners to come with me, John Redd and Greg Smith. They'd both graduated from Cass Tech with me in 1988. Carlita and I were technically on a date, but it felt casual enough to me. We clowned so badly, the staff threw us all out of the place.

Carlita was so embarrassed. She'd never been thrown out of a library before. I must not have offended her too much, though, because we still went to the movies the following night, and we haven't been apart since.

Developing the relationship was different for me. I still lived on campus. She lived off, but we spent a lot of time together. Tim and I later rented an off-campus house, but she and I basically

stayed together and did everything as a team. We bought grocer-
ies together. We bought a dog together, Hannibal, a rottweiler.
We both got food stamps. The food stamp game is an old hook-
up in neighborhoods from Detroit to Tallahassee. If you could
get them, especially as a struggling college student, then you did.

I also met her parents. I admit, few people would want to
make the first impression that I did. Remember, Carlita was the
good girl, and I was Kwam, the good guy who was still immersed
in college life. Her folks were in town, and I was supposed to
meet them for dinner… and I forgot. A few of my partners had
come over. We started hanging out, and things got a bit—how
should I say it—smokey. In fact, the house looked like a Cheech
& Chong movie scene by the time Carlita stopped by with her
father. To make things worse, we were playing Dr. Dre's album,
The Chronic, as they walked in.

One… two… three, and to the fo'. Only, this was Carlita's
father at the door. Wow!

Needless to say, they didn't appreciate my absentminded-
ness. As they stormed out, my friend Eiaon Conner looked at me.

"Hey, Brother," he said, "this probably don't look too good.
I mean, from my perspective, it don't look good. And I'm *in*
here." I had to sit through my friends' laughapalooza while Eiaon
continued. "If I was her daddy, I would beat her ass if she ever
mentioned you again!"

I took a shower and rushed over to meet them at Chi Chi's
restaurant. I'd eventually win them over… but not that night.

Carlita graduated in 1992, a semester before I did. I finished
my coursework in 1992, but completed a semester of student
teaching afterward. She returned to D.C., partly due to my urg-
ing. She wanted to stay in Tallahassee, and we had a big argument
about it. I knew that there was more opportunity for her in D.C.,
especially for someone with a journalism degree. The idea of living by myself one more time, during my last term, didn't seem
too bad, either.

It worked. She moved home. I was alone. And in no time, I
was miserable. I wanted my woman back. She was just as pitiful,

and I could hear it in her voice one day when we spoke on the phone.

It didn't make sense for us to be apart, so I told her, "I'm coming to get you. Pack." I jumped in my Bronco, drove to D.C., and called. "I'm on my way to your house."

"I'm packed and ready to go," she said.

Everyone was there when I arrived—her mother, father and brother. They weren't happy, and the situation was tense. It didn't help that I still hadn't gotten past that first impression I'd made on them. I greeted everyone, but none of them responded. Taking her bags and easing out the door, I decided to wait in the car.

The saga was crazy not by the audacity of the trip, but by the fact that I had a game the Saturday before I left. I flew out on Sunday, picked her up and returned for practice on Monday. Meanwhile, she had no job, nowhere to live, and no plan, or so I thought. We returned to my dorm room, and that's where she stayed for that first week back. We had an away game that weekend at Georgia Southern. I left on Friday, and when I returned, she'd found her own place, with furniture, *and* a job. She picked me up from the bus station in my car, and surprised me with all of it.

She got a job working for *The Tallahassee Democrat*, making about $20,000. We were rich! That was real money back then. We developed a rhythm in our relationship. I would come off the road from a game and go to my lady's house. I finished school that December and taught at Rickards High in Tallahassee through the Spring. FAMU only held Spring graduations, so I walked across the stage in 1993.

Everyone knew that we were Kwame and Carlita, campus couple. Our dynamic, however, was less glamorous. Our personalities have always been a study in contrast. I'm a people person. I like talking to people and meeting new faces. I like the socialization, the smiling. Politics, the public service end of it, thrills me. Carlita is much more insular. She's a loner. Spending a night curled up in bed with her favorite book and a cup of coffee is a perfect night for her. I'd slit my wrist if I had to do that for two or three nights. And she'd slit hers if she had to go a whole bunch of events.

I'm also more trusting of people, whereas you have to earn her trust. For years, we viewed and treated these differences as negatives in our relationship. They were natural traits, which meant they'd never go away. At one point, we'd have to face brutal realities, and deal with some brutal honesty, to turn them into positives. I'll state my belief right now that God had a plan in putting us together, because our relationship is not about opposites attracting. It's about the check-off and meeting in the middle. When Carlita and I do that—touch and agree—we make great decisions. Whether it's about finances, the kids, or the family, we always steer things in the best direction by coming to the table and exchanging our best selves. Our conscious and subconscious personalities are so opposite that coming to the center forces us both to give up something. That compromise brings greatness. That notion alone could teach many couples how to focus on the positives in their relationships.

Our family backgrounds also differ. Her family was nuclear—mother, father, brother and her. She had other relatives, but her family only gathered with them on holidays and major occasions. My family, on the other hand, will drop by because it's Wednesday or Tuesday, or because I was down the street. Aunts, uncles and cousins. I guess it was that black community ethos that says, *"Come on in!"* The Cheeks and Kilpatricks are heavily into that kind of flow. Family meetings would take place for all kinds of reasons—or no reason at all. And then there was Christmas, Kwanzaa, family picnics, family trips, bowling activities, and campaigns.

That dynamic caught Carlita off guard, because she was unaccustomed to sharing her personal space that way. And I would have to learn about boundaries, because I'd never had that in my life. These differences, in retrospect, ground themselves into the foundation of our relationship. We had no idea that they'd become buoys years later, when we'd go through storms the nature of which I wouldn't wish on my worst enemy.

Carlita actually had two jobs in Tallahassee—one at the newspaper, and another on campus. So she remained a presence on campus. She still came to my games and was active on some campus communities. I'd matured a lot, as well, and had stopped going to parties and hanging out. She became my social life. I'd also made the All-American Football Team that year (I was a two-time All-Conference player), which gave my sports career some forward movement. I attended some banquets and tried out for a couple of pro teams during the Spring while teaching school. My teaching job wrapped in June. I bid Rickards goodbye. I didn't make the teams I tried out for, so I took that as a clear sign that it was time for me to take the next step in my life. I decided to go home to Detroit.

My mother talked me into returning, and that decision placed the first strain on my relationship with Carlita. I'd gotten teaching offers in Austin and in West Palm Beach. I liked both places when I visited, and Carlita and I had discussed heading to West Palm and setting up shop. Detroit wasn't really in the equation. Carlita wasn't sure she wanted to come, and I wasn't sure that I *wanted* her to be there.

It's hard to articulate why I felt that way about her living in Detroit, but I'll try. Detroit represented my old world, the old Kwame. Carlita was a part of the Tallahassee world. She didn't quite seem to fit *Kwam B.T.* (Before Tallahassee). Still, Mom convinced me that there was not only opportunity in Detroit, but a chance for me to make a contribution to the city where I had been raised. She even had Dr. Cliff Watson, of Malcolm X Academy, call to talk to me about a series of all-male schools that had opened back home. All-male academies existed in Detroit, but not in the public school system. These were the first, and they were designed to benefit the city's population of youth who were considered to be at-risk. So I returned, and after being there for two months, I asked Carlita to come.

chapter 4

Startup Costs

I WENT BACK to Detroit in June 1993, found a house in August, and lived there for one week before asking Carlita to join me. She brought Hannibal, all her belongings, and we moved into the house I'd purchased on Santa Rosa Street, near 7 Mile Road and Livernois Avenue. Life in Detroit had begun. And it happened incredibly quickly.

I had decided to propose to her, and I had it all planned out. We traveled to Toronto by train the day after Christmas. We were broke, but there were packages available that allowed us to pay for the train, the hotel and a show, so I bought it. We stayed at the Sheraton, and went to see *Phantom of the Opera*. There's a restaurant called Hy's in Downtown Toronto, and we went there to eat. I'd been saving to pay for her ring, and I had it with me, hidden. When we got to Hy's, I gave it to the Maitre d' with specific instructions.

"Sir, will you bring this out at nine o' clock on the dot?" I asked.

"No problem, Sir," he responded. Now, I've got to give him credit, because that's all I asked. He had additional plans that would take my idea through the roof. So we sat down to dine, and I struck up a strategic conversation around 8:50 p.m.

"How'd we meet?" I asked. We love reminiscing, so down memory lane we went, laughing about the different events in our relationship. Like many couples, we had stories that benchmarked our development. We'd actually broken up once which, I suppose, is typical of young lovers. While we were apart, I went to a party on campus, not expecting to see her. But she was there, on the dance floor with some dude. In my mind, this wasn't acceptable, because we were only apart physically. So I walked onto the dance floor, cut the hell in and dragged her away. It was a young, brash move, and I manhandled her a little. It was nowhere near an Ike and Tina Turner moment, but way too much for our relationship. It was definitely stupid and childish of me, and she went off on me. But later, it was good to be able to laugh about it.

"You're just crazy as hell," she said, back at the dinner table.

"Yeah," I said, preparing to pivot. "Even through our break-ups, I always knew that we'd get to this moment right here."

"What are you talking about?" she said.

There it was, the perfect setup. Just at that moment, the Maitre d' approached our table with a big platter full of rose petals, and on one of the petals, he'd propped the ring. He laid it down in front of Carlita, and simply said, "Madame?" Man, that was so sweet.

I got on one knee, grabbed the ring, and asked her to marry me. She started boo-hooing. Hard! She had a hard time breathing, actually, so I decided to help her.

"Can I get an *answer?*" I said.

She said yes, and the restaurant erupted! We set September 9 as the wedding date, and the planning became as adventurous as the proposal. Carlita began planning a big ceremony and, in the spirit of custom, I called her father to break the news. As I told him of our decision, he listened quietly on the other line.

"Sir, as you know," I said, "it's tradition for the father of the bride to pay for the wedding. I'm not asking you to do that. I just want to see if you can help me out."

"Well, Kwame, I'm gonna send you $500. That's it." He was curt.

"Well, Sir," I said, "it's going to be a lot more than $500."

"I'm sending $500. You all want to get married, that's the decision you're making. My wife and I, we struggled. But we did it. That's all I'm sending you."

I thanked him, hung up the phone, and then cursed. "Damn that. We won't be having a big wedding."

On top of this wrinkle, Carlita had gotten pregnant with our twin boys early in 1995, but we didn't change our plans. She planned to walk down the aisle with babies on board.

My parents were absolutely thrilled to hear the news about the pregnancy. Ours would be their first grandchildren. They immediately began to brag to everyone, purchase things and ready themselves to be grandparents. Carlita's parents' reaction was the opposite. They were immediately unsupportive, and it hurt Carlita badly. Though her father's response was lukewarm at best, he remained respectful. Her mother dropped the phone upon receiving word of our news, and she didn't speak to Carlita for weeks. I don't know why she reacted that way. Carlita and her mother's relationship had always been a mystery to me. They have a great bond now, but in those days, they ran either hot or cold. I really love Mr. and Mrs. Poles. We get along very well now, and they have been amazing through our rough patches. It was just rough getting off the ground.

After that conversation with Mr. Poles, I resolved to handle the wedding plans myself, and I went to a travel agent named Patty Green who told me about group packages to the Atlantis resort in the Bahamas. Patty was the bomb! She discovered a deal for us by which Carlita and I could travel for free if we got twenty people to go with us. We decided to cruise to the island on Royal Caribbean and invited forty guests, including our minister.

The stage was set for a great trip, but Carlita's parents didn't want to come. They felt they shouldn't have to pay to attend their daughter's wedding. Money, however, was not their issue. They could afford it. They were just obstinate, and it was hard to contend with their feelings. Carlita almost lost her mind over the whole thing. And me? Well, I knew they weren't too fond of me at that point, but I still had a hard time understanding their rejection of everything.

Carlita wasn't completely without support from her family, though. Her grandmother, Laura Jayne, had been her rock throughout her life, and she had even visited us in Tallahassee. She loved whomever Carlita loved. Not only was she Carlita's favorite person in the world, she really liked me. Still, Laura Jayne was no substitute for her parents, and their attendance at our wedding was critical. So, I do what I sometimes do best—I got on the phone and *begged* them to come.

They relented, finally, but after the reservation deadline had passed, so they flew to the Bahamas for the wedding. We married at the Atlantis Resort on Paradise Island in the Bahamas. The ceremony was beautiful. Carlita was a stunning, pregnant bride. I sang a song to her that I'd written. Afterward, I secured permission from the ship's captain to bring Mr. and Mrs. Poles on board (Laura Jayne was on for the entire trip) so they could celebrate with everyone until we departed that night. Her parents had a great time once they arrived on board. They hit the buffet, danced and celebrated with everyone else as our families got to meet and spend time with each another. In fact, they were sorry that they hadn't taken the cruise with us. Somewhere in that scenario is a good sermon.

Real life, of course, was waiting at the end of our fantasy-like ceremony. Things were happening fast. Carlita was nearly six months pregnant when we married, and that shifted and narrowed my focus on my new family. We were young homeowners who became parents in a flash. The boys were born on January 1, 1996, and our lives changed from that day forward.

My focus had actually begun to change when Carlita originally informed me that she was going to have a baby. My priorities certainly transitioned at that point, and my family became my absolute priority. I entered Detroit College of Law at Michigan State University and, for the first time, began taking steps to firmly establish our future. The Kwame that most people would come to know publicly began to show himself. I conditioned myself to work feverishly for extended periods of time. Carlita certainly understood my new zeal. She and I had always agreed that we would never be broke. This became a conscious thought when we married and the boys were born. It triggered an urge in me to move constantly, to always be working on, or toward, something. It was all for the sake of my family, because I wanted to provide a better life for them.

I had no inclination then, but I'd actually begun establishing a frenetic work pace that wouldn't let up until the day I went to jail in October 2008. I started teaching by day, attending school in the evening and assuming "twin duty" at night (and the boys would not sleep). Within the next few years, I would add my first political campaign to the regimen.

Carlita, meanwhile, found Detroit difficult to embrace. She was used to having me to herself, but I was home, back in the midst of my family and ever-ready social circle. Carlita coveted her solitude, and didn't gibe with the intrusive revolving door of my family and friends.

On top of that a tension, the origin of which I still have difficulty pinpointing, began to develop between her and Ayanna. She and my mother didn't hit it off too easily, either. Theirs just wasn't the kind of warm, fuzzy rapport that spouses hope to develop with their in-laws.

My father, on the other hand, established a great rapport with her. Interestingly, her relations with both of my parents had been good when we lived in Tallahassee. I really believe the Detroit dynamic caused this adverse effect.

Building her own life in the city was hard, because Carlita didn't have many friends in the city, and it takes a long time for her to develop friendships due to her personal filters. Andrea Carroll, a great person, also became a great friend of Carlita's. Their relationship took a lot of pressure off me, but not all. She held to her nature just as fast as she did in college, securing employment at St. John's Hospital in their Community Relations department, and at Lerner's, a store in Oakland Mall, just outside Detroit. She'd also pledged Delta Sigma Theta sorority in 1995, which gave her a good social outlet and sense of sisterhood.

My situation was the antithesis of Carlita's. I was home *and* engaged in the community, but I was only twenty-five. We didn't know how to balance our perspectives in an environment in which we hadn't grown up together, but we were linked. So, like many married couples who find themselves in unchartered waters, we just began living this life together, doing our best, come what may.

As an educator, by then I was enlisted in the male academy movement. The three principal players, Dr. Cliff Watson, Ray Johnson and Harvey Hambrick, opened three male academies, Malcolm X, Paul Robeson and Marcus Garvey, respectively, the latter of which I taught at for three and a half years. The schools were part of the Detroit Public School system. They didn't remain all-male, however, because the National Organization of Women would soon win a suit filed in 1991 demanding that they admit female students. In my first class, however, I had just four girls in a group of thirty-two students. The development programs for boys remained strong, and I got a chance to positively influence many lives in that movement.

Harvey Hambrick was the principal at Marcus Garvey, and he was an excellent administrator! He didn't take crap from anyone. He was a hard-charging, proud educator who was born and raised in Mississippi and encouraged his staff to use unconventional teaching methods. His goal was to prepare our children, and that we did! I learned a lot from him.

I loved the work. To this day, it's still the best job I've ever had. I taught middle school, and it came very naturally to me. I know it's a cliché for educators to say they can see their direct influence on students on a daily basis, but I did see it over a two-year period. I worked with the same class, helping young boys bring their reading skills to the appropriate grade level. It was extremely gratifying to send fourteen-year-old young men to Cass Tech and Renaissance High School, both college preparatory schools considered to be the best in the Detroit Public School system. Marcus Garvey was an "at risk" school located in one of the most impoverished areas of Detroit. But together, the staff and students succeeded against amazing odds.

The job challenged me in new ways and altered my perception. For example, I stopped smoking weed because of my students. One day, a student came into my classroom high. He smelled like he'd smoked a joint for breakfast. His eyes were glazed. He wasn't ready for school, but I felt he was ready to be corrected by a strong male figure.

"Hey, man, you been smoking weed?" I said. "You can't come to class like that."

"Aw, Mr. Kil," he said. "I know you smoke, don't you? You too cool not to smoke."

"Man, naw!" I said. But I was lying. I wanted to set the right example, because it broke my heart to see where his priorities lay. I felt like a hypocrite. There was no way I could be an advocate for this boy's sobriety when I'd just gotten high a few days before. I quit at that very moment. I quit drinking also. That was music to Carlita's ears. She believed that crack, heroin and weed were all the same. Damn goodie two shoes! I love her so much!

I started a basketball team and a Boy Scout troop at Marcus Garvey, and I took kids to camp, although I'd never been myself. That experience, in fact, became one of the funniest and most fulfilling in my life. At the start of my second year as a teacher, I had the typical conversation with students about how they spent their summer, but when I asked if anyone went to camp, they gave terse responses.

"What? Camp?" they said.

I was a little surprised. "You don't go to camp?"

"You mean, go out in the woods?" they shot back. "Man, ain't nobody goin' to no camp."

I didn't like what I heard. They seemed too disconnected from traditional, edifying childhood experiences. So I got bold. "Y'all know what? If you do well this year, then next summer, I'm taking you all to *camp*." Mind you, this was the first day of school. By May, I'd forgotten I had put it out there, but they remembered. One of the kids approached me that Spring.

"Mr. Kil," he said, "Now, you *said* that you were gonna take us to camp this summer. We've been good, so you gotta take us."

"Yeah, yeah, I'll take you!" I quickly responded. I hadn't

done the first bit of research into camp sites. Moreover, I'd never been myself! "I didn't forget. I was just checking on *you*."

I had to do something, so I spent the entire week calling camps, only to find that they were all full. I tried the YMCA and 4-C with no luck. Then I realized the Boy Scouts had space in their D-Bar-A Camp, located about forty miles outside of Detroit. It was just past the Palace of Auburn Hills, where the Detroit Pistons play, but it was reserved for Boy Scout troops. I quickly called them, and a gentleman named Darryl Jones came over and helped us form an official troop. All I had to do next was make it to the campground.

Detroit Public School rules required a set number of chaperones, based on the number of students. But summer break was about to begin, and I couldn't find any chaperones to volunteer their time. I couldn't get one teacher to commit. I turned to my own circle of friends. Ibn Pitts, Carlita and Darryl committed. Darryl's girlfriend, Senita, also joined us.

chapter 5
Planting Seeds

TRY TO visualize a group of novice campers in the woods, preparing to fraternize with experienced Boy Scouts. We were an all-black troop, and every other group was white, and uniformed. That may not mean much in some parts of America, but Michigan is, to this day, one of the most racially polarized states in the Union. The other scouts knew drills, had formations and looked really organized. We wore t-shirts, cut-off shorts, sweat pants, jeans, whatever. No two people in our group were dressed alike. Even the adults in the other Scout Troops wore uniforms. And there were no other women present besides Carlita and Senita.

The first day was the worst. Isn't it always? It took us six hours just to pitch our tents. We fumbled with the equipment, managing to finish by dinner. A bell rang to signal all meal times. As the other troops grouped together in orderly lines, our kids made a mad dash to the front. Obviously, there was a protocol we knew nothing about. We looked bad. I mean, we looked *bad*.

We hardly looked any better the next morning. When the military revelry played to awaken everyone, we lined up late. We just had no procedure for anything. Adding insult to injury, we were unfamiliar with activities like archery and the three-legged race. People don't shoot arrows in the 'hood! So, the Boy Scout competitions that pit archers, swimmers and runners from different teams against each other started out embarrassingly for us.

Started embarrassingly. Once their timidity ebbed, my troop gained their footing. It's not like anyone offered to help us and, since the other troops were content to shake their heads and watch us flounder, we resolved to use what we knew to get what we wanted.

The week went from aimless to amazing after a few adjustments. We found loopholes in some of the competition's rules that allowed us to position the kids in our group who had talent in certain areas. One boy among us had a father who'd take him out to practice skeet shooting. The other kids in our group didn't know how, so we entered this youngster in the shooting competition. The camp asked each team to elect *three* shooters, but we changed that plan.

"He's going to shoot all of our shots," we said. They complained that we were breaking the camp rules but, of course, I started arguing the point.

"Where does it say that you have to have three shooters?" I asked. The rule wasn't written anywhere. "Where's that rule, since you're bringing up rules?" They were livid, but our boy represented us as our lone shooter and wiped out the competition. Needless to say, they didn't like us. To them, we may as well have been *homeboy* scouts.

The growing disdain boiled over toward the end of the week. Despite our newfound success in the skill events, we were still alienated. And we still managed to be late for meals. In fact, we'd eaten last at every chow up to that point. We weren't stampeding to the lines any more, but our punctuality needed work. Meanwhile, there was a rule that the first person from each troop to get in line could save a spot for the entire squad.

Well, we didn't have a punctual troop, but we did have Ralph, our "fast guy." We told Ralph, "When you hear that bell, run over there and get in line."

On the second-to-last day of camp, the revelry played and Ralph took off, arms pumping, high-stepping. He made it to the front of the line. The troop was right behind him, and I was walking. By the time I got close, a few of my boys came running back to me.

"Mr. Kil! Mr. Kil! You gotta come quick! Some white man pushed Ralph down!"

I'm thinking, "Awww… here we go." When I got to the meal tent, sure enough, Ralph was crying and angry.

"He pushed me! He pushed me!" Ralph screamed. I tried to calm him down, and then this guy approached me. He was my height, my build.

"Excuse me," I said. "Did you push this little kid?"

This joker got in my face and said, "You're goddamn right I pushed him! And I'll push him again if he gets disrespectful."

"Well, waitaminutewaitaminutewaitaminute," I said, keeping my composure, but feeling a volcanic anger inside. "What if I push *you?*"

The guy leaned into me. "Is that a threat?" He put his hand up toward me. That was all I needed to see. I clocked Mr. Pusher, busting him right in the mouth. He fell to the ground as everyone looked on. He writhed like a snake. The *police* came, of all things, and at this point, Mr. Pusher was crying, literally choking back tears and hyperventilating. "He-he-he…"

No one could believe it. Even the officer got sick of him. "Man, pull yourself together! What's wrong with you?" They ended up kicking both of us out of the camp. Carlita and the rest of my team stayed until the next day and helped get the boys home.

It was an experience for the ages. Corey Gilchrist, one of the scouts who would later work for my administration, tells the story in dramatic fashion. Those guys who've never camped join the Boy Scouts, led by a guy who'd never camped himself, and went from spectacle to spectacular. We were rudimentary from start to finish, but I was so proud of the way they figured things out as a team. By week's end, we out-ran, out-raced and out-swam the entire camp. We won medals in everything.

I think Mr. Pusher symbolized societal arrogance and condescension. But it goes to show that a rose, by any other name, is still a rose. That's one thing that children always show me—that

God gives us everything we need to thrive at birth. And those kids did.

Those kinds of experiences made teaching rich for me because, at every turn, groups of boys seemed to gel, and then excel. The basketball team had a 0-11 record in their first year. The same group went 10-1 in the second year. That year included a win over Hamilton, the best middle school team in the area. The victory included a comeback from sixteen points down. It was an incredible experience.

Let me digress a moment. I didn't explain the *detailed* chronology of events in my life at this time, and I think it's warranted. Teaching for a couple of years helped me see that service was my purpose. I fell in love with it because I loved helping people thrive. I also recognized that my life had been moving toward public service. My mother decided to run for Congress in 1996, and her seat in the Michigan House of Representatives was open. She'd had that seat for eighteen years, and she had always been an incredibly hard worker. She was dedicated to her constituency. The needs of the people she served always guided her political activity. And my values came from hers. I couldn't see anyone else in her seat. I'd worked in that ninth district—the neighborhoods surrounding three West Side high schools—Northwestern, Central and Chadsey—since I was six years old, passing out literature, going door-to-door. My grandfather, aunts and sister all lived in that area.

I seriously considered running for her seat around the time I was accepted to the College of Law in Detroit, now the Michigan State University College of Law. I'd just been accepted, and knew that would mean teaching and going to school at night. I didn't feel I could do it, though, because Marcus Garvey usually absorbed twelve hours of my day. I taught, tutored, drove kids home and picked them up. At one point, I leaned toward postponing my law pursuit, and *that's* when Carlita told me she was pregnant. This was all in 1995, and it made my decisions easier.

"Okay, you've gotta make a move," I told myself. I started law school that fall, the twins were born the following January, and I launched my first campaign for office. It was incredible. We were a group of young turks— Carlita, Derrick "Zeke" Miller and Christine Rowland (Beatty after she married) and me. Derrick and Christine were my best friends. I'd known them since high school. Zeke was a basketball and All-City baseball player, and we became friends during our sophomore year.

Christine managed the campaign while Zeke and I ran it. We crafted a campaign squadron by pulling Cass's 1988 graduation list, sending out a mass notice to our classmates, and inviting them to a meeting about my bid for office. We served chips and punch to all four of the people who showed up—me, Carlita, Zeke and Christine. *We're gonna be running this thing by ourselves,* we thought.

But off we went, walking through neighborhoods and knocking on doors. Our campaign theme was "Generation to Generation." We talked to people about how Detroit had always been about lifting up the next generation of leaders. The torch was now passing from Mom to me. And we didn't give up on the people who graduated with us. We got on the phones, called and asked them to join in Saturday literature drops in neighborhoods. Old folks from the Shrine and people from Cass showed up.

I had no money to fund the effort, not even enough for the literature, but we never let that stop us. Finally, we scored our first endorsement, from the Michigan Education Association in Lansing. They gave us $5,000. You'd have thought they'd given us a million, because we stretched it to its limits. It was just enough money to fund a mailing to the absentee voters, and we put together a piece that I still think is a classic work. We named it after the theme, and it bore a photo of my two grandfathers on the cover, holding my twin boys on their lap. The inside of the piece espoused the virtues of lifting up each other, and Detroit's complementary legacy. It focused on passing leadership down to new, younger generations, and I can't think of two men who embody the city's legacy more than my two grandfathers., Marvel Cheeks, Jr. and James B. Kilpatrick.

They were both amazing men. James Kilpatrick was incredibly well read. He factored into every report or paper I wrote from third grade until my college graduation, because I used the example of his life for research. He served in World War II, as did Marvel Cheeks, and later traveled with his wife all over the world, retracing his time in Europe. He held season tickets to the University of Michigan football games for more than forty years. Bo Schembechler was right up there with Jesus in his house. He never had a driver's license but knew every bus route in the city and the suburbs without a written schedule. We, and all of his friends, affectionately called him "The *Maestro.*"

After The Michigan Education Association made that meaningful mailing possible, the only other endorsement we scored came from the Detroit-based Fannie Lou Hamer political action committee. It was just as poignant and effective because my grandfathers were also very well known in those circles. James B. Kilpatrick worked at the post office for forty-two years. Marvel Cheeks, Jr., has lived in the same general neighborhood since the 1940s, and in the same house since 1953. So the mailout connected us to their communities, and it garnered a lot of votes. We certainly needed them because my opponent, a gentleman named Fred Durhal, who has been a member of the House since 2008, received several endorsements from police officers, firemen, and Dennis Archer, who preceded me as mayor. His support dwarfed mine. Though the MEA was not well known in Detroit, their financial support was critical to our success. And Fannie Lou requires candidates to pay *them* $500 for their support.

We won because of our refusal to be outworked, and our determination to win. I outlasted Fred by roughly 1,000 votes. That's a pretty wide margin for a district race. It was a nervous, exhilarating campaign (I'm always nervous when I'm campaigning), but I never felt I would lose. At the same time, however, I was surprised that anyone thought I would win. In all my campaigns, I would revisit that resolve—if we work hard, we'll win.

My greatest strength when campaigning is that extra gear that engages just when I need it. Somehow, I just don't get tired. I don't stop. I heard Kobe Bryant talk about something similar.

He said he goes into a zone where he just can't miss. I approach campaigns like an athletic competition. I listen to rap music on the way to a debate. I refuse to be outworked. If you beat me, it won't be because you worked harder than I did.

I was headed for a political career that would involve five campaigns, and that gear would drive each of them. Whether it was Buzz Thomas running against me for Floor Leader in the Michigan House, Gil Hill in my first mayoral campaign, or Freman Hendrix in my second, my will to outwork my opponent was the ticket. I can always see when my competition gets tired, when I got his ass, and I would always figure out a way to let him know I knew this. There's always a way to say, *Gil, you look like ya gettin' tired, baby. Hey, Fred, you're startin' to look old, baby. Lookin' like you can't hang. I'm about to go hit fifty or sixty doors. I'm telling let these folks what kinda campaign we're running. You goin'?*

We called this gear "campaign mode." I wasn't the only one who had it. Christine Beatty also had that wiring. She was right there with me, and that's how we connected. It never hit at the beginning of a campaign. Instead, we worked ourselves into it, getting to the point where debate answers just come to you, where speeches are flawless. You get so focused that it takes a while to come out of it. Even when exhaustion set in, we kept going.

My freshman year in the Michigan State House of Representatives was an incredible experience. I started on January 5, 1997. The State of Michigan had just enacted, through a statewide ballot initiative, term limits for legislators, which meant that my first term in the House would be the last time that anyone with more than six years of seniority would serve. I served with men and women who had made careers out of policy-making, and who built relationships out of trust, mutual interest and policy, rather than partisanship. I learned a lot.

At the time, Curtis Hertel was the Speaker of the House. He had served in the legislature for nearly twenty years. He had been Speaker before, then lost the majority and regained it. He was a native Detroiter with a long and rich political history on the East Side. His older brother, John, was chair of the Macomb County

Board of Commissioners (a suburban county east of Detroit) and is the director of the Michigan State Fair. Curtis appointed me as the only freshman legislator to chair a committee—Marine Affairs and Port Development, which wasn't exactly a heavy-weight group. As a matter of fact, only three bills were sent to my committee while I served as chairman, and two of them came from me. But I used that seat to hold hearings all over the state of Michigan, building relationships with truckers, shippers, road builders, environmentalists, port developers, elected officials, and most of all, my fellow legislators.

The Majority Floor Leader at that time was a man named Pat Gagliardi. I learned so much from him. He ran the Floor and House agenda with an iron fist. He was a yupper! (someone from Michigan's Upper Peninsula). The yuppers were my kind of people. They talked a lot of trash, drank a lot (which always made the people around me more fun), partied a lot and worked hard. Men after my own heart!

Pat was always looking for someone's ass to kick, but he would smile and talk nicely while he did it. I developed a relation-ship with him by sitting at his feet and learning the job of Floor Leader. I worked hard during that freshman year. I passed nu-merous bills, many of them becoming law. Most of all; however, I kept my mouth shut and learned. There was too much political and institutional knowledge not to take full advantage of the op-portunity. I learned policy, appropriations processes, committee structure, procurement, statewide campaign strategy and fund-raising, and most of all, how to position myself to help Detroit.

Many of the policies I supported or sponsored would later help me as mayor. In fact, I joined with Governor John Engler and Senator Spencer Abraham, both Republicans, to push a state-wide ballot initiative that we called the Clean Michigan Initiative. For lending my support to this initiative, I was able to negotiate over $100 million in allocations from that money for Detroit, in-cluding $10 million that we later used to build the new Detroit Riverwalk, which we completed during my time as mayor.

The Riverwalk was a more than three-mile stretch of Detroit

waterfront property that we redesigned beautifully. It became a tremendous example of cooperation and tenacity, truly a legacy project that rescued Detroit's riverfront from industrial dinosaurs and gave it back to the citizens. To get it done, we in City government had to do some heavy lifting, such as negotiating land deals and legal settlements, moving old companies and straight up hustlin', but it was truly a team effort that would only be topped by the Super Bowl. The City of Detroit, General Motors, the Kresge Foundation, and my mother, Congresswoman Carolyn Cheeks-Kilpatrick, were the major players, and an array of members from Detroit's business and philanthropic community lent their support as well.

Congresswoman Cheeks-Kilpatrick was a member of the United States House of Representatives Appropriations Committee. She sent significant dollars to the project, even reprogramming $5 million of unspent money and getting it to Detroit when we hit a funding snag. She'd done things like this for Detroit before, bringing more than half a billion dollars to her home district over a ten-year period, more than any Congresswoman in Michigan history. I know I digress, but hey, that's my Mama. The Riverwalk Project finished on time and on budget and Detroiters, for the first time, had an active place to engage in family fun. Skating, biking, running and walking became the norm. And the backdrop is the beautiful Detroit River and our Canadian neighbors across the waters.

We kept moving in a developmental direction, using more than $75 million of that money to clean up old brownfield environmental sites for new development. Brownfields are abandoned commercial and industrial facilities that are still available for use, and I later spent a lot of time at groundbreaking and ribbon-cutting ceremonies made possible by the money directed to their redevelopment.

An interesting thought related to this achievement is the wave of sentiment across the country that has often sullied the images of career public officials. I submit that this movement, as it would later involve me, has had a tremendously negative effect on public policy in Detroit, and throughout Michigan. Continuity and consistency has suffered, and people wonder why so many are hurting under the regime of the latest business executive to be elected mayor or governor. The answer is simple: They don't know what they are doing. It's not their profession. As for me, I didn't want to be the traditional black legislator from Detroit. I wanted to change the game. And that I did!

When I ran for Leader of the State House, my colleagues had to vote for me, so I literally had to travel across the state to get their votes. And I had a strategy: if I'm sitting in your living room, it's hard to say no to me. So I traveled, criss-crossing all these counties that sat on opposite sides of the Michigan mitten. I'd go from Houghton to Alpena, to Escanaba to Standish. My opponent was Mark Shauer, from Battle Creek. He later ran for Congress and won. Mark was and is a good guy. We were seat-mates during our freshman year in the State House.

Mark was in for one hell of a race, although I don't think he knew it. I went to places where I'd be the only black person for 600 miles, but I'd be in people's living rooms, talking to their wives. Often, these occasions would mark the first time many people had ever had a black man in their homes, but the camaraderie was nearly instant, almost all the time. They couldn't believe I'd travel all the way from Detroit to meet them. I went to an annual dogsled race in Escanaba, in Michigan's Upper Peninsula. The race goes through their streets, over a lake. People have died in this race, because the terrain is treacherous. I stood on stage and helped kick off the race. Getting in a car and driving to Alpena because I knew three representatives would mean everything, but it felt like second nature to me. I'd go deer hunting—hunting nothing—just to sit down and talk to them, and tell them how important an election was. And people truly appreciated it. They knew I wanted their votes. Mark began doing that toward the end, but it was already too late. I'd already been to all the homes!

I was the first black man to even run for this position. In fact, most people told me I'd lose on that fact alone. But again, that was nothing to me, because I've never run for an office that people thought I'd win. I love that! If anyone ever tells me at the beginning of a race that I'm predicted to win, I wouldn't know how to work.

I was the first African-American and youngest person to ever hold the position in the more than 175-year history of the institution. As Leader, I still had my northwest Detroit district, but my job description expanded considerably. I chose the Democrats I wanted to serve on committees, as well as the chairs for the Democratic side of the House. Managing the budget for the Democratic Caucus was also my responsibility, and travel came out of my office as well. We set policy direction, deciding what bills would be introduced. I led all negotiations with the governor and the Republicans on behalf of my Caucus. Essentially, I chose who got what, when. The Leader position in the Michigan House of Representatives carried a lot of responsibility, but it was so much fun, and a truly great experience.

chapter 6

The Pre-Season

CARLITA WAS excited, too, and very proud of me. She'd also begun to enjoy motherhood soon after the boys' first birthday. I say that because the first nine months with the twins was torture on us both! They were born while I was still teaching and attending law school, and they never slept through the night. Not once. They didn't sleep through the night until they turned three years old. It was unreal! For the first nine months, they would sleep in thirty- to forty-five-minute spurts, each twin waking up at a different time. One guy could be yelling at full decibel level while the other slept like, well, a *baby*. I'm talking deep sleep here. Carlita or I would get up and get milk or diapers. It was absolutely amazing. Then, thirty- to forty-five minutes after getting that twin to doze off, the sleeping twin would start.

We were both tired as hell, and we tried all the tricks. We put cereal in their milk and gave them "pot liquor," the juice that comes from cornbread and greens. *Everything*. Nothing worked. Just let them cry? We tried that, too. They would cry until we *had* to go in there to make sure they were okay. Man, it was such a rough nine months.

I still remind Jelani and Jalil, teenagers now, about how they were as babies. Of course, they find it hilarious. And it is kind of funny now, but it was not funny then at all. Carlita was miserable during this time. She was stressed and totally exhausted. She also experienced postpartum depression. I taught by day, attended school in the evening and came home to do baby work after that. My wife was usually exhausted by the time I arrived home at 9:30 p.m., so we would immediately bathe the boys and put them to bed. She'd then take a nap while I washed the bottles and prepared them for the night and the next day. Occasionally, I'd do some reading, but after bottle duty I usually fell asleep because the first shift for the twins' awakening was mine. Sometimes, I'd just stay awake until I heard the first loud cry, hurry and get whoever woke up first back down, and then go to sleep. Carlita would then take the second shift. Our system worked, but it just wore us out.

By January 1997, the boys were walking and sleeping more regularly, and they also began to go to daycare. Carlita found a job teaching non-violence and peer mediation courses in the Detroit Public Schools. She also wrote a column in the *Michigan Chronicle* for St. Johns Hospital's Community Affairs department.

I drove to Lansing, leaving at 6:30 a.m., but we only worked *in* Lansing on Tuesday, Wednesday and Thursday. That gave Carlita and I more time to be together, to go to movies, hang out with the boys and travel. Carlita loved my schedule then. Our lives were well balanced during that time.

My commute from Detroit was ninety minutes each way. I spent the night in hotels if we ran late, or during budget proceedings and negotiations. I never had an apartment or house in Lansing. Many reps do. Some come from as many as eight hours away. Others move their families to Lansing and travel back home on weekends.

Christine and I usually drove back and forth to Lansing together. As you may suspect, Carlita became more and more concerned about these times between Christine and me. She wasn't at all concerned for the first few years, but she definitely was toward the end of my time there, around 2000. She never said anything directly, but you know when your woman has a problem. I picked up on her body language, her facial expressions and that very suspicious silence that comes when certain subjects are brought up. I knew I had to make a change, because Christine was truly my friend. Heck, she was really my road dawg. Like we say in the 'hood, we were down like four flats and a spare. Plus, she did excellent work. But her name was becoming a buzzword to my wife.

Neither Christine nor I wanted any problems with our spouses, so we opened a district office in Detroit and decided that she would work there, in the community we served. It was a perfect arrangement for many reasons. First, she was pregnant with her second child, and the travel would have been too much for her. Plus, I needed someone on the ground in Detroit to help me raise my recognition in other parts of the city. And two, without Carlita having to say a word, I created the separation that she wanted. Zeke, who was then working in my mother's Congressional Office, came over to take Christine's place in Lansing.

Things were great! I graduated from law school in 1999 and took my seat as Leader in 2000. It was nice to put school behind me, because balancing my duties as Leader of the House with family and my education was grueling. But I had that hustle, and I got it done. In fact, I had fun doing all of that stuff, so much so that it wasn't hard to manage. These newlywed/rookie years revealed my true capabilities, and I was eager to continue to test my own limits. Adding to this self-discovery was the feeling that my work was helping people in the city that raised me. And though Carlita was still not happy living in Detroit, she was making the best out of the situation. It was the best of both worlds.

I was a member of AAMO, the African-American Men's Organization, a group of influential and dedicated Detroiters. My father and millionaire cable and casino magnate Don Barden were also members. During one of our meetings in 2001, a conversation arose regarding who should run for mayor. The members were dissatisfied with the job that the current Mayor, Dennis Archer, was doing, and sought to identify someone who would excite them enough to lend their support.

Specifically, they didn't like the way that deals for three new casinos built in downtown Detroit were handled. There was no substantial African-American ownership. In a city comprised of more than eighty percent African-Americans, black people had less than a five percent ownership stake. Barden, in particular, had been primed for ownership because of his track record, but he didn't obtain it.

At that time, many people also took umbrage with a mayoral candidate who hadn't been born and/or raised in the city. That has since changed with the election of Dave Bing, after my resignation in 2008, but Dennis Archer had to contend with it. Originally from Cassopolis, Michigan, he moved to the Detroit area after graduating from Western Michigan University to attend law school at the Detroit College of Law.

Dennis was the first mayor after the twenty-year reign of the City's legendary first African-American Mayor, Coleman Alexander Young. Mayor Young was truly one of the most brilliant political figures in American history. He was a public sector giant and also a polarizing figure. He exuded the spirit of an old-world statesman while using modern political theory to marshal support for a cause. And in the next moment, he could look you dead between your eyes with a sinister grin, and use the same eloquent language to call you a "motherfucker." He was celebrated and adored by most of the African-American community, just as he was vilified and despised by most of the white community. But overall, Detroiters felt an unbelievably strong bond and connection to him. He was our family. He was our leader. And like it or not, everyone who steps into the mayor's position in Detroit is immediately compared to him, seemingly by all.

Dennis was the first post-Young era mayor. People felt that he, as mayor, hadn't provided any significant opportunities for Detroiters to do business with the City of Detroit. This further exacerbated a feeling shared by many that their relationship with the mayor that they'd once perceived as good had deteriorated, or became nonexistent.

Bill Brooks, who'd recently retired as vice president of human resources for General Motors, had expressed his intent to run. Bill was a good guy with a great personality who'd helped many in the community while employed at GM. But the group and others felt that he couldn't garner the support to become mayor.

The group didn't identify a capable candidate during that meeting. Days later, I visited my father at his home. He'd been sitting with Archie Clark, one of his best friends who'd played in the NBA for eleven years, and was also a member of AMMO. They'd all rehashed the conversation about viable mayoral candidates. Among the names they considered was Dave Bing, the current mayor.

Jokes aside, my father then turned to me and said, "You know, *you're* the one who should run."

I looked at him as if I didn't hear him. "Man, *who?*" I said.

"You!" he said.

"Man, you're out your mind. Nobody knows me."

"Man, it's wide open. It's time!"

And so it began. My father was the first person to suggest that I take this step. The thought hadn't entered my mind. It even sounded crazy to me. But his initial suggestion became the first in a series of similar comments from random people. You know how a car you consider buying suddenly seems to pop up everywhere on the road, and it either strengthens or weakens your desire to go for it? That's what happened to me. It seemed like people in my life, friends and associates alike, began saying in passing or in conversation, "Man, you should run for mayor."

The comments moved from interesting to intriguing when, back in Lansing, I got a call from Freman Hendrix while I was on the House floor. Freman was deputy mayor for the Archer administration at the time. He called to inform me that he'd decided to leave the position, and wanted to know if I'd consider replacing him. He hadn't spoken to Archer about it, but he wanted to know if I was interested. I told him I was.

I drove to Detroit from Lansing that day, and talked to my father about it. He had a different take on the opportunity. "Man, that's some bullshit," he said. "Why would you take that? This guy's [Archer's] ship is sinking." He had a point. The Archer administration was dealing with two issues at the time that had upset the community, and parts of his own constituency. One was the casino matter. The deal brokered between the City and the gaming authorities designated room for three gaming houses, and Mayor Archer had a say in determining who would own them. Barden, a native Detroiter, had waged a public campaign that included bringing Michael Jackson to town as a show of support. His rejected bid set off the biggest recall effort in the city's history, amounting to well over 50,000 signatures. It failed by fewer than 500 but sent a clear message. It was a blow.

The second issue, slow response to a severe snowstorm a few months later, further tarnished his image, and his popularity declined from that point forward. He'd lost the people of the City of Detroit.

I actually think Dennis did a good job in some respects. I also feel there's an old *Dennis Archer vs. Kwame Kilpatrick* discussion that deserves clarification. Dennis would later come to feel that I was his opponent. I really wasn't. I think he labeled me as such because of my history with the Black Slate, a Detroit political action group. They were the ones who primarily pushed the recall effort. He was a different kind of cat, and a different kind of mayor than I would be. But we come from very different backgrounds, have different relationships with the city, and it with us. The city never did rise and fall with the personality, and the being, of Dennis Archer because he didn't embody the spirit of Detroit. He didn't embrace the ups, the downs, and the passion of the city. It just wasn't his style, and that kind of thing is reserved for very few men. Coleman Young was one, for sure—in fact, the biggest. And damn sure, Kwame Kilpatrick was another. People felt us the way they feel Detroit; therefore, they love us and hate us. But I have a tremendous amount of respect for Dennis Archer to this day, regardless of how he feels about me. I respect anyone who serves in that position for eight years and comes out with all his teeth still rooted in his gums.

My father, in debating whether I should work for the Archer Administration at that time, felt strongly about the position I'd put myself in by replacing Freman. "They'll isolate you." He then spoke to the bigger opportunity. "You could be *Mayor!*"

"Dad, why do you keep saying that?" I asked. I just didn't see it, but it was the second major mayoral hint to occur, behind the discussions launched at the AMMO meeting.

The third hint occurred when Christine came to my office days later. She simply walked in, brought up the subject, and said, "I think you should run."

My response remained the same. "You must've lost your mind." I'd actually begun thinking about how we could angle to get me on the ticket for lieutenant governor. I felt that state po- litical positions would bring a national focus that would allow me to move around the country. The thought of running for mayor hadn't taken, not with me.

But Christine wouldn't relent. "These Democrats are never going to pick you to be on their ticket," she said. "That'll never happen. You're too strong for them." And she was right. The Michigan Democratic Party likes and supports people they can control, particularly African-Americans. If you have the audacity to have your own ideas, and the courage to speak up about them, you will surely have to fight the party. The unions, and the people who control the Democratic process, who influence the place- ment of candidates on tickets, would not have supported it. She was absolutely right.

Christine never pulled punches with me, and her blunt hon- esty always helped my direction. She spoke the truth regarding my relationship with Michigan unions. They never really liked me. They'd opposed me for state rep, and for Leader. I always had to beat them, as opposed to gaining their support.

The mayoral conversations had now piled up like a stack of books. Christine's candor sat atop that pile. I began to explore the idea, and met with my parents to discuss it. My mother did not want me to run. She never liked the idea of me running for state rep. She'd never fully articulated her reasons for this, only stating that she didn't think it was my time. My mother is an old-school politician and, for some reason, she didn't think I was ready.

My father, who was assistant executive to the late, legendary Wayne County Executive Ed McNamara, was really for it. He told McNamara, who called and invited me to his office to discuss the possibility of my running. McNamara was an old warhorse in Michigan politics, and highly respected. I still remember my conversation with him.

"There are three things in politics that you always have to re-member," McNamara told me. "Number one is timing. Number two is timing. And number three is timing. This is the right time. I think if you run now, you'll win."

I balked, saying that the people wouldn't vote for another Kilpatrick, not with my mother already being in Congress. I was thinking of all the reasons not to do it. He said my argument was nonsense, that there were several Hathaways, McNamaras and other people whose entire families seemed to be involved in the political process. Mine was a crazy argument, he said.

Finally, while in Detroit preparing to head for Lansing, I lis-tened to a WJR Newsradio broadcast, as I often did while driving. A breaking story came on just as I arrived at the Capital building. Dennis Archer had announced that he would not seek another term as mayor of the City of Detroit.

"This guy's not even *running*," I thought. The news broad-cast immediately delved into a barrage of questions about who would run for office. They mentioned different people, can-didates who, at the time, were obvious considerations, such as Freman Hendrix and Gil Hill, then president of the Detroit City Council, who'd built his reputation by co-starring as Eddie Murphy's sergeant in the movie *48 Hrs.* Nicholas Hood, a pop-ular minister in the city whose family was also involved in the Detroit political process, was also mentioned. I thought no one could beat those guys. After a break in the newscast, they aired an interview with Ed McNamara. I sat in my car, in front of the Capital. Moments later, McNamara came on and said he thought that Kwame Kilpatrick was the guy who'd be the stalking horse in the race for Detroit's next mayor.

The reporter seemed surprised, and noted me as a name no one had considered. He mentioned my Lansing credentials, my standing as Democratic Leader in the House, and my youth. McNamara went on to say that listeners heard from him, first, that I'd be the man. And he didn't stop with WJR. He reiterated his feelings during an interview for WXYZ-TV. His verbal acknowledgments triggered widespread belief that I was *his guy.*

By the time I walked into the Capital building reporters from *The Detroit News* and *The Detroit Free Press* were looking for me. The question of the day quickly became whether I'd be running for mayor, to which I initially responded by saying that I hadn't thought about it. When asked whether I'd ruled it out, I said I hadn't ruled it in *or* out. These were obviously diversionary comments. Hell, I hadn't even secured my wife's blessing! But McNamara had effectively put me in the conversation. The idea of running for mayor then became a serious consideration. It was all so new, so sudden, but so seemingly inevitable.

I went home after answering the news questions, and later that evening I received what I believe to be one of the clearest messages from God that I've ever experienced. Carlita and I had moved to a house on Leslie Street, and after a restless night, I picked up my Bible and went to the basement. I was losing sleep due to my own thoughts, which were consumed with this mayoral discussion.

"God, you gotta help me with this one," I recall praying. "If you want me to do this, give me a word." I then opened the Bible. The page I opened was a chapter in the second Book of Samuel, which described King David's rule over Hebron, which had lasted for seven years and six months. The passage mentioned that David was then thirty years old. The Scripture said that David had sought and received the blessing of the elders to reign, and there was more than one mention of David's age. He was thirty years old, and so was I.

"Oh my God," I thought. I closed the Bible, ran upstairs and awakened Carlita. "Carlita! I just read this verse! You ain't gonna believe it!" I was all excited and screaming. She was fast asleep.

"Hu-what, what?" she said, startled.

"I just read this verse," I said. "This...this is...I gotta run for mayor! I gotta run! It just hit me. This thing was clear. I gotta run."

"Okay," she said. "Run." And she went back to sleep. There I was, astounded by my own revolutionary, spiritual experience. And there was my wife, succinct in her approval, and justifiably dismissive in her resolve. Hilarious.

chapter 7
Okay, Run!

I CALLED MY father, mother, Ayanna and Christine, the next morning. "Let's roll," I told them. "I'm running." We met to start putting the campaign together, and scheduled a kickoff press conference on the front porch of my mother's house.

All sorts of people gathered on Mom's porch that day. Dave Bing was there, as was Reverend Marvin Winans of the Winans gospel family, Reverend Wendell Anthony, president of the Detroit NAACP; and Willie Hampton, head of the SEIU, one of the unions that supported me. We also bused in groups of senior citizens. My entire family and extended family were there, as well as hundreds of people from my Detroit family. It was an amazing scene. We blocked the street, and news crews from all of Detroit's major news stations covered the event. Helicopters flew overhead, and cameras and reporters were everywhere.

I distinctly remember two things from that day. At one point, Carlita and I went to the back room of my mom's house. At least thirty people were inside the house, but we were alone. We sat down on an old couch and had a few moments of calm amid the frenzy. She looked at me, visibly nervous yet peaceful, and whispered how much she loved and supported me. She also said that she didn't want us to change. I told her that I loved her very much as well, kissed her softly, and told her that we wouldn't change.

That is a moment I will never forget because I would not

only fail to keep my promise, but I also had no idea what I was getting into. Carlita and I hugged one another and looked into each other's eyes one last time. Many nights when I lay in bed in the cold, damp, quiet solitude of my prison cell, my thoughts went back to that exact moment.

We were quickly brought back into the frenzy when a photographer snapped a shot of the two of us, and then Bob Berg, whom I had appointed my public relations and communications director for the campaign, told me that it was time to start. That moment was truly the beginning of a new life, and the end of the old one.

The second thing I remember is the end of my speech. I don't recall all the details of what I said to the people that day. Even though the speech was carried live on all of the local stations, everyone seems to remember the last part, because it became a legendary Detroit rallying theme.

"We can't wait four or eight more years for things to happen in Detroit," I said. "We can't just sit around and hope the future brings us great things. We need for our future to start RIGHT HERE and RIGHT NOW!" I repeated the question, "When do we want our future to start?" and the crowd responded almost as if we had planned the whole thing.

"RIGHT HERE, RIGHT NOW!" There it was, our campaign theme and rallying cry. Before anyone knew it, we'd planted that phrase throughout the city. You couldn't go anywhere in the Detroit in the summer and fall of 2001 without hearing the phrase "Right Here, Right Now!"

The election was grueling, but it was also the most fun I've ever had. I'd spent my entire life on the West Side of Detroit, and had represented about 90,000 people in my State House district, also on the West Side. When you run for mayor, though, you quickly learn that Detroit is a very large city. It's about 144 square miles, with a population at that time of about 950,000. I don't believe there is any part of that expanse that I didn't stomp through during that campaign. I also strongly believe that I engaged the overwhelming majority of all 950,000 Detroiters.

I was on a mission. I had experienced "campaign mode" be-fore, but never like this. The convergence of focus and commit-ment that led me through FAMU Football, teaching at Marcus Garvey, law school, and Leadership in the Michigan House of Representatives propelled me to new heights. It stretched me mentally, physically, spiritually and emotionally in ways that I didn't know were possible. We worked daily from 6:30 a.m. until well after midnight. Speaking engagements, debates, I was there. If individuals wanted to contribute to the campaign, I was there for the meeting. I refused to be outworked. The news did a poll on mayoral race after the May announcement at my mother's house. I polled at nine percent. By the time the primary election was held that September, I'd garnered fifty percent of the total vote among a field of twelve candidates.

We had an incredible campaign team. Christine ran the day-to-day campaign strategy and oversaw all implementation. She truly managed a great campaign. Alongside Christine was Conrad Mallett, former chief justice of the Michigan Supreme Court, who served as my campaign director. He gave us the sage wisdom and seasoned presence we needed. Bob Berg, my pub-lic relations and communications director, had also worked with Mayor Young for more than fifteen years. He is well known in Detroit media and communications circles, and he really helped me get on the radar in a strong and positive way. Derrick Miller was always there. He didn't have a title, but he worked diligently every day. He brought new people to the campaign, raised money and came up with new concepts and ideas. So many people helped, worked and supported that first campaign that I'd do a disservice to so many by naming some and inadvertently omitting others. I'll simply say that we had the best coalition of citizens, elected officials, business leaders and pastors that I have ever seen. Not only were these individuals well known, they worked hard for the victory.

On Election Day, we campaigned for twenty-four hours. In truth, it was really a forty eight-hour campaign, because we started on Monday afternoon, boarding an RV owned by my good friend, Bobby Ferguson, and making stops at various places throughout the city. I remember visiting work sites, auto plants and post offices. You name it, we hit it. We must have visited 100 places. And we didn't stop when the day shift ended. We fully embraced the youth movement that my campaign had energized, hitting clubs and social venues that night. It was football season, and a lot of clubs promoted Monday Night Football, so we went to those places. Zeke was with us, as were Bobby, my cousin Ajene Evans, my father, my uncle Raymond, and police officers Greg Jones, Mike Martin and Ron Fleming. The Black Slate also held a rally at the Shrine of the Black Madonna that evening. After that, we went to the casinos. The visits continued until Tuesday morning, which was shower time. We headed home, freshened up, and then I headed right back out to the polls to shake hands with the voters.

I was in the zone, barely thinking about anything beyond getting to as many people as possible. Churches. Senior citizen residences. Letting people see my bus. Checking in at headquarters.

The primary election was held on September 11, 2001. After campaigning for a couple of hours at polling sites, we heard the tragic news over the radio about a plane crashing into the World Trade Center. While heading to another poll to press the flesh, we heard more breaking news. Another plane had just slammed into another tower of the complex. We immediately went back to the headquarters, walked through the HQ doors, and stopped in our tracks as dozens of campaign workers huddled in front of several televisions scattered across the large room. People were crying, hugging one another, sitting on the floor and screaming for answers. The central hub that had produced so much energy and excitement for our campaign was suddenly gravely quiet and still. I gathered everyone in the large, open room. We hugged, held hands, and then we prayed.

I commend Dennis Archer for announcing soon after that the voting would continue and the election would continue on as planned. I believe then, and still do today, that there is no greater right that can be bestowed on a people by its own government than the right to your choice for your community's leadership, exercised by your right to vote. In the midst of one of our country's greatest tragedies, Equality Day, Election Day, marched on.

The atmosphere was festive, and victory was in the air. Everyone went to the Renaissance Center, where we had planned to wrap the campaign and wait for the results. In our hotel suite, family and friends buzzed with excitement. Ultimately, it didn't take long before we learned that we'd not only won, but we'd spent the day steadily inching away from my opponent. I took fifty-four percent of the vote to Gil Hill's forty-six percent. I was Mayor-Elect for the City of Detroit!

I had a lot of time to myself on election night, and several instances come to mind. One was shock and amazement over the fact that we had just won. Although it was expected, hearing the words, "You won" was a bit much. I had a huge suite at the Marriott Hotel in the Renaissance Center, in downtown Detroit. I sat on the bed with no one around, and took inventory of the moment.

"I'm actually the Mayor of Detroit?" I remember thinking. "This is *crazy.*" Christine and Derrick came in the room soon after, and we had a group hug. They looked just as shocked as I felt.

"We did some crazy stuff, didn't we?" I said. At thirty-one, all of us, we truly had.

I was nervous and overwhelmed with the responsibility, even though it would be nearly two more months before I'd actually start the job. When I review the footage of that night, my nervousness is visible, at least to me. Christine and Derrick? Same thing. I had no idea what I was really getting into, or how bright the spotlight would be. At that point, the inner workings of City government were foreign to me. And yet, the job was mine. The people had spoken, and it became apparent that I would soon have to bust my butt in order to be an effective leader. The stress was immediate.

The second instance I remember occurred just as we prepared to head downstairs and join the victory celebration. My mother came into the suite and said, "Can I talk to you, Son?" She took me into the bedroom to talk privately. She closed the door and said something to me that I'll never forget.

"Leadership is a very lonely position," she said. "The higher you go, Son, the fewer friends you're going to have. Remember this. It might sound harsh, but I want you to understand. Right now, while you have this position, you have all the friends you're ever going to have. And you're going to lose some of them."

I said, "Ma, nah, it'll be okay. We're going to be cool."

"Listen to me," she said. "You've got all the friends you're going to have—not all the *acquaintances*, but all the *friends*—right now." It would be one of the most profound things anyone would ever say to me. In those few words, she emphasized the loneliness, the realization that the buck stopped with me, and even the sense of alienation that the position creates.

chapter 8

No "I"

FOLLOWING THE election, we began putting together a transition committee, in which one side deals with the nuts and bolts of working City government while an inaugural committee deals with the actual swearing in of the new official.

I wanted to incorporate young people on both sides of the transition and make Detroit hot again, and to do that, we needed a different kind of spirit and energy. There were bad things happening. The economy was down. No one wanted to come to the city. The police department was in bad shape, and was under a federal investigation. The issues that needed to be tackled on the City side were typical governmental concerns, but the inaugural gave us a chance to send a positive message.

We brought in Detroit's biggest promoters to help organize the inaugural events. These weren't just typical event planners, but folks who kept Detroit's nightlife alive. We placed club owners on the committee, making it clear that we wanted to include the distinctly different parts of Detroit's community. The committee became a mix of traditionalists, celebrity hairstylists (hair shows were huge in Detroit at the time) and party promoters. Local stalwarts like Rufus Bartell and Moe Blackwell collaborated with municipal pillars like Tene Ramsey. The idea of community inaugurations was born out of this effort.

The swearing-in ceremony took place at the Fox Theater, instead of City Hall or in a judge's chamber, and we packed the

house. The room was full of City officials and employees, surrounded by people from the very neighborhoods they served. It
was an incredible sight. Judges Damon Keith and Conrad Mallett
led my oath of office. I remember my wife and my two boys
standing next to me. And I felt so full because once you take the
oath, you speak. Stepping to the podium, I looked out and saw my
mother and father, and how proud they were. They were crying.
Ayanna was crying. The city seemed so proud, and in that moment, it felt like we—Detroit—could do this. It took everything
in me to keep the floodgates from bursting open. I also felt like
we had to do this, like I had to make things happen for the city.

I then attended five different *community* inaugurations, which
gave people who couldn't get in the Fox an opportunity to be a
part of the inauguration. We went to Southwest Detroit, the hav-
en for the city's Latin and Hispanic community; to Northwestern
High School, near my mother's neighborhood; and to the East
Side of town, where most of the city's Southern immigrants settled. The venues in those areas were all packed, as well. We then
held a large inaugural for senior citizens.

Carlita got involved with the inauguration as well, coming
up with a great idea for a children's inaugural event. She spear-
headed it, and it was excellent. It took place at Cobo Hall, where
games and other activities for kids were available. We capped the
events with a nighttime club crawl to celebrate the *hotness* of the
city. We went to a house music club, back to the Southwest Side,
and to a few well-known bars. The night ended at the Charles H.
Wright Museum of African-American History. Bands performed,
and the legendary hip-hop artist Biz Markie DJ'd a party. The inauguration was revolutionary and innovative, and it pulled people
together.

The press trailed us during the entire evening in a bus that
we provided, documenting the events and capturing the energy
around town. It was good, although immediately afterward, the
news reports were critical, essentially saying, *Kilpatrick needs to
stop partying and get to work.* Well, the work was on its way. In
fact, it started with the inauguration and transition to office, so

the press needn't have worried. I was on my way to work, to the highest stress level of my life, and to a ballooned weight of 318 pounds, to boot!

I've been through hell in my life, and yet I've never felt as bad as I did during my first two years as mayor of the City of Detroit. Physically, mentally and spiritually, I was drained. My only encouragement came from the belief that I was doing what God wanted me to do.

My pastor at the time was Edgar Vann. He transformed a small church, the Second Ebenezer Baptist Church, into one of Detroit's most influential and largest congregations. He also built a good reputation around town in business and political circles. He was even the Chairman of the Baptist Pastor's Council in Detroit. The Council had once been a political force in the city, led by many Detroit legends like Reverend C.L. Franklin, Reverend Dr. Fredrick G. Sampson and Reverend Dr. Charles Adams. These men personified the transitioning role of the African-American pastor in our community. They were incredibly erudite community activists and also strong supporters of African-American leadership. When they spoke, everyone listened.

Reverend Vann was a transitional leader for the Baptist Pastor's Council because they had started to lose a lot of their clout in the community. He was appointed as leader to propel the political sway of the Council back the forefront of Detroit politics and connect with new views. Detroit's new generation didn't have a monolithic focus on race and politics. They were all over the place. The new Detroiter was more independent, instead of interdependent, and more individualistic in focus, as opposed to working from a purely community perspective.

Detroiters were moving into communities that had protested their presence just a decade before. Expanding ideas, creativity and multiple perspectives on issues created a new and vibrant culture in the city. On the negative side, Detroiters grew more and more self-serving, individualistic and open to being misled by those who didn't have the community's best interests at heart.

Reverend Vann increased the Council's relevance and political sway. He improved business relationships, organizational relationships and once again made the Baptist Pastor's Council a strong political voice in the city.

Shortly after stepping down from the presidency of that organization, Reverend Vann vigorously campaigned for me to be the City's sixtieth mayor. Unfortunately, he never stopped campaigning, even after I won. Our pastor/parishioner relationship had been destroyed in the throes of the campaign. And when I really needed my pastor, even when Reverend Vann was in the room, he was not there. He enjoyed the spotlight and the swagger he'd garnered. I was drying up spiritually and felt that I couldn't reach out to him. I felt alone and completely vulnerable. At a time when ninety-five percent of the people who approached me wanted something from me, most of our conversations were about community development and politics instead of what I really needed— a spiritual connection. But I was slowly and insidiously falling into neglect and avoidance of any real connection with God. And I would soon believe that the job was all that mattered.

Photo: Andre Smith

Hip-Hop Summit: Dr. Benjamin Chavis, Eminem, me and Nas. Get Out The Vote
Summit where Russell Simmons proclaimed me as "America's Hip-Hop Mayor."
The next day the media aggressively asked me to denounce the title. When I
wouldn't, they created and circulated "rumored" or "alleged" stories about me in
the company of strippers, excessively partying and even being late for meetings.
Of course none of it was true.

Photo: Andre Smith

**Me and Ernie
Harwell, the
legendary voice
of the Detroit
Tigers.** Many
of my favorite
childhood memo-
ries are of sitting
with my paternal
grandfather on a
hot summer day,
and listening to
Ernie calling the
Tigers game over
the radio.

Photo: Andre Smith

Ceremonial First Pitch. I threw the ceremonial first pitch at the opener of the Tigers baseball season. Jelani and Jalil also threw out the first pitch on different occasions as well.

Me and Detroit native Reverand Michael Eric Dyson. Dyson is off the hook! Good Brother.

Photo: Andre Smith

Tavis Smiley, Vivica A. Fox, Carlita and me. Get Out The Vote Rally in Detroit (2005).

Taking care of my senior citizens. I love senior citizens, and they always love me back. I always won the Senior Citizen Voting Block. We owe them so much for their struggle, sacrifice & courage.

Swearing-In: Fox Theater (2002). First day on the job. I had no idea what I was getting into!

The Late Edward McNamara speaking at my Mayoral Campaign Announcement (2001). He was a strong supporter, and a legendary political figure in Michigan.

Photo: Andre Smith

Carlita and KMK at my Mayoral campaign announcement (2001). Carlita and I in our final moments of life as we knew it. That moment was one of the most powerful moments of my life.

Photo: Andre Smith

Dave Bing, *above right* speaking on my behalf at my Mayoral Campaign Announcement (2001). He was a supporter from Day One.

Hosting Diahann Carroll and Dorothy I. Height at my home.

Presenting Detroit native and Superbowl XL champion Jerome Bettis with the Key to the City.

Photo: Andre Smith

Photo: Andre Smith

Roger Penske and me. I learned a lot from Roger. I have never met a more focused person in my life.

Annual State of the City Address at Detroit's Orchestra Hall. These annual speeches were carried live on network T.V., and became huge unprecedented events in Detroit.

Carlita, Lebron & me at the Palace (2004). A year later Lebron would put on his best playoff performance against the Pistons. After winning the series, I went back to the locker-room area and congratulated him. The Detroit Press called me a traitor.

NBA World Champion Detroit Piston Parade and Rally—downtown Detroit. You can never underestimate the incredible positive energy that invades a community after a championship. The Pistons and Red Wings had lifted Detroiter's spirits as we faced incredible daunting days.

Me and Freman Hendrix *(below)* in the second of our third televised Mayoral debates. These debates began to accelerate his undoing, and ultimate defeat.

DRAL DEBATE WAYNE STATE UNIVERSITY
LIVE FROM

Division 2005

Photo: Andre Smith

Me and Dallas Cowboy owner Jerry Jones *(above).* I had great conversations with Jerry while preparing for Superbowl XL in Detroit, and even during Superbowl week. His passion and energy is infectious.

Photo: Andre Smith

Ella Bully-Cummings being appointed to be the first woman to be Chief of Police in Detroit's history.

Reverend Jesse Jackson, Willis Edwards and me praying over the remains of Civil Rights Pioneer Rosa Parks. I was at her bedside soon after she passed away, and also had the humbling experience of saying thank you to her several times, while she lived.

Offering words on behalf of the City of Detroit at Rosa Park's funeral.

Victory 2005! Shocked and shook-up the establishment, We really pissed a lot of people off.

Me and Pete Karmanos at the Hard Rock Café opening in Downtown Detroit. Pete says what he means, and means what he says. He is a great guy, and an amazing business leader.

President Clinton and me. I had the opportunity to meet with President Clinton several times, including in the Oval office and aboard Air Force One.

Carlita, me and Russell Simmons. We registered over 3,000 voters at this summit, but the only news was that Russell called me the "Hip Hop Mayor," and how very negative that title was.

Photo: Andre Smith

At an Auto Show event in Detroit are Carlita, me, Detroit native recording artist Kem, and former NBA player John Sally and his wife.

Photo: Andre Smith

Detroit Pastors praying for me during one of our Inauguration events. It's been only God that has kept me.

Me and Minister Farrakhan. The title of this book comes from the words that he spoke to me.

My Pops and me. The second most misunderstood man in Detroit. He served in Public life, without a hint of impropriety for more than twenty years. He helped hundreds of people throughout our community.

LAW School GRAD

At the All-American Football Banquet in Baltimore, MD (1993).

Me after my law school graduation. Got it done, headed to master the Michigan Bar Examination.

Addressing the Democratic National Convention in Los Angeles at the Staples Center (2000). I also delivered a speech in 2004 at the Democratic National Convention held in Boston.

FAMU Rattlers Football.
Big Fella pulling around
the corner, on my way to
the All-American Trophy.

Me and my Mom in DC. My mom is the absolute epitome of a public servant. I have never seen anyone do it better. She didn't miss parent/teacher conferences, and made sure that our school-work was done. My Mom is simply an amazing woman!

The "Original Family": Mom, Dad, me and Ayanna (Christmas 1977). I was clean, even at seven years old.

(Below) **Ayanna, me, Diarra and Pop** at one of my annual Mayoral fundraisers.

Commitment! I purchased more new equipment, vehicles and technology for police officers and firefighters than any Mayor in the history of the City of Detroit. I also built several new facilities, precincts and communication centers for Detroit residents.

Our administration's Mayor's Time Initiative provided thousands of Detroit children with a variety of skilled program training and academic and social programs.

chapter 9
Hell and High Water

SOON, I was working from 8 a.m. until 2 a.m., daily. I made it a point to show up at every crime scene, every fire. If snow needed to be shoveled, I was at the Russell Ferry garage, making sure the trucks got out. I was killing myself. *We're not going to* not *shovel on my watch.* That was my thinking. I took things very personally, and it beat me down.

It also put an incredible strain on my marriage, and on Carlita. I was horrible, because my life became about the entire city. There was no room for God and no room for marriage. I didn't even create a space for my boys. It was like when the Lord made David a king and, faithful as David was, he allowed the throne to consume him. Everything came second to Detroit.

We've gotta get the parks built, 'cause they said we can't do it. We've gotta get the city cleaned for the Super Bowl. We've gotta build a recreation center. We've gotta manage this budget. Nobody thinks this young guy can manage a budget. You all need to stay overnight so we can do this.

I'd keep people in cabinet meetings until midnight. We'd order in food. Fishbone's restaurant handled several evening orders from us, because we were determined to stay until we solved every problem. And Lord, were there ever problems to be solved!

Municipal Parking was the only department that ran well when we arrived at the Mayor's office in January 2002. Much to the chagrin of many Detroiters and visitors, we wrote parking tickets in an amazingly effective and efficient manner. But that was the only thing we did well. Every other department was extremely dysfunctional, from Human Services to Human Resources and from Planning and Development to Recreation. The Water and Housing departments suffered, as well.

For example, one day in early March 2002, I was sitting in my office and opening a few pieces of mail. One of the letters was from the U.S. Housing and Urban Development Dept. (HUD). The letter wasn't rushed to me, or even given a high priority. It was just one of the things I needed to see. The letter referenced the previous six correspondences, over a six-year period, that had been sent to the mayor's office regarding issues the department was having with the City about our lack of communication about an $18 million low- and mixed-income housing grant that had been given to the City in 1996. HUD wanted a detailed report on how the City was planning to spend the money, along with our progress to date.

The letter also stated that this request had gone unanswered since 1998 and, due to the lack of communication, failure to submit a plan and the competition for these much-needed dollars around the country, we were to send our complete, detailed plan for our execution of the Hope 6 grant project, or return the funds within ten days.

As I read the letter, I realized I only had six days to solve the problem. This is how it always was in the beginning—one emergency after another. The City was going to lose $18 million of low-income housing money in six days if I didn't do something. So, I started making phone calls. First, I contacted our Detroit Housing Department, which was an organizational and financial nightmare. There were so many problems with that department, it needs its own book. Of course, during my urgent calls, I discovered that the City had indeed received the previous six letters from HUD, and did not respond. And we also had no plan for spending the money. No progress. Actually, I was really not surprised.

Next, I called Washington, D.C., to speak to Michael Liu,

who had sent the correspondence. As HUD's assistant secretary, responsible for our region of the country, he discussed the continuing frustration that the department had with the City. He'd given Detroit too many chances in the past. He apologized and told me that there was nothing that he could do, and that I should prepare to return the money or send a detailed plan within three days. I knew it would be impossible to send a detailed plan within that time frame, and after all the negative dealings that preceded me, I didn't want to send him unprofessional junk. And I damn sure wasn't sending the money back to HUD, so that was when I activated Plan C, which didn't exist yet. But I believed it would materialize.

And it did. The State Republican Party was holding a fundraiser in the Detroit metro area, and the keynote speaker for the event was President George W. Bush. I learned that he would be arriving in Detroit the following evening.

"Great!" I thought. "I'll have two days to save our money." I called my mother's congressional office, and we jointly worked on some credentials for me to meet the President at the airport when he exited Air Force One. He was set to arrive at 5 p.m. We got the approval in my office at about 3 p.m.

We raced down I-94 to Willow Run Airport. When we arrived, I was shocked at the size of the crowd. It was a very small, yet powerfully important group of people, at least to the Republican Party. All of the State's big-time Republicans were there. Big donors like Governor John Engler, Senator Spencer Abraham, and more of their peers.

Not so surprisingly, I was the only African-American in the bunch. You know the scene in movies when the black guy walks into the wrong party and the music screeches to a halt and everyone stares? That's exactly what happened, but without the music. I'm certain whiplash cases at the local hospital spiked that evening. I was also the only Democrat present. Because of this very odd combination of diversity that I brought to the mix, I was moved to the front of the receiving line, just behind Governor Engler. It was a perfect spot. When the President came down the steps, with the usual applause and small band playing "Hail to the Chief," all I was thinking about was saving my $18 million.

The President shook the Governor's hand, and then he immediately grabbed mine and said, "Hey, Mayor, how ya doing?"

"I'm just fine, Mr. President," I said, "but I do have one problem."

"What is it?" he replied. I truly thank God that this episode happened before Hurricane Katrina, Afghanistan, the housing market crashes and Wall Street pimpin'. Or before we learned of the dramatic fallout of the No Child Left Behind law and its continuing effects on public education.

"Mr. President," I said, "I have been mayor for less than three months, and HUD is attempting to take $18 million of much-needed low-income housing money from my city in two days. I really need some help from you to stop this from happening."

He immediately turned to a staffer and said, "Hook the Mayor up with Mel, ASAP." I thanked the President, and he moved on with the rest of his greetings. I stepped out of the long receiving line and huddled with his staffer. I gave him all of my contact information, and he gave me his. I then sought the nearest escape route before the President made some brief remarks.

I raced back to the office and, upon walking in, my secretary told me that I had just received a call from HUD Secretary Mel Martinez, and that he would like me to call him back ASAP. *Wow, the President works fast!* I quickly entered my office and called him. I told him about my problem in greater detail, and he listened carefully. He and I agreed on a date for me to go to Washington and meet with the department about an overall strategy to move forward in a positive relationship. He also agreed that we should disregard the previous letter and that no money would be taken from the City.

One month later, I flew to Washington, having saved $18 million. I met with Deputy HUD Secretary Alphonso Jackson and Asst. Secretary Liu. Liu was much more supportive and kind, as was Deputy Secretary Jackson, who was extremely supportive, encouraging and knowledgeable about the inner workings of government. President Bush later appointed him to HUD's top spot, and he remained very supportive throughout my time as mayor.

That wasn't the only time that President Bush helped get the City out of a bad situation involving federal departments and/ or federal dollars. It's funny, with all of the disagreements that I had with him and his administration on policy, politics and overall organizational strategy, he and his administration always helped when we called.

One problem solved, tons more to consider. The city was notorious for a couple of other things at that time. For one, more people died while in confinement in Detroit than in any other city in the county. Police officers would arrest people, put them in the city lockup, and they would die from suicide, stroke, and all kinds of reasons. It was a big issue. The Detroit Police Department was known throughout the land for using deadly force against its citizens. Police officers argued that they were bound in perform- ing their duties because they had few options to the use of tertiary force. They claimed that they either had to use mace or guns in difficult situations, and there was nothing in between. *Mace won't stop a crackhead.* I heard that argument several times.

Mayor Archer threw up his hands and called in the federal government. Without informing the Police Chief, he asked the Feds to take over the police force. This happened just before I was elected, and it was a live issue when I entered office. Detroit had a reputation of being the city where people got jacked, robbed and killed. And the Super Bowl was coming. The big thing for me was to get a handle on safety, to appoint a chief who had a national reputation and could start to hammer down the consent decree that the federal government had issued to the police department. I wanted to send the message that Detroit was becoming a safer place, so I conducted a national search and hired Jerry Oliver, who was then the chief of police in Richmond, Virginia.

Police officers rebelled against the new chief's leadership right away. I received several written threats to ruin my career.

Looking back on it, I guess they were more like promises than threats. But I stood by my decision, and to this day, I believe it was the right one. Ella Bully-Cummings, whom I appointed to succeed Jerry, was better received, because she came in and implemented many of the things he had begun to put in place. But they didn't like Jerry. Detroit has always had a closed culture, especially the police department. The police department was well on its way to becoming the bane of my existence as mayor.

When Jerry arrived, he decided that the best way to attack the deeply embedded negative culture of the police department was to completely change the organizational leadership structure, and to re-assign all of the people sitting in those positions. Many in the DPD saw this as an official declaration of war on the department. Lines were drawn, clearly defined battle groups started to form, and the enemies, Jerry Oliver and Kwame Kilpatrick, were clearly identified.

Jerry assembled an eleven-person team of deputy chiefs who helped him manage the day-to-day aspects of each division and section of the department. He developed a process that included oral and written examinations, and a personal interview with him. I made a decision very early in the transition period that I was not going to be involved in leadership's personnel decisions within the police department. Big mistake! Note to future mayors: vigorously and tenaciously study your police department! Understand the financial, business and operational elements of the entire force. And for God's sake, get to know the leadership before you hire them! I did take that advice later in my administration, and accomplished great things in law enforcement, such as grant writing, efforts for Homeland Security and overall police operational strategy. But I went through hell first. You live and learn.

Chief Oliver presented me with the list of names of those he wanted to see in the deputy chief positions. I didn't have a problem with any of them. Hell, I didn't even know them, for the most part. But one name in particular did stand out, and that was Gary Brown, in the leadership position at Internal Affairs.

I didn't know Gary Brown, but during the transition period, I received many negative comments about him. He was called "a snake" who shouldn't be trusted. Everyone acknowledged that he was smart, savvy and smooth, but they said that all of those qualities were most often used for deceitful activities.

I shook off the discussions because I wanted to give everyone an opportunity to present themselves. I didn't want anyone to be hampered or handicapped by rumor, speculation and innuendo. But I did not know enough to understand that the director of Internal Affairs is a very important position. The person in that position must understand confidentiality and trust. He must have the integrity to be sure and certain about an investigation, lest he recklessly pursue a brother officer. Also, considering the Department of Justice investigation, that person was the link between the City, our department and the federal government.

My immediate response to Jerry Oliver's list of eleven recommended individuals was "yes" to ten, but "no" on Gary Brown. I actually said, "Hell naw, not this guy," I explained that I had heard some bad things about him, and that he couldn't be trusted in that position.

"I really need him there," Jerry said. He said Brown would be helpful in dealing with the department of Justice. Now, my gut instinct has never failed me, but I've failed it plenty. And this time, I made a terrible decision. I told him to give me some time to think about it. After a week, I decided to approve Brown for the position. I made the decision to support Jerry. I'd brought Jerry to Detroit to help create positive and revolutionary change in the department, and I wanted to do whatever I could to support him in that effort. I trusted his experience and expertise in law enforcement. He was strong, committed and engaged. I appreciated his tenacity and focus, and I felt that it was time for me to stop stalling and allow him to continue to push forward.

I've often heard that the road to hell is paved with good intentions. I truly meant well, but this was really a bad decision. I approved Brown as the deputy chief over Internal Affairs, and when the rest of the team was announced, I received a call from

Benny Napoleon. Benny was a former Detroit police chief under Mayor Archer, and he is the current Wayne County Sheriff.

"You're making a big mistake," Benny said. "Don't put that guy there." He implored me, saying Brown was not the guy I needed to put in that position. I told Benny that I appreciated his advice, but I was loyal to Jerry. I've told Benny that he was absolutely correct several times over the years. Gary Brown is smart, and Jerry liked academically smart guys who can articulate law enforcement across a plethora of subjects. A lot of Detroiters are *street* smart. They come up a different way. They don't go before people and make presentations in a way that would please academia. Instead, they do it from a community perspective, in a way that makes others feel protected and secure.

There was a transition occurring in police work during this time, and it involved an influx of policemen as executives who had the demeanor that Jerry favored. It was a movement that was going on across the country, and it touted a new, "model" police chief. They were becoming more prevalent, especially in cities with high crime. Jerry was one of those guys. He was like Charles Ramsey in D.C., and Richard Pennington in New Orleans, and later Atlanta. They were counterculture, press conference guys. The movement started with William Bratton, who was New York's police chief before moving to Los Angeles. They represent the new pattern of a chief. You wear a suit, only wearing your uniform when attending official events.

It was the new thing, but it was the right thing. Jerry had the newspapers' confidence. He was able to raise money for police activities. He had different ideas about how to get support for the police department. He had tests to put people in positions that were based on merit, and not favoritism. But he kicked out the old-boy network.

With Jerry in place, we came up with a campaign named "Kids. Cops. Clean." Zeke, Christine, Carlita, Jerry and I sat down together and decided on this idea. We involved many creative minds in the project because we figured if we could get people more involved in helping clean up Detroit, we could make it a safer city, develop some activities for kids, and move the city farther than it had ever gone before.

The community embraced the idea. The first citywide cleanup we did, the Motor City Makeover, attracted 60,000 volunteers. City residents had gotten involved with the "Clean Sweep" project before my time in office, where they swept around their streets. But we thought, "Let's really give the city a makeover. We're getting abandoned cars off the street. We're doing demolitions, painting, and getting companies to support us." The initiative did more to clean the city in those first two years than anything that had been done in the past twenty. We cleaned vacant lots. We painted. We paved city streets. In fact, we would end up paving and resurfacing more streets in my first four years than had been done in the previous thirty years.

We were goal-oriented. I had decided that by the time Super Bowl XL got to Detroit, we were going to clean that sucker up. *This is going to look like a different place.* That was our opportunity to reintroduce ourselves to the world. So let's take four years to shine this bad boy (no pun intended) up as much as we possibly can.

We dangled the Super Bowl for constant public discussion. A popular response I'd get was that people didn't care about football. But I'd say, "Listen, you don't even have to like the sport *or* the Super Bowl. But *the world* is coming to your house! And they'll take away an *opinion* about Detroit that would last a generation."

Fortunately, we got people to buy into that argument, even City workers. They got things going, and they started early. By 2004, Detroit's crime statistics reached its lowest point since 1963. It had decreased consistently from the time we started, three years earlier. We rebuilt and redesigned thirty-seven parks in my first two years, complete with new playground equipment and a grass-cutting cycle to ensure it was cut in regular intervals. If that seems like a small thing to you, imagine what your child may come across while playing in a field in a large city, where the grass has grown a mere six inches taller than normal. Food. Cans. Dirty syringes. Animal waste. Sound more serious now? This is

what "Kids. Cops. Clean." was all about, seeing the vision for
people with short sight. Word on the street was that Kilpatrick, if
nothing else, was going to cut the grass.

The operational improvements that we made in our general
and overall maintenance program became our normal practice.
We were doing things on a regular basis that hadn't been done
in Detroit in more than a generation. The maintenance plan we
established for the city's roads resulted in consistent work over
a sustained period of time. People started calling my office to
complain that we were fixing roads *too much*, that there was always a construction project afoot. That was a great compliment, I
thought. We'd come out like gangbusters, and people were taking
notice.

Unfortunately, Jerry wouldn't last long enough to see the
"Cops" part of "Kids. Cops. Clean." through. While traveling on
official business in 2003, he packed a loaded gun into his luggage.
It was not his police-issued weapon. Of course, this was against
the law and the Detroit Police Department's rules. He was actually given a chance to remove the weapon from his bag before
takeoff, but he chose not to do it. The TSA recovered the gun
and immediately sought to arrest Chief Oliver.

The incident quickly became a fierce and aggressive media
story. The Detroit police unions and several officers called for his
resignation, or for me to fire him. The major issue was that Jerry
had suspended and fired officers for much less. He was a strong
advocate of a "zero tolerance" attitude toward police discipline.
He believed that one way to fix crime was to build trust in our police department, and the only way he saw to do this was to assure
confidence in our officers. So he'd harshly punished officers for
minor and major offenses. The unions, then, were vehemently
opposed to him and his style. This was the break they needed, and
they launched a campaign through the media, the police department and the community to get me to fire him.

I went to Jerry's home to speak with him and his wife, Felicia.
We discussed the circumstances and the next steps. I was willing
to support him and keep him on as chief. I did, however, need

him to truthfully tell me whether he believed he could still garner the community support and the confidence from his troops in the Detroit Police Department in order to lead them. After a few hours, Jerry decided that it would be best for him to step down. He, Felicia and their three children relocated back to his home in Arizona. I then changed the game again by appointing the first woman police chief in Detroit's history, Ella Bully-Cummings.

I've been asked if I consider any of our accomplishments during those first few years to be paramount, and I really don't. I do believe, however, that we achieved each of our three goal areas. We did a better job of protecting our children, we made Detroit safer and we cleaned up the town. The city had a new vibe.

By 2003, we were able to turn our attention toward economic development. We finalized the deals for three permanent land-based casinos in Detroit: MGM, Greektown, and Motor City (majority-owned at that time by Mandalay Bay) casinos. The casino activity had been stagnant since 1999. Part of the impasse was the desire to build the three gaming houses on the city's riverfront. We successfully changed that plan.

There's some behind-the-scenes history to note here. The three casinos had given the City of Detroit $50 million apiece—$150 million total—to buy land on the Riverfront on which to build their permanent locations. That was during Dennis Archer's time in office. Beth Duncumbe, Archer's sister-in-law, headed this project from her position as president of the Detroit Economic Growth Corporation. The DEGC is a quasi-public entity that spearheads a great deal of development for downtown projects. The leader is essentially hired by the mayor.

The DEGC spent nearly $120 million on twenty-five acres of land on Detroit's riverfront. That was it! It was the highest price for land ever paid in the history of the city. If I were still mayor, I'd probably be facing charges for that. Hell, General Motors bought the entire Renaissance Center development, including a hotel, for less than $80 million. The deafening silence around this mess was eerie. The DEGC carried out several disastrous and seemingly shady deals during that period. But hey, Kwame Kilpatrick wasn't involved, so it wasn't interesting.

By the time I arrived, there wasn't enough land to build one casino. The City had condemned some riverfront properties where businesses were still running, and a lawsuit hovered over this. This land-buying plan killed a thriving, growing riverfront business district. Some of the bar and restaurant owners in the area joined together and filed a suit against the City. On top of that, the casinos sued to get back their $150 million. The suit basically demanded either their land, or their money. To boot, the casinos no longer wanted to build permanent sites, because they were making so much money in their temporary spots. MGM had built theirs just off the Lodge/US-10 Expressway. Greektown had plopped down in Greektown, downtown, next to I-75. And Motor City had completely renovated the old Wagner Baking Company, where Wonder Bread was once made, on Grand River Avenue. As we say in the street, they were *straight*. For us, though, it meant that the City of Detroit needed to accomplish several things:

- resolve the issues with Riverfront landowners in order to get ownership and control of the land for future development,
- resolve the outstanding debt of $150 million to the three casino operators, and wisely spend the remaining dollars from the initial loan; and
- re-engage the casinos in discussions to move forward and build their multi-hundred-million-dollar permanent facilities.

This strategy required an incredible amount of skill, timing and pure *game*. Straight up, Detroit, West Side, ol'-school *game*. And I was just the man for the job. It took three phases, which had to occur nearly simultaneously, and with excellent execution. First, I assigned my Corporation Counsel, Ruth Carter, and my chief development officer, Walter Watkins, the task of settling all the claims of the Riverfront landowners. This included three cement companies, complete with their own silos. We also used a couple of private sector attorneys to help with this effort. The team did a great job, and their work alone became a historic project for Detroit.

Ruth Carter, now a sitting district court judge in Detroit, had been a prosecutor for many years. She was incredibly tough, but she always made you feel warm and comfortable even as she was kicking your ass. She was also hilarious, She always had a quick quip or witty comeback. And when it was time for business, she could focus and get great results.

Walt Watkins was the immediate past president of Bank One (which later became Chase Bank). He was a thirty-year veteran in the banking business, with deep ties to the development and general business communities. He was incredibly smart, focused, organized and savvy. And he was a fun guy also. Every now and then, that old Omega Psi Phi would jump out of him.

Ruth and Walt engaged the plaintiff's attorney, Al Ackerman, a longtime Detroit property and condemnation lawyer, and hammered out a deal that benefited the displaced Riverfront owners. The deal also moved Detroit's Riverfront development efforts forward, along with our overall downtown development plans. Especially exciting was the opportunity to plan and develop residential units along the waterfront.

Next, we tackled the cement silos. The City couldn't give the casinos the land because the $150 million was supposed to buy the cement companies, so the silos could be removed. Nearly $120 million had already been spent, and not one of the three cement silos had been purchased. Negotiations had taken place, but the City never bought anything from them. It was an all-talk/no-action situation. We somehow managed to buy them out with the $25 million we had left, *and* build them a new facility elsewhere.

The casinos' demands for their $150 million launched the third phase of our strategy. We met with them and offered some straight talk. Essentially, the several meetings that we held in both Detroit and Las Vegas merely echoed my position from the start. I made my argument clear. "You need to just write off that money," I said. "You're making $1 million a day. You're smashing records. And you don't want to be perceived in the City of Detroit as these monsters who are not good corporate citizens. You gave that money to us, essentially. It was squandered by the last administration, but you gave it to us. Let it go. And by the way, I need a little more money from you."

So, not only did I want them to forgive the $150 million debt and let us keep the land that we purchased with their money, I wanted some additional money. What a compromise, right? But at the end of the day, we got additional money from the casinos. We'd been getting nine percent of the gross receipts. I added two percent more for Parks and Recreation, and for the police. Because of the addition of a dedicated funding source from the casinos, we were able to build several new police buildings, purchase much-needed state-of-the-art equipment for police officers and build three new recreation centers for our senior citizens and children. These were the first new rec centers to be built in the city in more than twenty years.

We did a great job with that casino deal. In 2008 alone, the City got $190 million from that deal. In total, it was a $300 million switch. The City of Detroit owed the casinos $150 million. I negotiated us out of that debt, and then got $150 million. We negotiated agreements for permanent casinos. The only reason the City is surviving right now is because of that deal. Without it, Detroit would be bankrupt and in receivership.

We pulled off that third phase because I personally flew to Las Vegas, sat in the meeting and negotiated it myself. I did it without the lawyers. I always have hesitate to say how much I did, because I respect my team. But I took this negotiation personally. I was involved in every part of the strategy. I made sure that I stayed abreast of every detail in each part of this highly involved process. However, I saw the negotiations with the three casino operators a little differently. I truly believed that a positive result from these talks would be the catalyst to a new Detroit, and I was not going to come up short. So, I started attending all the meetings to be in on the negotiations. I stayed for as long as it took, unless it was better strategy to get up and walk out. You know, for effect.

In the last days of the negotiations at the Bellagio Hotel in Las Vegas, all of us—MGM, Motor City, Greektown and the City of Detroit—shared the same determination, and decided we would not leave Vegas without a deal.

I knew the deal was the fastest way to jumpstart development in the city in a way we hadn't seen before. It would put carpenters, electricians and laborers to work immediately. The result? Each entity built a mega casino and entertainment complex. Each spent well over $200 million. And MGM spent more than $400 million on its facility alone. Thousands of jobs were created for Detroiters. And we worked into the deal an agreement that fifty-five percent of the labor force had to be Detroiters. If you walk into any one of the casinos right now, you'll see brothers and sisters and other Detroit residents working there. That's the beautiful thing about it.

We knew we *had* to close that deal. That was the key to everything else. Having that kind of construction going on in Detroit also spurred construction on the Riverfront, because we'd cleared that land. Those silos had become an albatross around the neck of the city skyline. While other big cities had turned their Riverfronts into havens for residential and business development, Detroit's had, for too long, been dotted with abandoned warehouses and those terrible cement silos.

The casino development also ignited conversation about downtown development in general, both locally and nationally. The restaurants. The shops. It opened the door to build the Hard Rock Café. It even created the developmental energy that made the West Side Home Depot, on 7 Mile Road and Meyers Avenue, possible.

We were able to finish building Campus Martius, an area in the middle of downtown Detroit that boasts a concert pavilion with a stage that rises from underground. The Campus's lawn converts to an ice skating rink in the winter. Detroit 300, the City's tricentennial planning commission, had a plan for Campus

Martius that had been submitted to the Archer administration. But it hadn't moved by the time we came in. We drew the plan anew and re-engineered it. With the changed focus, we got it done. And it was possible because of the incredible energy created by our successful focus on basic City services and the casino deal.

The chain reaction continued with the news that Detroit would bring in hotels with showplaces. When Walt Watkins brought John Ferchill, a tough-talking, get-it-done developer out of Cleveland, to the table, and built the Hilton Garden Inn in Harmonie Park, downtown, we approached him and said, "Hey, why don't you take a look at the Book Cadillac?" This was an old downtown relic on Washington Avenue that was simply too expensive for most to fix, but too beautiful and historic to demolish. It had stood abandoned since 1984. The roof was open, exposing the building to the elements. That meant it had spent twenty years collecting rain and debris within its walls.

This all changed the energy downtown. General Motors remained a huge partner for my administration, but the new energy, new deals, restaurants, nightclubs, lofts and office towers began to divert the crux of Detroit's economic discussions away from the auto industry. Of course, the autos reclaimed that conversation years later when the economy went into decline, but I knew *then* that Detroit needed to get away from the auto industry as our "calling card," because it's a cyclical business. I never knew it would get as bad as it did, but we did figure it would encounter trouble. It always does. And because of the City's heavy reliance on it, when the automotive manufacturing industry catches a cold, Detroit catches pneumonia.

The signs had begun to show by 2002, and I said in what felt like 100 speeches that Detroit couldn't depend on the Big Three for economic survival. We had depended on the automotive manufacturing industry for nearly eighty years, but because of the cyclical nature of the business, bad times were always right around the corner.

The best thing about being mayor was the access to information through organizations like the U.S. Conference of Mayors.

You could get on a plane to go see different cities, projects, people and organizations that are thinking and acting in different ways to create change. There were always ways to satisfy my intellectual curiosity. In 2002, the gross metropolitan product (GMP), a term describing the economic output of cities and the metropolitan areas around them, was added to the lexicon of economic insiders. This was very interesting to me because, for the first time, cities were able to determine their economic importance to their states and the country.

The GMP fueled an interesting new paradigm of metro areas throughout the United States. I was named Chair of the New Economy Committee for the U.S. Conference of Mayors, where this study initiated. It offered incredible amounts of information, like shifts and trends in population, industry, economic output, forecasting and more. Unfortunately, the information presented zero or negative growth in population, jobs and economic output for Detroit. It also showed the tremendous shift in hiring for automotive manufacturing jobs throughout the United States. I began to see very quickly, from the data presented, that Detroit and Michigan needed to do something revolutionary to stop the certain economic tsunami that was on the way. Detroit no longer cornered the market in auto jobs. Therefore, as the City's leader, I felt we needed to move expeditiously to find and grow jobs in other economic and industry sectors.

Pete Karmanos' decision to move Compuware, his innovative technology services company, downtown was huge, in light of this, because it was the big first step toward moving Detroit out of its singular-focused dependency on GM, Ford and Chrysler. We actively pursued others in the technology, financial services and healthcare industries, and we were able to land several new companies in all of these growing industries. We explored ways to help the Detroit Medical Center grow. We actively weaned the city off the automobile industry's nipple, and the vision was becoming clearer and clearer to people each day. And we didn't stop there. We began cleaning storefronts to attract small business, and we focused on entertainment. We asked the right *ques-*

tions, like, what else do we have to do to make downtown Detroit *walkable*? All of this energy crackled because the casino deal went through. The city was beginning to show signs of life.

chapter 10
Who's the New Guy?

NOT EVERYONE was happy with me during those first two years. I had a chip on my shoulder, and I admit it. From the day my candidacy was announced, I heard that I wore the wrong suits, needed to wear red ties, trim my beard or remove my earring. To anyone reading this book who is not from Detroit, you wouldn't believe how big an issue this was. In the midst of poverty, crime, population decline, racial tension and failing schools, a diamond stud that I wore in one earlobe made the front-page news and a big story on local newscasts. Often!

The stud was made from my wife's first wedding ring. It was the one I'd paid for by layaway. After I became mayor, I bought her a new ring, but this first one represented a bond between Carlita and me. As trivial as it was to the public, she fought for me to keep it. My advisors, however, told me the day I announced my run to remove it.

It felt like people were trying to make me not me, and I constantly struggled with that. It sounds stupid to me when discussing it now, but it seemed like no one could move past the earring conversation during my first campaign! I mean, I was discussing policy, diversifying our industry base, exploring ways to better engage the appropriations processes in Washington, D.C., and in the State Capitol, and the next day's news would be all about my earring! During one campaign meeting with Conrad, Bob, Christine and Carlita, a debate ensued.

"Man, the people can't hear you," the advisors said. "Just take it out."

"No!" Carlita argued. "It's who he is! First, you tell him he can't wear the suits he wears. Now, he has to take it out? This is wrong!"

"Baby, this is nothing," I said. "It's just a damned earring. This ain't about our love for each other." I said the things men say to appease their women. I ultimately removed it, because it overshadowed the fact that I had a law degree and had led the Michigan State House. People responded like I'd won a prize or something, and the press wrote stories about it being gone. It was one of the first times I realized how much the media can drive public spectacle.

I don't think I could have ever trusted the media to tell this story in a way that accurately depicted its impact on my relationship with my wife. Like most politicians and public figures, I am protective of the little bit of personal space that I have. I have to be, because stories like this, stories that place perspective on public figures' lives, get trivialized. But it was real, and it drove a wedge between Carlita and me. She felt like I had chosen Detroit over her. I put the earring back in after the election, but she didn't care. Removing it made a much deeper statement to her. That was a major moment in our relationship, the first such moment in which Detroit's needs prevailed over my wife's. She would tell me, later, how deeply it affected her. Worse, every major crossroad after that required an immediate display of devotion toward the City or my wife, I'd choose Detroit.

Ah, stigma, stereotypes and me. Among the biggest stereotypes about me is the rumor that I spent a lot of time hanging out and partying while serving as mayor. That's frustrating, because I never did. But I *should* have.

Every now and then, I should have gone out, sat around, ate some good food and had a beer, even though I don't drink. I would have been much happier. My age, my maturity level and my demeanor were always the talk of the town. People drew opinions of my ability to lead based on these criteria. The talk shaped the

Kwame Kilpatrick aura, and it made me paranoid because it had such a strong undercurrent, such tidal potential. I felt like I was being controlled. *Yada-yada suit. Yada-yada earring. Gotta show up with this. Call so-and-so back. You can't go out, because they're going to blah-blah-blah.*

My whole life, I'd felt like a free man. As mayor, I felt like a slave, a puppet with a big-time job. As a result, I spent my time pent up at the Manoogian Mansion, the mayoral residence, or working very late with increasing regularity. Usually, Christine would stay late and work with me. Carlita hated my work schedule and the fact that I wasn't keeping my promises to be home on a particular day, or to attend an event completely separate from the job that we had agreed to earlier. She began to completely withdraw from me and the job. And she no longer questioned my schedule at all. She was just hurt and angry.

There was never a shortage of work. There's a saying that great things are done when men and mountains meet, but they rarely have time to waste in the street. If that's the case, then Detroit was my Mount Kilimanjaro, a mountain of issues surrounded by every climate in the political world. On one side, there was the economic development we'd successfully spurred. It started downtown, but it was beginning to move out to the neighborhoods in the form of new home building projects and other commercial activity, like that Home Depot on the city's Northwest Side. That was good. On the other hand, some of the toughest issues I'd ever face lurked in the darkness, just beyond my sight.

A string of Detroit youth murders that took place in 2002 tormented me. Twenty-two kids were killed in Detroit within the first six months of the year, with a rash of about nine occurring within days during that span. Each case was completely unrelated to the next, making it feel like a city that had existing issues with law enforcement was coming apart at the seams.

I had to do something, and I did, by personally visiting crime scenes or hospitals whenever an incident occurred, and offering condolences to the families. It told the community that I took these deaths personally, and kept investigators sharp. I viewed children's bodies on several of those occasions. On city streets. On hospital gurneys. It tore out my heart. Mothers and siblings would thank me for being there, while grabbing me and crying. They all told me that I had to do something about this, and I so wished that I could do more. I cared deeply. I wanted to ease their suffering. I wanted every perpetrator to pay. What I wanted can be described, but what I felt cannot. I can only suggest imagining a grieving parent clutching you while his dead child lies behind you. And everyone is emotional when you arrive.

Damn, Kwame! You gotta do something about this! What... the... hell? I didn't know what to do for them, except try to be strong. This, for me, was the other side of the mountain. I crashed headfirst into one of my job's brutal realities, one that ventures far beyond policy-making and business deals. I was expected to be the face, and the conscience, of an entire city. If I said I had a plan on how to contend with it, I'd be lying. I felt like, unless I worked my ass off, every day, all day, we would fail. And yet, I felt like it didn't matter how much work I did. We'd still fail. The pressure was incredible.

It's sad enough when a child is killed; it never makes sense. These kids, however, seemed to be dying for completely careless reasons. One child was shot while playing with a relative's gun. Another young girl was killed by a bullet intended for a man who bought defective radios from her uncle with counterfeit bills. If it sounds insane, that's because it was. What do you do about that? These scenes were just terrible! There was a guy who walked into a daycare center and opened fire where children were at play. Another case involved a child who was made to kneel as he was shot execution style.

Carlita saw me bringing this strain home, and wanted to get me away from it all. So we decided to have a family outing one evening. As we left with the boys, I received word that yet another child had been killed, and that the family was at Sinai-Grace Hospital. By now, the press had reported my presence at past scenes, and I felt obligated to go.

"I'll just stop by for a minute," I told Carlita.

"No problem, Baby," she said. She understood and support-ed me in these types of things. She loved when I extended myself to people. Yet it would be the very thing that caused her so much anger later, our shared feeling that "the people" didn't appreciate me for doing so, that they threw us away.

We arrived at the hospital, and I walked to the area where the boy's family had gathered. Sadly, a part of these visits had be-come routine. The family thanked me for coming, and I offered my condolences. Routine was then disrupted. I went to view the body. The child bore a striking resemblance to my son Jelani. I was stunned and dazed. I lost my balance, stumbled backwards, but played it cool enough for the family. It took everything I had to pull myself upright, but I spun toward the child's relatives, em-braced the family, and said that I had to leave.

The hallway was hazy, so I walked deliberately, acknowledg-ing no one. I made it back to the car and broke down crying as soon as I was inside. That was all I could take, and with the Police Chief's concern for my well being, that was the last scene I visited. Soon after, another child was killed. That time, I didn't go, but I watched the news coverage. The family, distraught, asked the press why I hadn't shown up and accused me of not caring. I was shocked.

I often try to identify the point at which I began to truly feel the strain of being mayor, and I always come back to those child murders. I wasn't quite myself after that. I should have talked to a psychiatrist.

It was also harder at home by now, because Carlita had dis-engaged from the job so much that I couldn't talk to her about it. I felt no support at home. None. Things had quickly gotten to the point where it was them, and me. No we. I tried to do a lot to hang out with the boys, but they always came back at me, saying, "You weren't there," or "You missed that, Dad." And me? I thought they were stingy. I was on this mission, trying to save a city and take care of my family. It was also important to protect my family by keeping them separated from the constant spotlight that shone on the job. I achieved that, absolutely. They were so separate that I created two separate lives.

I used to go home to my boys, hug them, tell them I loved them, and tell them about my day. But there was very little support from Carlita. I had pushed her away. I don't even think that she knew how to support me. Nor did I provide a way for her to do so. She detached and I allowed her to do so, emotionally and spiritually. She didn't like going to events with me, but those kinds of activities became an expectation, because she was the First Lady of the City of Detroit. Partnership between an elected official of a major metropolis and his or her spouse is important to both individuals' well being. But we'd never thoroughly discussed the expectations that would be placed on us as a first couple. And neither of us was emotionally prepared to shoulder it.

I began to do the job without her. She began living her life without me. We'd get together when it was time to do family activities away from the job. I was now twice married. Detroit was a second wife. Carlita and I barely crossed paths at home. We hadn't completely fallen out, but something about us had definitely changed.

I think Carlita was scared. She didn't know what to do, either as First Lady or as a wife, about a city that was taking her husband. And I get it. Her outsider's perspective of the city enabled her to see my situation objectively. She must have looked at how hard I was working for the City and thought, "What do y'all *like* about this damned city?" And she's got a point. Detroiters have a thing about the D that we can't get out of our system. The only thing I've seen that compares is the fanaticism New Yorkers have for Brooklyn. The chip on their shoulder, the way the pulse of the borough seems to beat on their sleeves. We boast the same pride. And I don't hear it from any other place. People say they're from certain places, but they don't fight for those places the way Detroiters do.

People who aren't from Detroit sometimes have a hard time seeing what we love about the place. And Detroiters sometimes fight for things that aren't worth saving. While I headed out to work every day trying to take care of the city, Carlita saw me failing to take care of myself. I gained weight. I was eating horribly and wasn't exercising. I was always stressed. I still didn't have a full staff, and I was barely six days into the job when the press began writing stories, inquiring about my plan.

One day, Carlita checked me. "You're never around," she said, stating the problem plainly. "I'm miserable. And I've got this baby (Jonas) to care for."

I knew I had to do something different. I remembered that during the campaign, I promised my wife that, if I won the election, I would set aside ten days every year, and we would go away as a family. Carlita actually reminded me of this promise after I became mayor.

"We'll take the entire ten days away from the job, the City, the politics and the problems. I'll just be Kwame and Daddy, and we'll just be family." We packed up and left town.

This was one of the very few promises that I kept during my time as mayor. And I thank God that I did. We were eventually able to reconnect, replenish and renew our energy and our family relationship. But with everything as a mayor in a major urban area, even the vacations would often get interrupted.

chapter 11

School of Duty

IN 2002, just before our ten days together as a family, I scheduled a few meetings before leaving Detroit to better educate
myself about what other cities were doing, and to also try to
recruit a public sector administrator from Florida. It was logical
enough for my line of work, except that it flew in the face of the
agreement I'd made with my wife. We did have a great time, despite my having to leave the vacation for a few days. But we had
planned to do it again in August 2003.

And then the Great Northeast Blackout occurred. We went
away, back to the Atlantis Resort in the Bahamas, where we'd
gotten married. That was special. On our second day there, I
went to the room while preparing to take the boys swimming.
I turned on the television as we changed into our bathing suits,
and saw a news crawler flashing across the screen, highlighting
cities that were experiencing a blackout. And then I saw images
of people walking in New York.

While I was away, I'd always give one person from my cabinet the number to the place where I was staying, as well as a cell
phone number to be used for emergencies only. As it turned out,
the cell didn't work in the Bahamas, so they couldn't get in touch
with me. And they had certainly tried. Fortunately, I happened
to return to my room from the beach, and decided to check in
about twenty minutes after the office had tried to call me. I used
the hotel phone and received the news: "Mayor, it's a blackout."

I called about thirty minutes after the Northeast United
States, Detroit included, lost power. I called everyone in by
phone, and gave instructions on the steps to take. Zeke took the
lead on the crisis management plan, along with the City's Fire
Chief, Tyrone Scott.

We were organized and ready for this situation. After the
tragedy of 9/11, the world had changed, and so did the United
States. The federal government took major strides to change
the way it gathered and shared important and vital communications. In doing so, the Homeland Security Department was established. One of the first priorities of its new director, former
Pennsylvania Governor Tom Ridge, was to have all the states and
major American cities submit an emergency plan to Washington,
D.C.

We'd begun working diligently on our plan early in 2002.
Detroit had unique qualities that presented gaping security
threats. Whether it was border issues with our Canadian neighbors, the City's incredibly large, conjoined water and waste system, which serviced more than nine counties in Michigan and
nearly half its citizenry, the global presence of General Motors,
America's largest automotive manufacturing corporation, or our
hospitals, and universities, security was an issue. So we developed
a plan that would assure our readiness in the event of an attack
by weapons of mass destruction, chemical or biological outbreak,
disease pandemics, acts of God, and yes, even a blackout.

Ours was a solid, smart and agile plan, and it was the first to
be delivered to Homeland Security. I wanted Detroit to be the
national leader in this new area, and we took a step toward that
goal in delivering that plan. The development of the Emergency
Operations Center, or EOC, was one of the key elements of that
plan. This would be the nerve center for the entire plan, an offsite
facility that could be set up in minutes and be a fully operational
command center in the event of any crisis. We could uplink technology and effectively communicate with all the relevant parties
involved, including the public, in real time. All employees would
know their emergency assignments, and whether they should re-

port to the EOC or another assigned post.

We even planned a way to set up a secondary facility if the EOC were ever compromised. We ran mock crisis and emergency response training modules, discussed assignments to the staff, and communicated our plan to City stakeholders. Hospitals, neighboring governmental entities, businesses and even the Canadian government offices knew that we were thoroughly organized and ready.

The EOC sprang into action when the blackout occurred. All parties reported to their assigned areas, and we were fully operational in twenty-eight minutes. Meanwhile, we found a private plane so I could fly back. I hadn't even been away for a full twenty-four hours. Carlita and the boys stayed in the Bahamas.

The plane took me straight from Nassau to Detroit City Airport. From there, we went right to work. I walked the streets, inspected neighborhoods and conducted interviews. It was the biggest emergency of its kind, an entire region of the country losing power in one instant! Panic had set in throughout metro Detroit. Gas stations had no power, and the few that did have it had such long lines that many ran out of fuel. Food was spoiling on grocery store shelves. Television stations were temporarily knocked off the air. Water supplies were disrupted because the electric pumps failed. There were numerous threats to peoples' health, including flood warnings due to heavy rainfall and broken sewage pumps. It forced some freeways to close.

It was August, the hottest time of the year, and the Detroit area was also enduring a mighty heat wave. Folks were already scrambling to parts of the state that still had power, crowding stores and filling hotels. They needed assurance before the panic became widespread.

Detroit shined in the midst of all of this. The EOC was very effective, and I was in the neighborhoods just hours after the lights went out. From making the call twenty-seven minutes after the city lost power, to finding a plane within thirty minutes, and making the two-hour trip to our city airport, which sits smack in the middle of a residential area, I was walking the East Side in little more than the time it takes to watch a movie.

I was up for two days straight. There would not be riots, looting, or any other foolishness in my city, on my watch. CNN reported a disturbance at one point. I ran to the news crew's truck and told them that their information was absolutely erroneous, and to stop broadcasting. I assured them that people were active, but civil. I kept talking to brothers in the street. "This is our city," I said to everyone who would listen. "Let's show 'em what we can do."

The City was recognized nationally for its handling of the blackout, so in one respect, yes, we shined. People also got a chance to see that I knew how to operate as mayor. I was invited to speak at several forums around the country, including giving formal testimony in Senate Committee hearings in Washington, D.C. I also participated in several meetings directed toward raising awareness of the importance of police and firefighters in defending our homeland, and specifically our hometowns. Detroit did become a national leader on that issue, particularly in the areas of border security, law enforcement coordination and city emergency preparedness. Those efforts improved our ability to obtain more appropriations to outfit our police force, fire, water and Homeland Security departments. We got better equipment, radios, and capital for construction. Good changes were happening.

On the other hand, my wife was again left feeling deserted, knowing that I couldn't keep any promise. Not because I was some horrible guy, but because I wasn't in the position to make those kinds of promises. The City won every time. Carlita understood the magnitude of the blackout, but her sentiment still mounted. When would we be a family again?

It took four days to deal with the blackout issue, and then I flew back to the Bahamas. I got to spend four of the ten days with the family. It was enjoyable, but each call to duty was like a hammer, driving the wedge between us deeper and deeper, farther and farther apart.

However, our handling of the blackout, and my presence

during those tragic times convinced the people of Detroit that I was not a novelty mayor. My youth, size and familiarity with pop culture had created that stigma, and I loathed it. For instance, co-median Chris Rock jokingly called me "the hip-hop mayor" when I was elected. He even said I influenced the creation of Mays Gilliams, the character he played in the 2003 movie *Head of State*. Flattering as it was, he branded me a gimmick. Hip-hop pioneer Russell Simmons would echo that nickname soon after, when his Hip-Hop Summit came to Detroit in 2003. It was a tremendous event, but it also branded me.

I'd been quietly fighting the "hip-hop mayor" tag. Meanwhile, the Summit made history by registering 17,000 people, the larg-est number of registrants in its short history, to attend the event at Cobo Arena, downtown. Popular artists like Eminem, his group D12, Nas, Doug E. Fresh, Detroit rap group Slum Village and Simmons headed a panel to discuss voter registration and educa-tion. Khary Turner, this book's co-writer, was also a panelist. I was thrilled when Russell invited me to speak. Not only did this happen early in my first term, but the young audience boasted a lot of people in my age group, and we were notorious for having some of the lowest turnouts in recent elections. I had a chance to connect to them and mobilize that part of my constituency.

Now remember, while it was true that I was raised on the streets of Detroit, I was also raised running the halls of the Michigan State Legislature while tagging along to work with my mother, which speaks to my diverse perspectives on numer-ous issues. But I am hip-hop. Damn, I said it! And I'll say it for the thousandth time. I love all kinds of music, including rap. But that's the beauty of being real hip-hop. You can flow to Coltrane or Jay-Z. You can listen to "Ready or Not" by the Fugees on your way to work, and "Ready or Not" by After 7 when you chill with your lady that night. The hip-hop generation is not some mono-lithic culture tied to any one genre of music. It is a multicultural, multidimensional plethora of sights and sounds, joys, pain, hap-piness, sorrow, hatred and love—an ugly, beautiful collage of the American landscape set to the world stage. It's too big to be tied

144 ■ SURRENDERED ■

to any one thing, and it was a shortsighted disservice to American pop culture for anyone to think it simple to tie me to it, as if it were a shoelace. To the conservative media, it was a bad label. And unfortunately, many of my constituents believe anything the media tells them. Anything!

I did get to meet Russell Simmons at the Cobo Center, along with Eminem and his manager, Paul Rosenburg. Proof, Eminem's friend and a member of his rap group D12, was also there. He was killed in a shooting years later, but I remember him as being very affable. I also struck up a friendship with Rosenberg.

On the dais, Russell introduced me, imploring the audience to lift me up because hip-hop had its own mayor. It felt incredible hearing everyone cheer for me. I thought to myself that these were the people who were going to change Detroit, make the city a world-class town. And they were depending on my leadership to get us there! I stepped up to the podium.

"Who remembers this song," I asked the crowd. "I'm the king of... !"

"Rock!" they all shouted, finishing the line from an old Run-DMC song. It was a rush, doing a traditional call-and-response with the crowd. I felt like I connected on a plane that few politicians get to experience. This experience transcended the restraints of politics... and branded me.

I had no way of knowing that the nickname "Hip-Hop Mayor" would stay around to haunt me, preventing large segments of my constituency from taking me seriously. The hip-hop stigma sometimes crept into my thoughts, but there's nothing I would have changed. The hip-hop generation's vote is just as valid as anyone else's. The only thing I could do was work and maintain a presence in the city for child murders, blackouts, and fallen officers.

In retrospect, even if I had wanted to change my ways, there's nothing I could have done differently during those times to assuage the tension between Carlita and me, except discuss the demands of the job with my wife before I ran, so we'd both have a better understanding. But I didn't know. I was thirty-one, and I had never been mayor. I had no idea what I was getting into, and this job doesn't come with a rule book or a job description. And I'll back off the age reference, because I don't care how old you are. You could be Coleman Young's age, or Dennis Archer's. No one is immediately *prepared* to be the mayor of Detroit. Nobody!

The mayor is seen as the savior by some, and as the barometer for failure by others. It's like there's no responsibility on the greater community's part. Everyone points the finger of blame toward the mayor. I don't know if there is any other community in America where the mayor is so personally connected to individuals' attitudes, successes and emotional well-being. In many cities, residents often can't even recall their mayor's name. In Detroit, not only do you know the mayor's name, you also have a very strong emotional response to that person's position. It's love or hate—gray areas just don't exist. And while that passion drives the determination, perseverance and courage of Detroiters, it's unfortunately the same passion that drives the culture of hate.

chapter 12
Out of Nowhere

I WAS TIRED, had a headache every day without fail, and was working my ass off. Plus, I was constantly fighting bullshit rumors about me. One that began to spread alleged that a party had taken place at the mayoral residence, the Manoogian Mansion. The rumor had it that the party, which was said to be so wild that it involved strippers, occurred during the fall of my first year in office.

We were still living in our own home during that time. Carlita was renovating the Manoogian and forbade me or the boys from entering the mansion until it was completed. It was the one thing that made her happy at that time, so I dared not dishonor her request.

Still, the rumor gained momentum. Barbershops, nightclubs and neighborhood gathering spots buzzed about it. In fact, people spreading the story began to *place* themselves, their close friends or family members there, as well. And because I was known as "the Hip-Hop Mayor," it was perfectly believable that I had a party at my home—where my wife and children live—with strippers and complete mayhem. Before we knew it, the press picked it up and began reporting it as though it were factual. One facet of the reports suggested that Carlita crashed it, breaking it up and even assaulting one of the dancers. As hard as I was working, and considering the discord between me and Carlita *because* of my work for the City, this struck me as complete bullshit. I believed, at first, that most people felt the same way. But I was completely wrong. I don't know when it actually happened, but during this time, Detroiters' perception of me as the young attorney and family man committed to serving the City eroded, and was replaced with a media-crafted perception of me as an arrogant, hedonistic, immature asshole that didn't give a damn about anyone but myself.

Noted business leaders, pastors and community stalwarts asked me to admit that there had indeed been such a party, as if offering me their sage wisdom. One Detroit pastor even told me he was told it happened by someone who attended it. Of course, he wouldn't say the person's name.

The entire episode quickly depressed and angered me. I was completely undone. While we, as a city, were experiencing paradigm shifts in City services, economic development, crime reduction and our ability to recruit and land huge national and international events, I was reduced to a partying hooligan.

Attorney General Mike Cox, a Republican, announced plans to investigate the rumor in 2004. He rushed to get involved because he really believed that it had happened, and the story stood to advance his own political career by becoming the man who got to the bottom of it. He spent more than $4 million of the State taxpayers' money on the probe. He subpoenaed cops, my neighbors, hospital workers, the administrative staff in the Mayor's Office, and others. He pulled 911 tapes, hospital entrance reports, EMS run sheets, police run sheets, and video footage from the house. No real date for the party ever materialized (not even a calendar month) during his query, nor a credible witness or attendee. He never even found one person who *knew* someone who had attended it. He even interviewed me! It was the biggest news in the city, bigger than the G-8 Energy Summit and the Major League Baseball All-Star Game that was coming to town. And it turned up nothing.

Cox eventually concluded that it never happened, dismissing it as an "urban legend." But the press weren't convinced and kept pressing the issue. They deduced that the Attorney General was really a friend of mine who was actually helping me, so they vowed to stay on the investigation. Note that my "friend" the Attorney General would later join the Wayne County prosecution team against me, just to show that he was not my friend. He then would run for governor and air campaign commercials saying that he was the reason Kwame Kilpatrick went to prison, and that's why people should vote for him. He would lose because the ridiculous rumor would spread and include *him* as a partygoer. I wish I were making this up. That is funny to me.

What's not funny is the fact that the rumor still lives, nine years later. The newspapers and news stations have made a massive amount of money on the story, and have managed to implore other law enforcement agencies to get involved. The only question that I still ponder is why? Why am I still on the news about it, after eight years and nearly three years removed from being mayor?

A second issue that plagued me toward the end of my first term was the City's lease of a Lincoln Navigator for the purpose of transporting my wife and children. This became a national story, one that could have been avoided. But we *were* unorganized in this instance, and our bad decision-making delayed communication of the truth, thus propelling it forward.

The Navigator issue was big to me, because it rose from a conflict between Carlita and Christine. We'd entered the administration already owning a Navigator. It was the vehicle my wife and children used. When I entered office, Jerry Oliver insisted that Carlita and the boys have some form of security with them at all times. He preferred that she not drive her own vehicle unless is it was necessary. I completely agreed, so a Detroit police officer was assigned to be with Carlita and the boys on a daily basis.

We planned for the officer to drive our Navigator, but Detroit Police rules prohibit officers from using private vehicles. They must drive a police vehicle. The City's insurance policy wouldn't cover any other kind of situation, so it provided the Detroit Police Executive Protection Unit with a Ford Expedition to transport my family. It was an existing vehicle in the City's police fleet, and it did just fine. Carlita preferred the Navigator, and asked to be assigned one when the City renewed its fleet. I didn't touch those smaller issues. That was Christine's job. So I hardly thought about it, although my first response to Carlita's request was that I thought we should get a Chevy Suburban, because I'd just asked my entire staff to take a pay cut, myself included. Plus, the police already had those. So, I did disagree with her about it, but under what I felt were reasonable terms, and then moved on.

I had no further communication with my wife, Christine or the Chief of Police until Steve Wilson, a reporter at the time for Detroit's ABC affiliate, heard the story about a month later and confronted me at the U.S. Council of Mayors conference in Washington, D.C. A member of my security detail, Mike Martin, pushed Wilson, and it became a big story.

Upon my return to Detroit, the Police Chief told me the Navigator had already been leased, a *special* one leased outside the fleet of other City vehicles. *Damn! Here we go again,* I thought.

"Well, *we* don't need it," I said. "We're already driving the Suburban." But the dealership wouldn't take it back. Christine then got upset because she felt we never should have ordered it in the first place.

Cooler heads ultimately prevailed. Both the Navigator and Suburban were police vehicles, so Carlita never drove either. But the press behaved as if it were hers. We failed to get in front of the story, and it became far bigger than it ever should have. In context, it wasn't that far out of the ordinary. Mayor Archer's wife was escorted in an SUV for eight years. Positioned properly, I could have asked the public why an escort for one mayor's wife was no good for another's. But because we failed to get ahead of it that way, it ended up looking like another mayoral blunder, one in a line of PR miscues. It was as interesting a phenomenon to watch as it was unnerving, because it furthered the negative perceptions about me, and it helped put me on a collision course with a saga of epic proportions. Sensing this, or something like it, I had a headache all the time. My political career had become a huge roller coaster. My marriage had become an even bigger one.

chapter 13
Friendship and Loyalty

T HE MOST riveting controversy of my career is also the most intensely personal, and it requires a step back in time.

As I mentioned earlier in this book, I met Christine Beatty at Cass Technical High. As a teenager, she was a somewhat popular girl who didn't get too close to guys. She was known as the girl who intended to abstain from sex until she was married. In high school, if a girl wasn't having sex, guys generally weren't interested in her. I hate to sound cold, but most men can think back and associate this with their own hormonal years.

Christine, whom I call "Chris," was in my tenth grade chemistry class. She had a strong personality, and always thought she knew everything, a trait that continued well into her adult years. In class, we'd talk casually about whatever classmates discuss in high school. That was the extent of our interaction. I was playing football, and Lou Beatty, the man Chris would later marry, was on the team with me. One day in the locker room, the fellas were talking trash about who had this, who had that, who had the finest woman, and so on. Guy stuff. Lou always bragged about having the finest women, and Chris was his girlfriend.

"Whatever," I said, "Chris ain't fine! She ain't fine at all, man. She's *funny* lookin'."

Lou said something back, I'm sure, because I really don't commit those kinds of conversations to memory, and we carried on, talking junk and teasing each other. But the next day, he told her what I had said. She was offended and cold toward me for a while after that. About a year later, she cooled off. We had many of the same friends, and had plenty of opportunities to hash things out. In fact, we became good friends by senior year.

Ours was a platonic relationship, although as platonic friendships sometimes go, we did share an underlying attraction. We just channeled it. I considered asking her to our prom, but I didn't, because I wanted to have sex after prom. Again, the guy thing.

We began dating after graduation. *Kinda.* She and Lou had broken up, so we started hanging out, going to movies, things like that. We'd kiss and hug. It was an innocent relationship.

We broke up during a graduation party at my house. I'd been listening to people who suggested that since I was leaving early to start football camp, I'd want to date at FAMU. We agreed that we should break up while we were apart, and just keep in touch. She'd write three-, five-, and ten-page letters to me, and I learned that she'd gotten back together with Lou. Oh well, I thought. We had tried to turn a true friendship into something romantic, and it never worked. Something always interrupted our would-be romantic moments. So, we remained friends throughout college. In fact, I dated her friend Alexis during the summer after my freshman year, and continued to date her until I met Carlita.

During these times, I'd take trips to D.C. to hang out with Chris and her friends. We developed a deep trust in each other. If there was anyone in the world I could talk to about personal matters, besides Carlita and my closest partners, it was Chris. We were very much like Dre' and Syd, the main characters in the movie *Brown Sugar* whose connection was complicated by Reese, Dre's fiancé, who was a new and disconnected love interest.

Chris and I know each other like the backs of our hands. The only difference in our relationship from the movie was that Carlita wasn't a new entry in my life. I'd grown up with her, too, just at a different phase, and in a very different way. Carlita and I nurtured an adult, romantic relationship, while Chris was my *dawg.*

This aspect of my relationship with Chris has always challenged my wife and I more than anything, and yet it's the truth. When Carlita moved to Detroit, Chris and I naturally saw less of one another. But we'd see each other around. In 1994, when I was back in Detroit with Carlita, my mother ran a write-in campaign after Michigan State Senator David Holmes died, even after the filing deadline. Sen. Holmes is a legend. He once hit a man on the floor of the Lansing legislature for making a racist remark toward him. He was so revered that his people filed for him to run for re-election while he was on his deathbed.

To aid the campaign, Chris and Zeke helped me organize a youth mobilization effort. We got more young people to participate in the campaign and write in Mom's name than any other youth voting movement in the city's history. That was the first time I'd worked with Chris, and she caught the political bug soon afterward. Running my 1996 campaign was the next thing for her.

I hired Chris as my first chief of staff when we won and went to Lansing in 1997, thus morphing our friendship into a working relationship. We watched each other grow. She was excellent at her job, and became a legitimate policy shaper and chief. That underlying flirtatiousness, however, the "what if" factor, never went away. It was still the one thing we'd refused to act on. She was close enough to be my sister at this point, only she wasn't. Plus, she was with Lou, and I was with Carlita.

As I mentioned earlier, when Christine got pregnant and returned to Detroit to work and get ready to be a mom, those were good times. We were angling for a run at a new State ticket but knew, in all the time that I was a State Representative, Democratic leader and mayor, that the party never fully embraced me. The party's movers and shakers were always opposed to me. In fact, I've always taken the most heat from my fellow Democrats. We realized early in the game that we couldn't rely on them to help position us. We'd have to shape our own destiny. In fact, when I took the stage and spoke at the 2000 and 2004 Democratic National Conventions in both Los Angeles and Boston, we secured those slots without the Michigan Democratic Party's knowledge. They would have never suggested that I speak. I had to go behind them and use national organizations to get that done. It was always constant work, and I'm telling you this because, when we were working, it wasn't a movement. It was Kwame and Chris.

Angling. Working. Deciding whom to write for letters of support. It was deep. There were only three of us in my first office —me, Christine and Sharon Solomon. Sharon was a gifted writer. She could make a letter sound like I was the president of the United States. We may have numbered too few to call ourselves a movement, but we moved things. And through it all, the person who remained strongly and deeply engaged through those tough days on the House floor, through excruciating votes on issues like the Detroit school takeover, or City budget issues and during the campaigns when no one thought I would win, was Chris.

Our work styles were complementary, as well. My decision-making style is thorough, but fast. I'll listen to all opinions in a discussion, consider them all within a few minutes, and make a sound decision on an issue. I process information quickly. Plus, I rarely forget a name or a detail once I hone in on it. Christine drives for a methodology, a process. So once I decided something, she could take over and engage the staff, identify the action steps, and implement them.

We built a tangible *and* intangible love. When you go through those kinds of trials with someone who stays in the trenches with you, you come to expect that support and loyalty. That's a rare relationship in this line of work, but we had it—a kinship, a fondness. Tupac Shakur released an album called *Me Against the World*, and that title accurately describes our shared stance. At work, it was Chris and me against the world.

The problem, though, was that I was slowly creating two separate and imbalanced worlds.

It was in Lansing that I first started to separate my home life from my professional life. And yes, Carlita was affected. At work, life was about Chris and me. At home, it was about Carlita and my family. Because Carlita didn't like to engage the political process, I always felt she didn't want to be involved unless it was something fun. But I also separated her from it because I honestly felt that things worked more smoothly when she was absent. I was free to go work, get out there and do what I do. I understand when I see these Hollywood marriages, or guys married to people outside their profession, and you never see their wives, unless they're at an event. I see how such marriages can work, but I also see how it causes an incredible strain when contending with the separate nature of the relationship.

Christine was working in Detroit in 2001 when we started putting together the pieces for my mayoral run. Once I decided to do it, Christine jumped into her usual role. She'd already managed three campaigns for me, but for the first time, I saw her get nervous. She tried to defer and give the position to someone else, so I brought in another woman, Pam Jackson, to manage the campaign. Pam, a Ph D., is just brilliant. But Pam and Chris worked together about as smoothly as oil and vinegar. Also, Pam didn't match the campaign's general vibe. But I'm partly guilty of setting Chris up, because I knew she'd assume managerial duties as soon as she saw someone else attempting to run things. And that's exactly what happened. I just never called her the campaign manager.

Pam left after just a few weeks, and Conrad Mallet stepped in. Chris had the final say on media—editing and commercials. She met with the field staff and assigned everyone to their respective posts, approved all literature, and ordered posters and lawn signs. After watching her work, I felt she was ready to be chief of staff for the City, and I hired her for that position.

The same reason that I didn't hire her for the campaign manager's job was the precise thing that inspired me to make her chief of staff. Many people suggested during the campaign that the manager's job was too much for her, and I think even she bought into it. And so did I. Christine never really saw herself as talented, per se. She just got the job done. She was good at identifying problems, delegating and motivating people, and putting out fires. She used the same approach whether she was involved in labor negotiations or campaigning. *Ok, we've got to win. Let's figure out how to win. How do we get in the community and stay in the community?* I knew she would take that same approach to solving the City's problems when we took office. Community policing. Illegal dumping. *How do we fix it?* was her first question to everything. I believe hiring her for that position was the right thing to do, but we engaged our personal relationship the wrong way.

And here's where that starts.

Just before the transition period, after winning the mayoral election, we started acquiring books and documents from Dennis Archer's administration and began to go over the vast nature of City government. It was the very first time that I really looked at the massive organization that was City government.

We were suddenly administrators of a company consisting of about 17,000 employees, more than forty departments, an incredible amount of appointees, and a $3 billion budget. Just to grasp it, I had to study it with the intensity of my bar exam preparation. The job required that I dedicate all of my time to it, and I felt there was no room for negotiation. That's what I mean when I say my stress started right away. I refused to be an unprepared mayor. People thought I had energy, and some ideas. I knew that. But I felt the bigger issue I faced was how to manage this organization. I needed to know it inside and out. I wanted to meet with employees, and I wanted to see everyone face-to-face. That became an overwhelming prospect. But to get it done, I immersed myself in the work.

It was late 2001. Jonas was born during this time and, though I was probably the most doting father in the world when his older brothers were born, I hardly did anything to help Carlita with Jonas. I believe her depression and loneliness was deepest at that time. I was completely absent, heading to the transition office at 7:30 a.m. and returning home well after midnight. I hadn't even been inaugurated yet. I'd promised Carlita a trip, but we cancelled it due to her pregnancy. We just went right from the campaign, to the transition, to the inauguration, to the heat of public office.

At the inauguration, Carlita had Jonas in a stroller, at less than a month old. She gave birth to him through an emergency Caesarian, and she had not yet properly healed. I was pushing myself in multiple directions, trying to be a good father, husband, and a good new mayor. But all of my attention started moving toward being the latter. Christine and I hopped planes and took trips around the country trying to find a police chief and a chief operating officer. If I needed someone to stay until 2 a.m., she was the first person I asked. We just became each other's everything.

The stress was incredible, and we all suffered under it. Zeke's hair began falling out. He gained twenty pounds and had to see a doctor. Christine became anemic. She'd later develop cancer. The strain was nothing short of incredible. And I don't think anyone can understand it unless they've been through it, but I do believe the people in Detroit can truly see and feel the effects of people in office who are not working as hard as we were. It takes a tremendous amount of energy, persistence and tenacity to move anything in Detroit. No one wants to go there. No one wants to spend money for the City. There's no one knocking on doors to participate. Everything you get, you have to wrangle it by the sweat of your brow. And it's a hard... ass... job. When nationally-syndicated radio host Tom Joyner interviewed me two years ago, I told him that it's the second-hardest job in the United States, behind the presidency.

But it's no excuse for being absent from marriage and family. The Bible says that when a man marries, he leaves his father and mother, and cleaves to his wife. Well, I didn't heed the wisdom of the inspired word of God. I cleaved to Christine. It wasn't a wham-bam-thank-you-ma'am relationship. It started with us trying to prevent sex; taking time to calm each other's nerves due to the frenzied work environment. The discussions and reminders about our aspirations deepened our professional interdependence, and our friendship felt even more significant because neither Lou nor Carlita were prepared to provide the kind of support we needed. And how could they? I didn't know how to support Carlita, either. None of us had any inkling what we were getting into.

Christine and I wrestled with this frustration together. We lifted one another up and reminded ourselves why we had aggressively sought these positions. We felt that God truly wanted us to be there to serve His people. Through it all, though, we lost our focus on the anointing that had been placed on us, and turned our attention toward each other.

We were in the transition office late one night, talking. The holidays were approaching, as was the inauguration. We'd submitted our transition report and hired our police chief, and we decided to take a break for Christmas. After doing some cleanup work, we were standing by a window when the moment grew emotional. From the third-floor windows of the small building on the corner of Larned and Washington Boulevard in Downtown Detroit, we could see the dazzling Christmas lights in front of the Cobo Hall Convention Center. A fresh layer of snow coated the ground, and reflections of the Canadian skyline danced on the surface of the Detroit River. It was serene and awesome. I had what I'd wanted since age nine. I was proud, excited and extremely thankful.

Key cliché's apply here, from lives flashing before our eyes, to feeling like we had our backs against the wall. The moment was revelatory, and it seemed to hit Chris and me simultaneously. We turned to each other and hugged. And then we kissed. And then, we looked at each other.

"What the hell are we doing?" we said.

chapter 14
Forsaking All Others

I DON'T REMEMBER who said it, but we had to acknowledge what had just happened. We both admitted that we loved one another, and always had. We acknowledged our underlying feelings. And then we both said, aloud, that we couldn't go to that place. It wasn't our path.

But we did. The kiss ignited something, and it wouldn't go away. It lurked as we tried to settle for intimate conversation, but we eventually had sex.

I know my actions were absolutely wrong. There are no excuses for it. My grandfather used to say, "When you point your finger at someone, there are three more pointing right back at you." I reflect now on the moment I could have stopped it. I could have stood firm and listened to the still voice in my spirit. I just didn't.

The press would later use words like "torrid," "salacious" and "steamy" to describe what happened between Christine and me. Had those simple adjectives adequately described it, however, it might have been easier for us and our spouses to confront. But it was, by all measures of the word, a love affair. We began handling our business differently. We might take a trip to recruit a possible new hire or appointee, and we'd make it an overnight trip. We went to movies, clearly indicating to each other that ours had moved from a working relationship to something deeper. We discussed our children, and talked about our homes, compromising the sanctity of our households. We began to share everything with one another—our hopes and dreams, our deepest fears, our bodies. We scheduled time to be with one another, away from our families, the job and Detroit. We shared secrets of our past, and had profound moments in which we genuinely released past hurts, pains and demons. We grew closer and closer, all the while knowing we were wrong. We crossed the line long before sex became a factor. We built up that passion through our mutual respect, and our shared atmosphere until our emotional maturity escaped us.

The spiritual growth, maturation and girding that had protected me through a hard-fought election was damaged. My relationship with Christine broke the vital spiritual foundation of both our households. We had conversations about the pain we were causing our families, and the further pain we'd cause if they knew, and I felt tremendous guilt.

At this point, I believe you should know that my wife is not a shrinking violet by any stretch of the imagination. Her spirit told her that I was no longer the man she had married, and she didn't know what to do. But she didn't remain quiet. *You've got to come home sometimes. You haven't been here for dinner in a month. You have to take time to do some things with us! Go to a movie with us!*

"What the *hell?*" I'd respond. "I ain't got no time for no *movies!* I'm trying to make some revolutionary changes in the city! This city's been down on its blah-blah-blah… !" I still hedged on the lack of support, and started making speeches to her. I turned her into a constituent to be won over.

It's amazing how early in my administration this all happened. Looking back, I realize that Carlita tried to get involved on several occasions. She'd offer advice at times, and I would disregard it. I decided that she just wasn't going to be involved. She still knocked, but I shunned her. The job became my personal life, my hobby and my identity. And I hated it! I woke up unhappy every day, feeling burdened, in danger, and fretful in my mission. Between the mayorship and my home life, I was in a war of wills, and worked as if I were surrounded by enemies. My age. Racism.

The press. The city's depressed spirit. Principalities. They were all enemies to me, devils to fight daily.

But I wasn't equipped to wage those battles. I didn't have the spiritual and familial balance. Sure, I knew politics. I had tenacity and energy. And I had pride. But the Bible says that "pride goeth before the fall." It would take a few years before I realized that the pursuit of wisdom should be every person's constant act, especially for a leader.

I love my wife, and I love my sons. I never stopped loving them. And I regret that they became a separate entity from the job, a group of people I needed for occasional photo ops. I've learned since that fatherhood and being a husband is so much more than purchased happiness through an occasional vacation, toy or gift. I would, at some point, come back to myself, realizing that I couldn't do this whole life thing without my family. It would be years, however, before I truly saw how much I needed Carlita to be by my side and with me in my career. By then, I'd let some things go too far.

That shift occurred within Christine's household, as well, but the dynamic was different because she was a mother. She spent most of her time learning to be chief of staff, learning about the city, the budget and helping hire people. This thrust her husband into the caretaker's role. I'm sure there were some ego and manhood issues that her husband had to deal with behind the scenes. It can be hard on men when they are not the ones with the more "important" occupations, or the ones bringing the most money home. I believe that started to be a problem for Lou. It strained them. Neither of their daughters had even reached age four, and they weren't ready to be away from their mother so much.

On top of that, Chris was hanging around me 24/7. She was supporting my every need, professionally. And soon after that, as Lou suspected, we had an affair. Neither he nor Carlita were ever comfortable with our relationship. They tolerated it, and we'd even vacationed together in the past. But they never developed a comfort level about it because at the time, Christine and I were closer to each other than we were to them.

Those vacations stopped when I became mayor. We also stopped hanging around each other as couples. At events, I'd try to avoid them, and Christine would try to avoid us. The tension was obvious, and we knew that suspicion was a contributing factor.

I've been asked why, after evaluating the city's needs during the transition, we didn't just step back and tell the people of Detroit that we could only handle so much at a time without jeopardizing our households. All I knew, in my spirit, was that I didn't like to fail at anything, and to me, that kind of announcement would have signified failure. FAMU's Alpha Phi Alpha chapter, Beta Nu, has a motto: "Tenacity, above all, tenacity." My football coach in college would always say, "If you make a mistake, make an aggressive mistake. If you jump off sides, damn it, kill the guy on the other side. Don't jump off sides and stand up and look around you. *Hit* that MF in front of you!" That's how I learned. If I'm gonna make a mistake, it's going to be an aggressive one. I won't fail for lack of trying.

The other reason I didn't step back and say, "Hey, enough for now" is the pride that comes from believing your own speeches. I really believed that we could bring change to Detroit. I believed in a rebirth, a renaissance. I believed we had the right people at the right time to create the city that God had intended. I was, and still am, a true believer. But I had to learn patience, and that comes from wisdom and experience. I've learned more about those qualities in the past three years, by experiencing a purification process by fire, than in my first three years as mayor.

I've often thought about what I would say to Lou, now Christine's ex-husband, if I had a chance to speak to him. I've wanted to reach out and tell him that I'm sorry. But I didn't because if he wanted to hit me, I would have to let him. I completely disrespected that man and his household. I disrespected his daughters. Early on, a friend asked me to look at this from Lou's perspective. He came to me when the affair was still going on and said that while he wasn't sure about what I was doing, I was clearly disrespecting Lou. He pushed me to look at things from his point of view. And when I did, I saw that I broke up their marriage. Though one single thing doesn't always ruin a union between two people, it can be the straw that breaks the camel's back. I've wanted to write to him, to speak to him, but I stopped because, if I were him, I wouldn't want to hear *anything* from me. And though an apology may not be enough, I want him to know that I am sorry. I loved his wife, but I had no business occupying that air, taking her away from home and husband. I, as the man in that relationship, had the responsibility to do the right thing. And I didn't. And I'm sorry. And I'm suffering for it. And so is he.

Only time heals those kinds of wounds. I've sat on the jail-house floor and asked for Lou's forgiveness, and asked God to help heal his heart, because he's one of the people I truly feel guilty about hurting. Lou's grandfather and uncles were close to my grandfather and great-uncles. His parents are pretty close to my parents. His aunt's house is a few doors away from my sister Ayanna's home. I've known the Beatty family my whole life, and I knew Lou Beatty before I even knew Christine. He and Ayanna graduated together, and it's only recently that they've begun to talk again, but I really screwed up their relationship. Lou would hang out at my house a lot when we were growing up. We'd shoot hoops in my backyard. He took Christine to his prom, and they came to my house to take pictures with Ayanna and her date. I was there, too, home for the summer, acting silly. The family relationships alone should have drawn a thick enough line between Christine and me.

Christine and I have discussed the reasons that we drifted away from our spouses. I won't go into those details. I'll just say that everyone has his or her own reasons to explain why things don't work out in a marriage. But it's even more difficult when that marriage has to stand against negative outside forces and distractions, particularly when said forces—emotions, urges, relationships—appear to be safe, secure provisions. It's a constant illusion that makes it easy to avoid dealing with serious issues in your own marriage. And I was the distraction. I was the safety and comfort for Christine. Knowing that still sickens me, and I still atone for it.

chapter 15

Controlled Chaos

B Y JANUARY 2005, I was at my lowest point emotionally, physically and mentally during my tenure as mayor. Too much work. Too many problems and lies. Too much on my mind. I was completely unhappy and devoid of energy. No one cared, and I wanted to quit.

The press was feasting on the Navigator story, the City's budget deficit climbed over $100 million, and all the prognosticators were preaching gloom and doom for any re-election bid that I would inevitably seek. For the record, I never believed that I could lose an election to anyone at any time. I just have that much confidence. But I and those closest to me knew we had serious problems.

I decided not to focus on re-election at all, and just try to be the best mayor I possibly could. I wasn't even certain that I'd seek re-election. It would take months, and the media's anointing of Freman Hendrix as mayor apparent, to spark enough ego, competition and pride to fuel another run. I would run, but first, I had to repair some things in my life.

I had to speak with Christine first, and tell her that it was time to stop. Honestly, this was at least the fifth time we had had this conversation, and I don't know why this time was any different, except that I cared less about my job then than at any other time in our relationship. I wanted Kwame back.

Next, I had to talk with Carlita. Whew! This was surely the

most difficult thing that I had to do. I was prepared to be honest, but not completely transparent. Not yet. Still, I was going to try, because I couldn't be me without her. Renewing my commitment to her was non-negotiable.

Finally, I had to figure out how to fix a $100 million deficit in the City's budget, while keeping the City moving forward. The Super Bowl was right around the corner. My options were to lay off cops and firefighters, close recreation centers, eliminate bulk trash pickup, or do nothing and let the next mayor handle it. If you don't get me by now, though, you never will. Shifting responsibility, passing the buck or cowering under harsh decisions and circumstances is not my style. Decision made, I went to work after speaking with Christine. I went to her house in February 2005, after the Navigator fiasco began to subside. We were in her basement. Her daughters were sleeping upstairs. I sat down next to her.

"Oh, boy," she immediately said. "I guess this is 'the talk,' huh?"

"The Talk" is what we'd come to call our inevitable break-up conversation. I told her that I felt like a complete mess, that my life was in turmoil, and that I needed to focus on my family first. What we were doing had clearly taken a heavy toll on both of our lives and our families. Nothing good would ever come from it. The affair was dishonest and whimsical at best, and we owed each other more than that. She cried, and I cried a little, too. We hugged and I left her house. I felt saddened, but lighter. I was ready for the second conversation. Or so I thought.

A few days later, in early March, I found myself alone with Carlita in the kitchen of the Manoogian Mansion. She was finishing dinner and was still wearing her workout clothes. I watched her for a few seconds as she walked around the kitchen making her final preparations for the evening meal. Although my 310-pound self was in the room, she moved around the area as if no one were there but her.

To break the silence, I asked her if she wanted me to seek re-election.

"I don't know," she said. "That's up to you." She didn't even look at me—she just grabbed a washcloth and wiped down the oven area and adjacent counters. I needed to say something to get her attention.

"I don't want to do anything without you," I said. "I don't want to be mayor. I don't want to run for re-election. I don't want to do *anything* without you. I need you all the way in, or I'm out." And then, I shouted, with an honesty and passion that surprised even myself, "I want my family back!"

Carlita abruptly stopped what she was doing and looked me right in my eyes. And with all the pain, anger, passion and courage she could muster, she said, "Your family hasn't gone anywhere! You left *us!* You chose everything else over us! The job! The 'people!' The movement! The so-called mission! Over *us*! And I'm so damned tired of it. I don't like this job, this city, these bloodsucking people, or you! I don't like you anymore! I do still love you, but I don't *like* you!"

It wasn't the first time that I'd heard some of those things. But on this day, at that moment, there was a certain air of finality and decisiveness in her tone that made this conversation more serious than any other. I could tell she had more to say, so I measured myself carefully. I was scared—truly afraid that my wife would decide to leave me. "You're right," I replied. I told her that I was tired, and that I needed her to help me. She said that she was tired as well, and that she just didn't know if she could.

We talked a lot more that day, and the more we did, the layers of fatigue and years of bad communication began to melt away. We talked more and more about everything, even Christine. She told me how much I hurt her by apparently choosing Christine over her, by taking her side in disagreements, and by spending entirely too much time with her. I told her that my relationship with Christine had gone too far, and that I was definitely going to change. She didn't ask me if we were having an affair, and I didn't offer that information. I was still trying to save my own ass.

She did say that she thought it would be best if I would let Christine go, and I agreed. But I wanted to make sure she had somewhere to go, and that she would be financially secure. Carlita agreed.

Carlita then got behind me. She said I should be the man and the mayor I was destined to be, and that she was with me 100 percent. That is a moment I will never forget, because after our long discussion that evening, she became a real force in the next campaign. She held meetings, made speeches, joined community boards, raised a little money and even did radio and television commercials. She... did... her... thing!

I knew that Carlita always supported my aspirations, but that was the only reason she supported the first campaign. She got behind the re-election idea because she didn't like the way I was portrayed in the media. In fact, she was outdone. She fought to show the people who the Kilpatricks really were.

Conversations about Christine's exit didn't come up again until 2006. She moved over to manage the campaign. By then, Carlita and I were back in like, and in love. We laughed, joked, went over strategy and even hung out together. The Bible says a husband and wife should not be unevenly yoked in the presence of unbelievers. In other words, Carlita and I needed to come to-gether through our misery and help each other shoulder our bur-dens. I'd stopped doing that, and before I knew it, she was bearing her own cross. Neither of us wanted that to happen again. I found the time to dedicate to Carlita and the boys. But I had to take care of one more thing before I could fully mature into the man I knew I should be. It was an absolute necessity to reconcile my relationship with God.

The City of Detroit comprises 139 square miles, and boasts more than 3,000 churches. I believe I visited about half of them during my tenure. But one pastor was always a little different to me. His name is J. Drew Sheard, and he pastors the Greater Emmanuel Institutional Church of God in Christ. Bishop Sheard is a strong, confident man, the kind of guy who can walk with kings, yet never lose the common touch. He was always positive, always had an uplifting word to offer, and was always very honest with me. I decided to talk with him not long after Carlita and I had our reconciliatory conversation. I actually visited him more than once, but during our first conversation, he read me like a book. He seemed to have a direct line into my thoughts. I seriously wondered if he had talked to my wife before talking to me. He was open, and real. He told me things I needed to hear, not what I wanted to hear. It was the first time that I felt *pastored* by a real man of God, but also by a brother who'd lived and experienced bumps and blows in his own life. I connected with him immediately.

I spoke with him again about a week later and told him about my intention to attend church with my family. We also discussed other matters, and he kept calling me out! So I just gave up, and decided I would really talk to him. And I did. And he told me something I remind myself of, even today. He told me I needed to move Christine out of my administration. He didn't want to know any details, but he told me that her presence there was a problem for me, and that my wife was hurting because of it. He appreciated her talent and intelligence, but implored me to make a spiritual decision.

Of course, since you know where I ended up, you can surmise that I didn't take his godly advice. In fact, I lied to him, telling him that everything was fine. He knew I was lying, too, but he never stopped praying for me.

Bishop Sheard is too young to be my father, but he supported me like one from the first day we talked. Even today, he supports me. Although my family now lives in Dallas, and attends the Potter's House, where Bishop T.D. Jakes is my current pastor (he has truly been a godsend for my family, as well), Bishop Sheard is the man who truly helped me begin my walk back Home. I and my family joined Greater Emmanuel the following Sunday. Our new church family welcomed us with open arms, and Karen Clarke-Sheard, Bishop Sheard's wife and a famed gospel singer, reached out and pulled Carlita close.

They say the journey of a thousand miles begins with a single step. Well, the short steps toward the altar at Greater Emmanuel were quantum leaps for me. I didn't know it then, but that simple

gesture immediately positioned me to stand in the midst of whatever would come next. I marvel at how awesome a visionary God
is, because I believe He knew that strife was on its way to meet
me. I needed years to prepare for it, because the guy I was before
would have crumbled under that *international* pressure. As a weed
does a rose, that Kwame dug some deep roots, and wrapped some
ugly habits around my spirit. It would take fertilizer, donkey dung
and a good tug from God to rid me of him.

chapter 16
The Do-over

THE LAST problem to fix was the City. I was making final preparations on the City's budget. I also needed to restructure my team. I hired Anthony Adams to be deputy mayor, and moved several City departments under his immediate supervision, including Police and Fire.

Anthony was a Detroit political veteran. He worked in the Coleman Young administration before opening his own law firm in the 1980s. After Dennis Archer became mayor, his successful practice took a financial hit because of his longstanding relationship with the Young regime. Politics is truly a contact sport in that regard. I saw Anthony a lot on the campaign trail, and I really liked his style. He was serious, yet funny. Polished, yet he had street cred. A real Detroiter, yet as conservative on policy as Newt Gingrich. Perfect for my new team! He came over to the City from the Detroit Board of Education, leaving a post as general counsel to the school board. He is now back there as president. Anthony stays in the mix.

After the election, I also added former Detroit City Councilwoman Sharon McPhail. She replaced Ruth Carter, who received a judicial appointment, as my general counsel. I split Ruth's job in two. Sharon handled the counsel aspect, generally serving as my lawyer, while attorney John Johnson was appointed to handle the day-to-day management of the Law Department. Interesting histories preceded both appointments.

John's wife is a District Court judge, and at the time, he was chairman of the Fannie Lou Hamer Political Action Committee. The committee was founded by the Reverend Wendell Anthony, president of the Detroit Branch of the NAACP, and a pillar in Detroit's activist community.

Reverend Anthony and I had a hot and cold relationship. He supported me in my first election, but believed that he never received any benefit for that support. He voiced his concern to several individuals, including me, when I sought the organization's support in my re-election bid. As a matter of fact, many of the traditional politicos and their organizations felt this way.

I was extremely independent. I was never into political pay-offs or the typical wash-my-back-I'll-wash-yours style of politics. I just worked hard. That's why all the media-driven rumors and speculation about my being corrupt bothered me so much. I truly believed, with all my heart, that if you work hard on a creative and focused strategy that produced positive results, everyone would benefit. The traditional political organizations didn't operate that way. They saw it as me shunning them and ignoring their so-called political power.

One thing was definitely true—not issuing consistent perks to political organizations and catering to the inflected egos of political leaders in Detroit—unions, clergy, and political action committees—left me open to attack, because very few community leaders were willing to stand by me during my most difficult times. I appointed John to mend some of these fences, but unfortunately, he was overmatched by the demands of the job from the first day, and many knew it.

Sharon's appointment came from an altogether different place. Before President Roosevelt's concept of a "team of rivals" was re-introduced to the American political population in Barack Obama's 2008 campaign rhetoric, I had already fully bought into the theory. The best political decisions come from strong people who bring ideas and philosophies to the table through debate, deliberation and passion. A consensus of decision makers boasts the collective concept mastery necessary to make an informed decision. Anthony Adams's conservative ideals matched Christine's fiercely liberal ones, and Sean Werdlow, our chief financial officer, matched wits with Chief Ella Bully-Cummings.

Sharon was just the catalyst we needed to take debate, strategic planning and consensus building to the next level. She'd worked her way up the Detroit political ladder from the Wayne County Prosecutor's office and, at one point, lost a close race for mayor to Dennis Archer. She ran for two other Wayne County posts and ultimately won a City Council seat in 2001, before running once more for mayor, against me!

Sharon was the most active and dominant personality on the Council. She championed causes like wars against topless bars, and was a consistent thorn in my side. She forced us to work. She was focused, aggressive and very intentional. She is also very smart, and a very sweet person, but only if she likes you. And back then, she didn't like me.

When Sharon ran against me, I listened to many of her ideas throughout the campaign, particularly the ones that focused on improved community outreach and citizen empowerment. She put to rest any preconceived notions I had about her. I found her to be bright, tenacious and determined, attributes that I wanted on my team. I wanted her support for my run-off campaign. I also wanted to incorporate some of her ideas into my own administration. She gave me her unequivocal support, ideas, and even some camera footage that we used for our final, and finest, campaign television commercial. The footage showed a woman who was older than seventy being dragged out of a school board meeting by a small gang of cops as board President, Freman Hendrix, ferociously yelled, "Get her out of here now! NOW!" It was political mettle at its best, and it shredded Freman's golden image. Sharon joined the team and later fought to protect me when we began to suspect that business and governmental powers were coming for me. I'm grateful for her help to this day.

I continued to make key changes in numerous City departments. There were individuals who were on the team, but not committed to the mission, and after lightening so much of my personal and professional baggage, it was easier to see why I'd been working so hard. People were just going through the motions on my watch. I was serious about creating change, and that meant it was time for everyone to crap or get off the pot. Some left willingly. Others were encouraged to leave, fired or relieved of their appointments.

It was a new day. I began to be the mayor I'd intended to become in 2005—focused, experienced, and engaged with my personal life in order. I was ready to lead the greatest turnaround in the country, and I had no need for anyone who did not share that belief. The re-election campaign seemed to parallel the renewal that Carlita and I were undergoing at home. The team now had energy, experience and attitude. Unfortunately, some relationships withered during this process, the most important of which was my twenty-year friendship with Derrick "Zeke" Miller.

Other than my wife and Christine, I trusted no one more than Zeke. Unfortunately, that trust, and our friendship, waned after I became mayor. It happened early in the first term. I appointed Derrick Chief Administrative Officer and charged him with honing the City's outdated administrative processes. He was good at his job, and generated some innovative ideas. He also worked on an as-needed basis on special needs projects, like the casino development agreements, the Port Authority, and the Cobo Hall Convention Center expansion. I saw Derrick's other role as the nice guy who could politically corral business and elected officials and forge elusive relationships. You know, political reconnaissance.

Derrick and I often talked on a daily basis during my first two years in office, and usually several times each day. But the frequency of his conversations with me and the rest of my cabinet members decreased. The cabinet developed a running joke that no one knew what Zeke was doing, or many times, where he was. He became a mystery man. I'd raise this issue at cabinet meetings and Derrick would defend himself vehemently, often enough to make others back down. Everyone, that is, except Christine and, later, Anthony. Their clashes fit the team dynamic, because we encouraged a hard defense of each person's opinions. The process produced some of our most progressive policies, and the most sound financial decisions and community strategies. We came up with the first property tax cuts in the city's history, modernized communications for the police department, and sold pension obligation certificates to infuse more than $80 million in cash into the City's budget. And we built more recreation centers and parks. We were working with limited resources and abundant need, so everyone had to bring their "A" game to the table.

That's why it stood out so much when Derrick began to deliver weak reports from his area. It was odd because Derrick always believed he was the smartest person in the room. He always had an opinion, even if he chose not to share it at a given time, so his silence spoke volumes. I knew he was distancing himself. I'd seen it as a political practice before, and I was seeing it in him. It pricked me, though, because Derrick wasn't a random politico. This was my friend since age fourteen, the one I met in Mrs. Cunningham's ninth grade English class at Cass Tech. This was the guy who got drunk at a gathering of high school students at my mother's house, and broke the glass pane from an antique door in Mom's dining room. She's still pissed at me about that, and I still owe Derrick for it! This is the guy who traveled the State of Michigan with me as we worked to lead the State House of Representatives. For God's sake, he was in my wedding, and I was in his. And now, he was strategically and meticulously distancing himself from me. I knew it, because I knew him.

After one cabinet meeting, I asked Christine and Derrick to step into my office for a quick conversation. She'd suggested the day before that I speak with Derrick because she'd picked up on his strange vibe, too. He was cold upon entry. I'd never seen him like that.

"What's on your mind, man?" I said. "What's the problem?"

An uncomfortable silence and some jittery body movements seemed to last forever before Zeke launched into a lament. He was tired of being tied to Christine in newspapers, and tired of being packaged as part of my crew of buddies from high school.

He believed he brought skill and professionalism to the job, and that was being overshadowed. He wanted to be judged on his own merit, he said.

I appreciated his honesty, and understood his position. But I was surprised that he'd kept all that bottled up inside. It didn't seem like a big deal to me. He and I had far more serious conversations. He, *Christine* and I had overcome bigger obstacles. This was like the scene in the movie *New Jack City* where G. Money gets mad because Nino Brown's attention is diverted away from him by some random chick. Trivial. And bitchy!

Derrick wasn't telling me everything. Maybe he thought the grass was greener on the other side, or outside of the administration. Maybe he felt he'd find the kind of acceptance and recognition he desired by being elsewhere.

Christine remained quiet during the discussion. She was as close to him as I was, but she'd just taken a beating on the Navigator story, and thought he was angry with her about it. So when she walked out of the room, I asked him what was going on for real. He began to tell me about the word on the street, that I was going to lose the next election. He also suggested that I should sever my relationships with several people both on and off the staff. He'd received some information from Sheila Cockrel, a City councilwoman who fraternized with a lot of the folks who despised me. Derrick had begun to socialize with that group. It never bothered me because the places they hung out, like certain bars in the area, were great places for information. Drunk people don't lie. I told him that while I appreciated the insight, I was concerned about him. His mindset. His whereabouts. His focus. He said he was well, and ready to move forward.

"Okay," I said. We gave each other a hug and he left my office. I didn't have another serious or private conversation with him. That was the beginning of the end of our friendship.

My team of rivals were quite a special crew. We revamped the way the City approached workforce development, moving people from unemployment to focused, multi-industry training, to jobs. We saw a record number of building permits submitted to the City. This led to the city being regularly cleaned, mowed and shoveled. Through our efforts, the City hosted world-class events like the Major League Baseball All-Star Game, the Detroit Grand Prix, the Red Bull Air Races, and Super Bowl XL. We also added jobs and recruited several companies to relocate to Detroit.

Detroit was moving forward in ways people hadn't seen in decades. Not just aesthetically, but internally, economically. Every area of City government had tremendously improved during the time we were in office. Though we started some good projects, I would have to win a second term before I could make the team fully operational. We also had to pass a budget, the one that was $100 million in the hole. Big-City mayors earn their keep during times like these.

The modern mayor is more like a public sector CEO. Gone are the days of surplus, inexhaustible revenue streams and tax increases to cover debt. Today, cities must exist within their means, and the Mayor's job is as simple as it is profound: show growth while remaining fiscally solvent. You also have to maintain your customers' (residents and taxpayers') confidence. It's a customer service job.

Budget balancing is, in fact, an exercise in revenue and expenditure management, and it calls for quality customer service. It takes smart, gifted people to be able to do that. Most private sector leaders miss the mark when they apply themselves to the public sector because they lack the charisma, people skills and pure game to pull this off. And most public sector leaders lack business acumen, financial expertise and, frankly, the balls to say "no" when they need to. It's a blessing when a city has a leader who can strike that balance between worlds. Not to toot my own horn, but I fared well in this effort.

I was blessed with the opportunity to meet and study leaders from the public and private sectors. Ones who exemplified this leadership approach. In the private sector, I'm talking about people like Pete Karmanos, CEO of Karmanos Cancer Institute;

Roger Penske of Penske Automotive Group; Jim Nicholson, head of PVS Chemicals; and adept public sector gurus like Richard Daley, Willie Brown and Maynard Jackson. These men gave me wisdom that still drives my passion for leadership, and fuels my intellectual curiosity.

So it was that, in April 2005, when I made some tough choices while putting together the budget, we did it. What made it huge was the fact that, facing re-election and sagging approval ratings, I proposed to lay off cops, firefighters and other City workers. I also proposed a new bulk trash pickup fee, something the citizens had never had. But what residents didn't realize is that they were paying trash pickup fees through their taxes based on a thirty-year-old financial picture. They were *underpaying* the cost of service provision, and suffering with substandard service as a result.

Proposing this was like going one more round in a losing fight. But Detroit needed to live within its means. Businesses responded well. Residents went crazy. We held community meetings from churches to peoples' homes. I met with any group, anywhere. If you wanted to talk to the mayor, I was there—I not only loved it, I thrived on it.

My supporters worried that I was addressing all these issues when I should have been campaigning. They feared I would further decrease my chances of winning. But I would never get anything done if I worked just to get re-elected. I never ran for the position to have it for a long time. You see, I loved the city more than the job, and this was my chance to prove it, face-to-face with people. We won a lot of people over with that road show, and many who remained opposed at least understood my position. We mended the budget. After a few typically misplaced and misguided shenanigans from the City Council, they passed it. They were up for re-election, too, and played their own brand of politics.

And I could move on to my re-election campaign. I was still tired, but I was willing.

chapter 17

Not *This* Negro

M Y COMPETITIVE spirit was back by the time the re-election season arrived. Freman Hendrix had gone from offering me a job before my first term to placing me at the root of the city's problems while, of course, promoting himself as the answer. He'd pushed me, and I thought, *Hell naw, this dude ain't about to beat me. I'm about to whup him.*

What bothered me about Freman was what he represented. He was the alternative to what many metro Detroiters saw as this sorry, self-indulging Mayor, "King Kwame." I could *feel* people thinking I was dumb, hip-hop and horrible. *I'm smarter than this empty suit ever will be*, I was thinking. This race was not about who was most qualified. It was about who you liked the most.

The thing is, Freman *had* come to fight, and he spent the majority of the campaign in the lead. He and Sharon McPhail were the biggest threats, prior to her joining my administration, so the primary campaign was energetic. Freman surfed a wave of scrutiny over my first-term mistakes. When stories emerged questioning whether I was attached to the murder of a stripper who was said to have danced at the supposed Manoogian Mansion party, I realized matters had gone from worse to ridiculous. They were actually hinting on TV that I was a murderer! Reporters chased me down to question me about it. It was crazy! And yet, I felt called to move beyond it all and keenly refocus.

I lost the primary. It was the first election I'd ever lost, and

I was not gaining on him. But that was okay because my resolve was firm, and so was my team's. Except Derrick. He disappeared after the primary. I didn't see him again until election night.

We moved on. The campaign had been organized to achieve two goals: confront the issues of the first term, and refocus Detroiters on the city's future. People needed to be reminded that their city was being rebuilt right before their eyes. Their streets were clean. Their parks were new. Their waterfront was undergoing a transformation.

With Carlita in full support of the effort, we hit the streets. We visited barbershops and senior residences. I sat in families' living rooms and backyards. We rode buses, taking the conversation away from the news cameras, and directly to the people. Many gained clarity. Others expressed frustration. And I made apologies for some of my first-term decisions. My contrition created the atmosphere for balanced perspectives. It was a very, very tall order, but people slowly returned to discussing our record. We still faced an onslaught on my character, and it looked grim. The television stations, *The Detroit News* and *Free Press* endorsed my opponent. It was the first time that I had seen the television media endorse a candidate. Still, we were undeterred.

The momentum started to build once we got a good group of young, energetic people who saw our vision to start walking the neighborhoods. Working that closely with us gave them a chance to see firsthand that I was *working*. I wasn't at the club, like the rumors said. I was at community meetings. They sucked up this truth, bought in and decided to get me re-elected. They were bright and driven, and did much more working than talking, neighborhood by neighborhood. And people responded. People may have heard the rumors, but they could *see* their grass being cut. They could *see* consistent trash pick-up. And they could *see* that people weren't attacking my job, but me. Fortunately, enough people were willing to stand up that they energized the campaign. It was amazing to hear people say, "That's our guy. They're not going to run him out of here."

Home visits became one of our strongest driving forces.

Once again, we sat in people's living rooms and discussed their concerns about me, their mayor. My sister Ayanna and many others did a magnificent job of pulling the volunteers together to make these kinds of events successful. We'd ask people to assemble their loved ones, and I would go to their house and sit and talk. The gatherings grew, and we didn't filter conversations or duck questions. People asked me to explain the various controversies, or Gary Brown's removal from his appointment, which took place earlier in my first term. But they also asked about common City issues, like, "Why y'all so heavy with the parking meters?" Our goal was to elicit those kinds of questions. All of Detroit's people had concerns, and we addressed them at well over 100 such meetings.

In fact, the meetings worked so well that we began hosting evening conversations—open to the public—at the Manoogian Mansion. We held gatherings for artists, for business and civic leaders, and for barber and beauty shop owners and their employees. Despite our efforts, Freman Hendrix was still considered a shoe-in by the press. But we kept our sleeves rolled up and did what we had to do.

At one point, to drive the sentiment in the neighborhoods, we ordered green wristbands and stuck them inside a mailer. The mailer had printed quotes from Malcolm X and Martin Luther King, Jr., noting similarities between their causes and ours. People could read the mailer and wear the wristbands as a show of support. Thousands went out to likely and unlikely voters. The reaction was immediate, and we were re-energized even more. It was a timely outreach project, because it happened just as the campaign was getting ready to head to the polls. I was hungry, and we had momentum.

I fasted for eleven days just after the primary, and was on my seventh day when the first debate took place at Cobo Hall. My campaign team assembled and kept shouting at me, "You've gotta eat! This is ridiculous! You look tired!"

"I'm fine," I told them. "I'm just focused." I was ready. Not ready to run, but ready to be mayor. My strength was renewed.

From that point, even being down in the polls, I sensed that we were going to win. "Campaign Mode" was back.

The deeper thing I had was a relationship with the people of Detroit. I was family. And nobody messes with family. There was a connection between me and the citizens of Detroit that I call *Detroit Love*. It's the love of everything that defines us. The Bad Boys. Belle Isle. The Joe Louis Fist. The old Boblo Boats. Coney Island restaurants. Coleman Young. Motown. Love is the most powerful force in the universe. This city defined itself through it, and looked to me to uphold it through my service.

My opponent didn't fit into any part of this image, and had no relationship with the people beyond the City's aristocracy. I, on the other hand, embodied it. I was a true son of the city. And the race was about community pride and active participation in revolutionary change. It was about kinship and action. In the final analysis, spirit and connectivity would decide the race. After that, the guy with those connections had better have the chops for the job. I did.

Freman attacked my mistakes in the debates. His strategy was to hammer in all of the things that had run in the news. But hammering an already-driven nail just creates noise. The attacks were just that… attacks. I deflected them by apologizing and admitting I could have done some things differently. I also made it clear that we had accomplished a great deal despite the controversies, and that I deserved a chance to finish what my administration had started. Freman, meanwhile, couldn't articulate a clearer vision than ours. He was too vested in the past, my past, when the people wanted forward-thinking leadership. By the time he outlined his own plan, I'd driven ours home.

I killed Freman in the debates. They were not even close, plus, his cognitive skills were questioned for the first time. I relished opportunities to not only outsmart so-called socially acceptable negroes whenever I had the opportunity, but to also leave them appearing cognitively deficient. Freman lost credibility, and the press couldn't rescue him. He was simply underwhelming. His supporters wavered a bit in the aftermath, swayed by the hole we'd poked in the proverbial hot air balloon.

Election day was intense. We were confident that we'd reached enough people to get the vote out and win. We had the Fruit of Islam, the Nation of Islam's security detail, come out to help at the polls, because there was some tension at the locations. We wanted to ensure that no tampering took place, and their well-groomed, stern presence said a lot.

Young voters also turned out in impressive fashion. The eighteen-to-thirty-five bracket, historically Detroit's largest and most evasive demographic, seemed to arrive in droves, and constituted the largest youth voter turnout in the city's history up to that point. And man, were they colorful! Some were well mannered, but we did see a few blunt smokers and rolling twenty-two-inch rims. They cared enough to cast their ballots, and I was happy to see them all. The black bourgeoisie showed up right alongside the 'hood. The Latino community, which was growing and thriving, voted in heavy numbers. The eyes of the state were focused on Detroit, and everyone picked a side.

The race was emotionally and racially charged, but I'm proud to say that my support base was very diverse from the first day. My supporters lived all over the metropolitan area, and came in all shapes, sizes and colors. Interestingly, I was blamed for stoking the flames of race throughout the campaign. Though I didn't, it helped sell papers.

We gathered at our campaign headquarters at day's end to watch the results. Freman's numbers came in early and fast—so quickly, in fact, that Channel 4 (NBC) declared him the winner early in the evening, minutes after the polls closed.

"Wow!" Ayanna kept saying. "That is not the sentiment we got at the polls today. And we were *all over the city*." The early reports threatened to dampen our spirits. But I called Ayanna before anyone got a chance to wallow in any bad news.

"Don't worry about that," I said. "I know what they said, 'Yann, but all the numbers aren't in. Just hold tight."

We moved to the hotel and sat around, waiting for news. The mood went from low to tentative. Out of nowhere, Derrick entered the room, wearing a sad expression that I'll never forget. He thought we'd lost the election. I couldn't blame him. The media had already reported it, and the pollsters on Channel 4 called to tell him we'd lost the race. They'd done live shots from his headquarters, proclaiming him victorious. And here was my old friend who, over the course of a few years, had become very good friends with people who couldn't stand me, people who would later work to remove me from office and imprison me. Even now, it still stings.

I went to the hotel ballroom and talked to my supporters, who were actually ignoring the numbers and were in a festive mood. I told them we were still waiting for the rest of the numbers to roll in.

"Be patient and watch God work," I said. "There is no way that we lost this election. The streets have not spoken yet." The numbers finally came in well after midnight, and we won! I went back out elated and, in a speech that became famous, declared that "the streets spoke."

In the end, the race wasn't that close. People can tell you who they're voting for, but you never know what they'll do until they step in that voting booth. We'd worked and prayed, collectively and actively. Even today, I believe God is still responding to that prayer. Before the re-election campaign, my life had reached its true nadir. But I hadn't seen anything yet. My saga was about to take on epic proportions.

chapter 18
The Calm Before

IT FELT LIKE life was beginning anew in 2006. Carlita and I were enjoying each other, reconnecting through the ability to communicate that has, historically, been one of our hallmarks. We strengthen each other when our rapport is strong. We were happy to move past the period between 2003 and 2005. I also began to spend more time with Jelani, Jalil and Jonas. All they ever wanted was to see their father in the morning and at night on a more regular basis. It was hard for them to go to bed so many nights before I got home, and I know they were disappointed whenever I failed to make a game, or an event.

The family thoroughly enjoyed attending church together, and Pastor Sheard and Karen's consistency and connection with Godly living was huge for us. We needed that. Strong leadership spurs copycat behavior. We'd never experienced balanced living as a married couple until that point. The year 2006 was the closest we'd come to some semblance of it.

Unfortunately, Carlita's active support of my mayoral duties would be short-lived. She soon withdrew again because I did not fire Christine. Carlita knew what she didn't know, that my connection to Christine was inappropriate. She didn't need details to feel that my best friend was the bane of her existence. I hated everything about that, the torn sense of loyalty, the position I put Carlita in, not knowing how to handle it, and not being willing to make the right choice for my family. Christine had remained my most trusted advisor after we stopped seeing each other. Our friendship stood as intact as it had been before our affair. And it was critical now, because it was time for me to grow up in my position, to step it up even more. One could argue that I was again putting the city before my wife.

We'd overseen this immense corporation for four years, learned it inside and out, made allies and enemies, and now, we were ready to make it run efficiently. I'd begun to focus the City's attention on the Super Bowl's impending Detroit touchdown early in 2002, soon after I took office. With this being the most watched spectacle in the world, it meant the world was coming to Detroit. We had to be prepared to make a great impression, especially since history had stacked the deck against the city.

The NFL had brought the Super Bowl to the Pontiac Silverdome a little more than twenty years earlier, for Super Bowl XVI. It was an abysmal failure for our state. Horrible articles ran about how bad people's experiences were, about dirty streets, dirty snow, a winter wasteland, crime and poverty. Many articles implored the NFL to leave Detroit and never return. Well, that pissed me off, because the press clippings roundly referred to Pontiac as Detroit. It was an unfair comparison. Plus, I was twelve years old when all of that happened. I pulled my cabinet members and appointees and made the message clear. For this thing to succeed, we had to first believe! I wanted people to see, feel and sense a new city, a renaissance city.

Getting City employees on the same page was task number one. I spent weeks meeting with hundreds of employees from different departments. The message was simple. In 2006, hundreds of national and international media outlets, and hundreds of thousands of visitors would descend on our city, and they would proceed to tell the world what they saw. What they said could create or damage our opportunities. The spectacle was also expected to bring about $500 million to Metro Detroit's economy. This was bigger than all of us, individually. But collectively, we could determine the course of the city for our families. Let's pull together and show the world who we really are. I answered their questions and came away from those meetings with firm commitments.

As part of our planning to create a more appealing and visitor-friendly downtown, I and Walt Watkins and his team launched the Gateway Project. The venture's intent was to beautify the streets that served as the main corridors to the Downtown Detroit area, and later branch out to other streets. Gratiot, Woodward and Michigan Avenues, Jefferson Avenue and Washington Boulevard were all lined up for facelifts. They'd be resurfaced, and each would have a specific beautification plan. It was a major project, and it had a very short timeline. We actually completed this project the previous Summer, before the Major League All-Star Game hit town, by re-engineering underground water lines, lighting, developing a master landscaping plan and creating walkable areas.

This became one of the first major assignments where major City departments—Water and Sewage, Public Works, Safety and Engineering—collaborated successfully with our economic experts. We finished on time and on budget, and Downtown swiftly took on a new visage.

We took this success one step further by redesigning an old railway that had been once used to bring cement, coal and other materials to the old industry on our Riverfront (before the Riverwalk). Today, this corridor is the Dequindre Cut, a beautiful walking and jogging trail that extends from the waterfront to Detroit's world-famous farmer's market, the Eastern Market.

These developments were all ready for the press to pick and prick by Super Bowl time. The press are treated like gods during Super Bowl week. And when they are not, the host city and the NFL surely read about it. We got this fact, and understood that the city would need nothing short of a spring cleaning, a complete renovation, and some potpourri to pull this off. Every Super Bowl host city puts together a Host Committee to better enhance the visitor experience. The committee spends years scouting Super Bowls in preceding host towns, and then coordinates activities with the NFL, as well as essential government services.

The NFL's Special Events team does an amazing job producing these events. They're also responsible for the league playoffs, and the NFL Pro-Bowl.

The Chairman of Ford Motor Company and owner of the Detroit Lions, Bill Ford, Jr., asked billionaire businessman and racing legend Roger Penske to chair the Detroit host committee. This turned out, I believe, to be one of the best decisions Bill Ford ever made. Roger is an incredible leader with uncanny focus and consistency. He could oversee and diagram an overall logistics plan for Super Bowl transportation, and in the next moment, walk to the site and share stories and laughs with the bus drivers. All the while, he never lost sight of the ultimate goal. He was sharp, quick-witted, patient, charismatic and stern. Such qualities helped him build his empire, multibillion dollar businesses whose services ranged from auto supply to NASCAR racing, and global logistics to trucking. I learned a great deal from him over the four years I spent working with him on the Super Bowl plan.

Roger tapped Susan Sherer, another awesome mind, as executive director of the Host Committee. She'd worked with the Detroit Convention and Visitors Bureau, and had the ability to seemingly get anyone to do anything she wanted. Her infectious laugh and unique voice contrasted with a strong sense of organization and acute business acumen. Susan's task was Herculean, because she handled business leaders, politicos, community leaders, Democrats and Republicans, urbanites and soccer moms.

I think Detroit's was the best Host Committee in Super Bowl history, at that point, and yes, I am biased. I have attended about ten Super Bowls. I have gone officially as mayor, and as Super Bowl committeeperson, to five. I've been fan and prospector, and I've studied, taken notes and supervised activities. No other city put in the work that Detroit did, from official business to quality control. And none had to battle the Detroit stigma.

At one point, in my first term, I pitched the Detroit Renaissance Board, the City's corporate roundtable, to help raise cash for gap financing for these new projects. Member companies include GM, Ford and Compuware, and they do a great deal

of development in Detroit. But somehow, they hadn't had a collective impact on the city. They'd become more political than
business-oriented. But when I pitched them with the same speech
I gave the City workforce, they raised over $23 million to help
provide financing to close residential and commercial development deals in and around Downtown Detroit. It was the first time
they had raised that much money, and their achievement sent the
message that everyone was on board for the Super Bowl.

Super Bowl Week progressed wonderfully. The press wrote
such unbelievably positive things about Detroit for the entire
week that it felt like a miracle. Even *The Detroit News* and *Free
Press*, papers that have insatiable appetites for circling the wag-
ons and shooting into Detroit, wrote positive stories. I'd never
witnessed the level of regional support, kindness and camaraderie
that the area received during this week. And I take pride in how
organized the City received it. Even God was on our side, because the weather was above fifty degrees all week. The only day
it snowed was on game day, a light fall while the game was played
indoors!

The sights, sounds, energy and love were something to treasure, especially in a region as fractured as ours. For the first time
in quite a while, we felt like we could play big. And we felt a real
connection to one another. The event was the sum of its parts,
and the greatest unsung heroes were the Detroit City employees.
The police, fire and EMS teams, the bus drivers and transportation workers, the mechanics, the Public Works employees who
kept the town clean pulled together in a team effort and made a
tremendous impact.

The event became a catalyst like no other. After the event,
downtown development continued, and neighborhood development picked up. Housing development sprouted, and we removed
65,000 abandoned cars from city streets over a two-year period.
We bolstered the annual neighborhood City clean-up, and would
see five straight years of 60,000 or more volunteers.

The positive energy in the city was tremendous. I began
touting the new movement in Detroit around the country. We

were being *covered favorably in newspapers from* The Los Angeles Times to *USA Today.* The *New York Times* ran full-page spreads. The Super Bowl had come to us, and left Detroit sparkling-clean.

I benefited personally when my approval ratings soared. At more than sixty percent by 2007, they were highest of any I'd had, far exceeding even then-Governor Jennifer Granholm's. The negative press about me simmered during this time, which freed us to focus on City affairs. I revamped my communications team, adding Ceeon Quiett as my communications director. Ceeon brought focus and professionalism to my Communications endeavors, which had been lacking previously. Ceeon had actually started in 2005 but left the next year, following Hurricane Katrina. New Orleans was her hometown, and she felt called to return. I truly respected her for that, and appreciated the communications plan she left. We followed it long after her departure.

chapter 19
Snake Pit

MAYBE WE should have forecasted trouble brewing when, earlier in my first term, the police chief shared a couple of awkward memos with Christine. The first, which was written by Gary Brown, my Internal Affairs director, notified the chief that he was investigating an auto accident that involved a member of the Executive Protection Unit. It was a basic memo, the kind that usually wouldn't leave a department, so Christine received it with curiosity, but didn't see why it should make its way to me. A second memo, an anonymous warning about Brown's investigation that followed just days later, warranted more concern.

Christine showed it to me, mainly so I could see what the guy I'd instructed to clear up our backlog of more than 500 unsolved, uninvestigated matters of police misconduct per the federal consent decree, was doing with his time. We looked deeper and saw that, a full year after receiving his charge, Brown had solved *not one* of the crimes in that backlog. I was disappointed to say the least, so I removed Brown from his appointed position. In these cases, removed appointees have the option to return to their original positions, but he surprisingly opted to retire. He then wrote one more memo, a much lengthier one, accusing me of "firing" him for investigating matters involving me and my Executive Protection Unit.

Brown didn't do the job he had been asked to do, and that's

why I removed him from his duties. The Justice Department was to revisit the backlog he had been assigned to solve during my first term, so I needed results. Instead, he piddled over things that should have been handled at the supervisory level. He then began a sinister political exercise that targeted me. It was like working with J. Edgar Hoover. People think I removed him to cover my own ass, but I did it to get the Detroit Police Department's butt out of a sling.

I did what any boss would do with Brown. And it was the right decision, because those cases were solved after he was gone. Ralph Godbee, the current chief of police in Detroit, moved over to lead after Brown's exit. He did an excellent job, and also helped regain the Feds' confidence in our department.

I'd never encountered the level of treachery that Gary Brown displayed, and to this day, I have no idea what I did to warrant it. He was deceitful, shrewd and prepared. But for what he was planning, he needed a team. So he hired his friend, Michael Stefani, as his lawyer. And with that, they set out to find people who would help them build a case against me and the City of Detroit. Harold Nelthrope became his crony.

Nelthrope was known as a mediocre officer. He had a history of alcohol abuse and psychological issues, had been in drunk driving accidents, and never should have been placed on my Executive Protection team. In my first term, though, I didn't select the EPU. The unit's leader, Ron Fleming, introduced them to me. Ron had run Executive Protection for Coleman Young's administration, so I took his expertise for granted. That was a mistake, because Nelthrope was his friend, and Ron knew of Nelthrope's history. Still, he gave Nelthrope a cushy job on my team—to watch the Manoogian. So, he spent most of his days at the house, monitoring the cameras and ensuring that the people working in the home during that first year—2002—moved in and out smoothly.

That was when Carlita and a local designer, Roxanne Taylor, were renovating the official residence. The traffic in the house at that time consisted of painters, craftsman and other construction workers. As I mentioned earlier in this book, because Carlita wanted the new look at the Manoogian to be a surprise for me and the boys, she ordered us to stay away, which we did until it was completed.

Carlita and Nelthrope communicated a lot and became friendly. Our children even participated in activities with his kids. But he developed a problem with two other EPU officers, Greg Jones and Mike Martin. They disliked Nelthrope. Why, I'm not sure. But Nelthrope told Carlita one day that he was leaving the unit. We were a little sad, but we shook his hand and wished him well. At that time, the EPU had high turnover for reasons outside the Mayor's office, so I made it a point to never get involved with personal matters. As long as my wife and children were safe, I was good.

Nelthrope and I remained casual acquaintances, and still saw each other at the boys' events. Months after Nelthrope's departure, I learned that Brown had interviewed him about an alleged car accident involving one of the EPU officers. He also asked him about overtime abuse and, of course, the party rumor. It surprised me that Brown used Nelthrope as his main source of information. It shocked me further when, checking the interview dates, I realized that one took place just days before Nelthrope and I marched together in the Rosedale Park parade, with our children! He had smiled and behaved normally that day, but had already begun conspiring with Brown.

In his statement, Nelthrope said he went to work one morning and saw cups and trash on the floor that indicated a party had taken place. I was speechless. He never specified a day, or even a month, but said it was "probably the fall of 2002," smack in the middle of Carlita's renovation project. She was floored. When the media reported on his statement, some City contractors who were hired to clean the Manoogian a few times a week told Carlita that, on several occasions, they'd seen him in my private clothes closet, upstairs, in our living quarters. They said he was going through my drawers and "looking around." They thought he had permission, because he was a police officer. I can't over-

state the importance of trust between a principal and his pro-
tector. Men in Nelthrope's position are privy to a family's most
private moments, and your life is in their hands. They *have* to be
trustworthy. Hearing about this pissed me off and made Carlita
very uncomfortable. Hell, I was gone for long hours many days,
and God knows what this man was doing around my family. And
who else was involved? One thing was certain—he was playing
for Brown and Stefani's team.

Stefani spent a few years building his case against the City.
He deposed me, Christine, and other members of my administration about Brown's allegation. He also pulled a trick. Walt Harris,
a former EPU member, had filed his own lawsuit, claiming that
I abused time by having him drive me around town to meet and
have sex with women. One tryst happened, he said, in the back
room of a barbershop, while other people were present. Another
involved me meeting a young lady at a downtown apartment
building who came out to meet me wearing a full-length mink
coat with nothing on under it. His stories were sexy and descrip-
tive, but why was he the only apparent witness to these kinds of
supposed activities?

Stefani used Harris's suit to spice up his, which had grown
stale after the Attorney General's expensive investigation turned
up nothing, and the car accidents failed to interest anyone. Stefani
deposed Harris with a court reporter present and no opposing
counsel, and then handed the document to the *Detroit Free Press*
who, moving forward, developed a relationship with him and
reported whatever he gave them with factual overtones. It gave
Stefani's pursuit new appeal.

Harris did say one thing that troubled me. He said Christine
and I communicated on our two-way pagers "all the time." It was
a random statement, but it marked the first time our text messages were discussed. To me, it stuck out like a sore thumb. And
it would change the complexion of their case and the way it was
reported, because the public fodder would slowly switch from
wrongful termination to sex, affairs and cover-ups. There was
never a mention of this stuff in their pleadings, but to this day,

people in Detroit believe the case was about sex. By the time he deposed my staff and me, Brown's probes evolved from termination talk to include the affairs, the party and Harris's *sexual chauffeur* tales.

When Stefani took his act to the Wayne County Courthouse for the pre-trial hearing, I found him to be remarkably unorganized. But I was also wary that he had my image, and Detroit's century-old history of polarizing race relations, on his side. He could have litigated in Bermuda shorts and would still have a chance to win.

Judge William Callahan presided, and Stefani made an early motion to subpoena Christine's text messages from the Skytel Corporation to use as evidence. Callahan ruled that *he'd* subpoena the messages, and hold them in his chambers. He did, and later he ruled that they could not be used.

The trial officially began in August 2007. While the City approached the suit like any other—cities get sued all the time—the TV networks pre-empted programming and ran it live. We felt the City had a very good case. Our legal team, which included Sam McCargo, Wilson Copeland and Valerie Colbert-Osamuede, felt it would be hard to prove that I had abused anything. First, security had to be with me wherever I went. If anyone's time was abused, it was *mine*.

Daytime television was pre-empted for the duration of the proceedings. My testimony was highly anticipated. That morning, I wore traditional corporate attire. Dark suit. White shirt. Red tie.

I was comfortable and confident taking the stand, but I was not comfortable with the jury, which was made up of eleven whites and one black woman, all non-Detroiters. That was ominous, because publicity around the suit carried a *me vs. them* kind of tone. It felt like the jury was judging not just the facts, but me.

Stefani examined Christine first, and asked her a battery of questions about the affair, and the text messages. We were surprised that he brought them up, despite Callahan's ruling. But he did, and we offered no objections. I was not prepared to divulge my personal secret to the public, and I had very little time to think about how I would answer if he took me through a similar line of questioning. He was within his rights to ask about it, and we should have anticipated the weasel to come out of him. At least, our attorneys should have. In the movies, our attorneys would have jumped up and objected before I got a chance to answer the question, and they probably should have.

Stefani had gone around rules, orders and the law since 2004. He was a street fighter, and our lawyers were erudite and appropriate. They ran up against a guy who'd do anything to win. When he examined me and asked the same question, there was again no objection, and I answered quickly and stoically, hoping I wouldn't regret what I'd done. I denied the affair, and lied on the witness stand.

He continued, probing social meetings between us, intimate messages; text messages again, conversations about the alleged party, and nude dancers. He even asked if she ever told me that she wanted to leave her husband. The questions were so specific, I could tell that he'd probably seen the texts. Judge Callahan was supposedly the only one who had them. And, per his order, they were sealed and would not be used. I was concerned.

Stefani finally moved on to questions about Brown and Nelthrope, but the underhanded and tangential tone had been established. Stefani had cornered us with irrelevant, and supposedly protected, information.

Sam and Valerie tried to reposition our argument in cross-examination. They asked questions about Internal Affairs, Gary Brown, and Harold Nelthrope. I regained my composure and reiterated my original position, focusing on my core concerns about Brown and the reason I removed him.

At the end of it all, the jury made a decision in just over twenty minutes. They awarded Brown, Nelthrope and Stefani $8 million, much more than they had demanded. We were shocked that they won, and that Stefani's strategy worked. I immediately vowed to file an appeal as I believed—and still believe— that we'd done nothing wrong to those officers.

Stefani, meanwhile, agreed to have a settlement conference to prevent a costly, and possibly protracted, appellate process. All the attorneys agreed on a mediator, and my attorneys kept me abreast of the progress. In the meantime, I went back to work and allowed the City's legal process to run its course. After a week or so, the story disappeared from the newspapers and newscasts. The holidays were approaching, and the city began gearing up for its annual festivities.

I was thankful to get back to *mayoring*. I'd begun serious talks with the City of Windsor, Ontario, Canada, to consummate a lease deal on the tunnel between our two cities, which would bring the City of Detroit $75 million. Dan Gilbert, owner of Quicken Loans, had also closed a deal to move their headquarters to downtown Detroit from the suburbs. We were also working with General Motors and the NCAA to create a great visitor experience for the upcoming NCAA Regional Final, which was set to be held at Ford Field that following March. The Final Four was coming to the same venue the following year. The City was moving forward, downtown and in the neighborhoods. It wasn't too long before I forgot about Brown, Nelthrope and Stefani…

…until I got a call from my attorney, Sam McCargo, just weeks later while traveling back from Washington, D.C. He told me that Stefani had just shown him several text messages Christine and I had exchanged, messages "of a very personal nature."

"Damn!" I shouted, cutting him off. Stefani used a subpoena that Judge Callahan had not approved, which made it illegal (he would later admit this), and retrieved about 6,000 texts, purportedly pulled from a Skytel pager Christine used. We'd learn later, by Skytel Corp's admission, that they came directly from the company's server. Skytel would also admit to violating at least one federal law by giving them to Stefani. We'd have to deal with that later because, presently, *Stefani* had them. That was bad news.

We were 24-hour employees and, for that reason, the City allowed us to use the pagers for business *and* personal purposes. The majority of the messages were about City business, but exchanges with spouses, children, physicians, parents, pastors, friends and lovers were considered private. Even the messages between Christine and me qualified. There were, however, some pretty lewd messages.

I met with Sam, and then we spoke with Carlita and the boys. Next, we huddled in a small room to talk privately, where Sam proceeded to describe what he read in detail. He suggested that Stefani didn't want to release the texts, because of the way he'd gotten them. He suggested we settle the case, include Walt Harris in the agreement, and put it all behind us. My concern was the settlement cost, and whether I could be certain the messages wouldn't go public. Sam suggested a confidentiality agreement in which both parties would exchange private documents as part of a trial and settlement strategy. In other words, we'd have something on them, and they'd have something on us. Wilson Copeland and Billy Mitchell, two conferring attorneys, echoed the sentiment as standard practice. So I thought about it overnight and decided to go with it. The attorneys exchanged private documents that could prove damaging to both sides. We were given the texts, and we gave up Harold Nelthrope's incredible mental health history, as well as Gary Brown's history as a narcotics officer. *The Detroit Free Press* soon referred to this as a "secret deal" that I negotiated, as if I acted alone, and did something illegal.

With that, I put it behind us. I reasoned that they hadn't won, but just cornered me. My job was to get Detroit past it. Detroit's Risk Management fund would pay the settlement, so the City's budget wouldn't be affected. And though I was pissed at having to pay for something so illegal, I was comfortable with the decision. Stefani got $2.2 million, Nelthrope $2.6 million, and Gary Brown $3.2 million. Walt Harris got $400,000. It was robbery, a jack move, and both sides knew it. Of course, my critics were giddy to see *me* lose.

One caveat that really bothered me, enough that I shouldn't have signed that version of the agreement, was the wording in the agreement that categorically released all attorneys involved from any liability if any other contents exchanged in the agreement became public. They covered themselves. My attorneys advised me that this was standard practice and, despite a sinking feeling that I shouldn't do it, I did. I still kick myself for that.

Stefani also signed a statement claiming that we had the only copy of the texts but, with no liability to be concerned about, he was able to confidently sign off on an untrue declaration.

I knew I'd see those messages again. So did Christine. She came to my office in December 2007 and implored me to come forward and tell the truth about everything. Brown and Stefani were both snakes in our eyes. The thought of "coming clean" was daunting, and I wanted time to think about it. A few weeks later, we talked and started planning how we would break it all to our families. We also planned her exit from the administration. We'd replace Christine with Kandia Milton as chief of staff. Kandia didn't know why she was leaving, but worked with her to effect a smooth transition.

Stefani, meanwhile, slithered as expected. He'd given the texts to a *Detroit Free Press* reporter weeks earlier. A thread in my life's fabric was being secretly tugged. And a yank was coming.

chapter 20

Hoofbeats

I LOVE WHEN horses prance. Clydesdales are my favorite, with the whisking, powerful *cl-cloomp-cl-cloomp-cl-cloomp* of their hooves. They move with force, power and direction, and their hoofbeats serve as a symbolic clarion.

I'm convinced that hoofbeats of a political nature mobilized and barreled toward me as early as my first term. Unseen, unreported tangents to my public controversies, they possessed disdain for my administration, our vision for Detroit, and for me. Warnings about growing loathing, of certain forces that wanted me out of the way, came my way soon after my re-election. Hoofbeats in City and State politics; in business, in the media.

"They're coming to get you," were Sharon's exact words, spoken privately in my office one day. I probably didn't take her as seriously as I should have. I believed I had solid relationships with key people, at least solid enough to ward off any detractors with malicious intent. I believed my work would be my voice. I believed in my team. I was wrong.

At the beginning of term two, we sought to change the way the City of Detroit brought new dollars in, created jobs and encouraged tourism. We wanted to reintroduce Detroit to the world and put Detroiters to work. The people needed employment. I even created an Executive Order to expedite it.

This order protected workers from any ulterior motives by businesspeople, because it wasn't racially driven, and it was mandatory. It reinforced requirements that were previously too flexible to have an impact to grant Detroiters access to economic activity in the city. My focus was clear, and my objectives were known. If you wanted to participate in the hundreds of millions of dollars in construction and development projects that were going on in the City at that time, then you'd better hire Detroiters.

Employment is priceless. It breeds self-determination, confidence and hope. The community deserved to see their dollars exchanged among residents and commercial business in their backyards.

Members of the business community received this move like a punch in the face. Detroit is full of old-school economic thinking and traditional business dinosaurs who relish control. But the younger business culture brimmed with innovative ideas and a twenty-first century vision. A new undercurrent of positive energy and activity brewed in the mid-market and small business area, but it hadn't impressed most of Detroit's business fixtures.

We were simultaneously mobilizing community outreach efforts, and one of our biggest opportunities lay with the then-new Workforce Development Initiative. This department funded well over 100 community organizations and mandated them to educate and train Detroiters to enter the workforce. We'd long known that Detroiters had few opportunities to find work outside the city limits. So, Workforce Development, as an organization and a philosophy, was critical. Yet most of the organizations getting money from the initiative possessed a grotesque lack of urgency. Their collective job placement rate of five percent fell well below the mandated fifty percent average.

Sharon presented a concept to me, and I granted her permission to implement it. She notified 135 of the funded service providers that their contracts would end in eighteen months, and that they'd have to not only reapply for their funding, but would also have to include a detailed strategy to improve their placement rates. Several organizations, including one called Jewish Vocational Services, railed against the notice. JVS received about $25 million from the City, and their placement rate was two percent. I was told that their leadership, when challenged, actually admitted to feeling that they couldn't prepare the people they served to enter the workforce. That was their argument, to blame it on the people. It was also an admission that they couldn't do their jobs, but expected to get their $25 million. Well, we were no longer in the business of pouring money down the toilet. Everyone was accountable.

The Workforce Development initiative ultimately proved as divisive as it was noble. I was offended by these organizations' willingness to pretend to help Detroit communities. People languished in poverty while those with money and a mandate to develop their resources shunned them. We started to change that. The initiatives we launched drove increases in medical and dental assistance programs and other skills. Students gained clinical experience by working in state-of-the-art labs and classrooms. It was gratifying to see people go from struggling to donning scrubs and white jackets, while learning to draw blood or clean teeth.

We were creating household educational environments, and our data suggested that the children of parents enrolled in Workforce Development programs improved their own grades. Today, career education is growing exponentially across the country. Well, we foresaw this day coming, and took advantage of it, and it was exciting! But the consensus among funding recipients was that we were endangering their bottom line. Prominent board members on some of those organizations began to whisper.

I starting getting phone calls and visits from individuals imploring me to reconsider my strategy. One visit came from Reggie Turner, a Detroit attorney who seemed to be involved in a great deal of Detroit activity. He told me, "Sharon and her Workforce Development moves are causing major problems for you, Mr. Mayor." He suggested that my administration was enjoying its first real peace, its first absence of negative press in a while, and that I should get Sharon to "chill out." *Cl-cloomp.*

Gary Torgow, a very influential member of the Jewish community, and a supporter since I'd been in the State House, also visited me. He and I had a great business and personal relationship. I even attended his son's wedding and purchased my infamous earring from his brother-in-law, a New York jeweler. Gary came to talk to me about the concerns in the Jewish community about Sharon's apparent "attack" on JVC. He also wanted to let me know about the growing concern regarding my relationship with the Nation of Islam and, particularly, Min. Louis Farrakhan. *Cl-cloomp.*

Our Workforce Development efforts paralleled other attempts to bring national events to the city. The Detroit Convention and Visitors Bureau was working overtime. That's how we got the Final Four and other events, like the Nation of Islam's Saviour's Day celebration. Saviour's Day falls on the birthday of the religious organization's founder, Wallace Fard Muhammad, February 26, and celebrates the organization's history. The Nation of Islam's leader usually delivers the keynote address, which meant Louis Farrakhan would be speaking in 2007, the year it came to Detroit. It was held at Ford Field, the home of the Detroit Lions, and it was huge.

Minister Farrakhan is a master orator and defender of people of African descent whose rhetoric has been a thorn in mainstream's society's side for decades, and this event provided a very large platform. He's also been publicly called "anti-Semitic" by organizations like the Anti-Defamation League for critical comments he made about Jewish people almost twenty years ago. But he is still considered a hero by African-Americans.

I was truly excited to welcome the thousands of visitors who would come to eat, spend money and enjoy our city during the Saviour's Day event. But Gary told me that the Jewish community viewed the event as a personal affront.

Josh Opperer, another longtime supporter I had also known since my days in the Michigan House, expressed similar disdain. "Minister Farrakhan hates Jews," he told me, adding that he didn't see how he could be my friend if I had friends like that. Gary was less succinct and dramatic, but that was the last real communication I had with either of them. After his warning, he left my office and never returned. Josh resigned from a board to which I had appointed him, and never spoke to me again.

I knew I was treading on thin ice with some powerful people, but I felt it was critical to ensure that our citizens were nurtured, and given access to their hometown. Further, the business community was a part of the citizenry, and their hotels, restaurants, shops, and so forth, needed patronage. These events serviced those needs, and helped brand the city. I believe our community's diversity and tolerance *must* be celebrated and acknowledged. Especially after hosting the Super Bowl, it was important to continue to welcome the world to Detroit.

We all benefit from that energy, and Saviour's Day was only one contributor. No one was offended when I supported and the LGBTQ (Lesbian, Gay, Bisexual, Transgender and Questioning) community's "Hotter than July" event every year at Palmer Park, on Detroit's Northwest Side, and spoke at a large sit-down dinner that the same community organized in conjunction with State and national groups. I participated every year in the *Cinco De Mayo* celebrations, and invested millions of dollars in a project called the Mexicantown Development. We did this to celebrate Detroit's rich Hispanic and Latino population, culture and history. Recognizing this as a strong, diverse branch on Detroit's family tree, I instructed an entire section of my staff to focus on this part of the population; one person for business outreach, another for community outreach, and one more for ecumenical outreach. In fact, Fred Feliciano, the president of the Hispanic Business Association, was on my staff.

We didn't stop there. I also worked with Bishop Andrew Merritt, pastor of Straight Gate, a West Side church, when he hosted the "One in Worship" celebration, a global Christian event that brought in nationally known pastors, ministers and gospel artists. When I say we wanted to reintroduce Detroit to the world, we meant it literally, and we didn't just expect the world to come to us.

I also traveled to Dubai on a trip sponsored by the Arab-American Chamber of Commerce to market Detroit as a destination place for Arab business and commerce. While there, I courted leaders from their government to come to Detroit for the

American-Arab Summit. Delightfully, they accepted, and when the Summit was held at the Renaissance Center in Downtown Detroit, it became an international event covered extensively by international press outlets, including Al Jazeera. We'd trumpeted in Dubai that Detroit has the largest Middle-Eastern community in the world outside the Middle East. The Arab World was welcomed in Detroit. We also worked extensively with the Arab Community to raise money to build the National Arab Museum in Dearborn, Michigan. The Museum project was a big enough deal that Dubai leadership also supported it.

Numerous Arab periodicals featured this connection in their cover stories, capturing my meeting with Dubai leader Sheik Hamdaan, when he spoke in Detroit at the Summit.

In a perfect world, the people who hated me for supporting the Nation of Islam and Minister Farrakhan would have opened their eyes and ears enough to see that I gave a platform to people based on the fact that they had as much of a stake in Detroit's vitality as I did. Some say I was naïve and idealistic. I say, okay! Nations are built on idealistic foundations. It's better than hate! Unfortunately, my naiveté inspired an army, and my next move would give it urgency.

Comerica Bank, Detroit's homegrown, hometown depository for more than a century, decided to move its headquarters from Detroit to Texas in 2007. The bank didn't inform me, the Governor, the press or its own workforce of this decision until the day of the announcement. They told everyone at a big press conference. In fact, Ralph Babb, Comerica's chairman and CEO, made the announcement *from* Texas. He'd already moved. He called both me and the governor just minutes before the press event took place.

That year was marked by changes in the banking industry. Banks were relocating, merging with other banks, and some went out of business. But Comerica had maintained its Downtown Detroit presence and prospered through all of the industry transitions. They were a Michigan success story. And they happened to be the City of Detroit's primary banker. Hundreds of millions of the City's dollars were kept in numerous Comerica accounts. That translated to hundreds of thousands of transactions, for which Comerica received millions in transaction fees. Most of the City of Detroit's 15,000 employees kept their money in Comerica accounts and, although the bank charged us ridiculous amounts in fees, most people stuck with them. It was, after all, the home-town bank. Until they moved. Discreetly.

I was nervous about the loss of employees and tax revenue, but their CEO assuaged those concerns by confirming that a full staff of employees would be staying in Detroit. He said there would be a staff reduction, but nothing drastic.

I saw the move as an opportunity to create competition within the banking industry for Detroit's dollars. It was time to maximize the opportunities that other financial institutions might offer. Detroit was big business with financial power. In the past, Detroit had largely kept money in Comerica and executed ele-mentary transactions through that relationship, never attempting to demand or leverage anything from it. The City didn't recog-nize its power. Well, that was about to change.

The City's annual budget was approximately $3 billion. But when we pooled all of our money, the sum total of which was held in several banks outside Comerica, we became a $14 billion powerhouse. That kind of money moving daily through those ac-counts helped create a more competitive creative environment for Detroit's banking business. There were better banking prod-ucts out there, and they could save the City tens of millions in transaction fees, while producing some creative lending oppor-tunities for our residents and businesses. I moved on the oppor-tunity, tapping my Deputy Mayor, Anthony Adams, to lead the strategic implementation of a new Banking Consolidation Plan. We sent RFQs (request for quotes) to several local banks, and the response was overwhelming. We received strong statements of interest from the Royal Bank of Scotland, Bank of America, National City and others. And, of course, Comerica. I met with several of the CEOs from these financial institutions, and they all wanted our business.

We enforced a deadline in which to receive responses, and announced our process to everyone who expressed interest in the business. We set up an extensive proposal review process, and brought in several financial and banking experts to assist us in information gathering and processing. It was truly an exciting undertaking. It became very obvious, fairly early in our evaluation of the different proposals, that for years, Comerica had been overcharging the City severely, while providing terrible, substandard banking services.

It is also noteworthy to mention that Bank One, which was in the process of being absorbed by Chase Bank, held the second-highest amount of the City's cash at the time. They didn't respond to the RFQ until well after the cutoff date. However, we still allowed them to submit their proposal, and it was absolutely horrible. It was a true reflection of the Detroit business community's old economy arrogance. So much for home court advantage. We moved forward, and each bank made an oral presentation. I was very impressed with how well prepared the institutions were. I asked questions, and discovered a plethora of opportunities available for better management of City dollars. In return, they offered better ways to leverage our dollars and provide our citizens with opportunities for small business development. The process was exciting, and felt revolutionary. We were positioning Detroit to become a player in the global banking economy, and break from the ways of the old, traditionalist economy.

Our committee met to bring back a recommendation. Meanwhile, Anthony recommended to me that we take some of the City's money out of Comerica and put it in a smaller bank. We looked at First Independence, a small bank that happened to be historic, given that it was Detroit's first African-American-owned institution. It didn't hurt that the headquarters were local, either. Anthony suggested that this move could substantially strengthen one bank without hurting the other. I agreed, feeling that First Independence, with its good track record and corporate citizenship, would greatly benefit. I also thought Comerica would hardly flinch, given that we were talking out a relatively small amount, compared to the much larger City sums they still held.

After First Independence confirmed that they were prepared to handle the deposit, I agreed to move $90 million from a
Comerica account to our new banking partner. It was the single
largest deposit in the bank's history. The confidence and opportunities that sprang from that deposit afforded First Independence
the ability to compete and thrive in new, wider areas of the market.
I was so proud to be associated with that process. But Comerica's
leaders were not happy. In fact, they were enraged.

The majority of Comerica's board members were elite
members of Detroit's business and corporate community. Reggie
Turner, who was a new Comerica board member, hustled back
over to my office to give me the news, telling me that his fellow
members "were pissed." I explained the entire thought process
around the Banking Consolidation Plan, and also how creating
competition significantly helped the City. But he was the mes-
senger, there to warn me about the anger and contempt that was
brewing toward my office. I told Reggie that I was really surprised. I was a public sector CEO charged with the task of providing optimum levels of city services, while continuing to drive
down costs. In addition, I had to keep finding ways to cut grass,
provide for adequate trash pick-up, shovel snow, build homes,
repair streets, run buses on time, put out fires and keep people
safe without spending any more money than I had the previous
year. People wanted me to do more, but with less money. Now
that I'd found a way to save millions—tens of millions—for the
City and create additional resources, while working from within
homebound networks, the business community was mad. At me.
For conducting business. Incredible.

It would take a few more years for me to fully comprehend
such a collectively draconian mindset. It was selfish. The sense
of entitlement was foreign and uncomfortable to me. I wanted
nothing to do with it. I thanked Reggie and told him that we were
marching forward. There would be no publicity around who I
pissed off, but I heard the hoofbeats. There were grumblings
at this point, but I would feel a complete withdrawal of support
when the rumors began to eat at my reputation.

My Family! Four Generations of descendants of Marvell and Bessie Cheeks (MBC). Still Standing Strong!

Me and my niece, Anaya. The first girl Grandchild for my parents. She is our Princess!

Keeping the City Safe. We had a forty year low for crime in Detroit, during my tenure as Mayor. We also were the first city to deliver our Homeland Security Plan to then Homeland Security Secretary Tom Ridge.

Call to Action. The Black Slate, the Shrine of the Black Madonna's political and community organizing arm, along with many other organizations and individuals assisted our efforts to keep our schools and community safe.

President Barack Obama and me. We knew each other before his meteoric political rise. Here we share a moment in my office in 2007.

Me and my sons out front of our home in Texas. After a record snow storm in Dallas, we made a snowman, and named him "Motown."

16th Anniversary of my pledge line, The Nubians of the Nu Dynasty (Chicago 2000). I love my bruhs! (David Wells, Joel Johnson, Pat Scott, Byron White, Rich McCloud, Derrick McCants, Ted Gilmore, Robert Flakes, Joe Youngblood, David Askew, Mike Bonds, Mike Hargrett, KMK and Vince Adams.) Regie Wynn, not pictured.

Carlton & Pamela Poles, Carlita, me and Laura Jayne (Granny). We all love Miss Granny. The Poles—my in-laws—are two of my favorite people in the world. Their union represents the epitome of a great marriage. They did it right. They played by the rules, and I admire, respect and love them dearly.

Motor City Makeover. We renovated dozens of parks and recreation centers. During our annual clean-up in Detroit, we marshalled the forces of over 60,000 volunteers, with additional volunteer businesses to scour the city clean. We demolished structures, removed abandoned cars, and thoroughly cleaned streets. The City was cleaner during my administration than it had been in more than a generation.

Me and Liberian President Ellen Johnson-Sirleaf. The first woman to be democratically elected as President on the continent of Africa. The hope and pride that I saw and experienced, during my time with the Liberian people, was unlike anything that I ever felt or seen before. I had the great pleasure and honor of meeting with the Presidents of Ghana (John Kufur) and South Africa (Thambo Mbeki), during visits to those countries as well.

(Above) **Mom, me and Former House Speaker Nancy Pelosi.** I was a part of a Speaker Pelosi lead, Nine Country Fact Finding mission. We visited Countries, and met with leaders in Europe and throughout Africa.

(Inset above) **Me, a tour guide and Congressman Jim Clyburn (South Carolina).** On tour at Robben Island Prison, of the coast of Capetown, South Africa. Standing in the cell where Nelson Mandela was housed for so many years was, both, a tremendously humbling and hopeful experience. That day reinforced the biblical truth that "With God, all things are possible."

Me and Bishop J. Drew Sheard. One of the greatest men alive. I thank him so much for Pastoring me through incredibly difficult times.

Christine, me and Derrick...the original Three Amigos! We worked, prayed and created a movement. But, unfortunately in the end, none of us could spiritually handle the enormous and tenacious assault that came against it.

(Opposite page, bottom) **Force Commander, Major General Cru Ihekire: African Union Mission in Darfur, Sudan.** One of the most profoundly painful, gut-wrenching and spiritually draining experiences of my life was the day that I spent at a refugee camp in Darfur. The sadness, confusion and fear in the faces of so many women and children will haunt me forever. And the feeling of absolute powerlessness was even worse.

Me and Bobby Ferguson. My Main Man! One of the hardest working men that I have ever met. Completely unafraid and unabashed to be who he is. If he wasn't so success-ful, that might have been a very positive thing.

The Kilpatrick Crew! The family on one of our many vacations. These were truly the best of times. I love being with the four of them more than anything. We have a hilariously knee slapping, fun and wonderful time together. You have to have thick skin in our crew. Nobody is off limits to be slammed. Not even Mama!

(Top) **Me and Wifey stepping out.** The Big Fella in the picture, always stayed clean.

(Bottom) **Dyson, Reverend Al Sharpton, me and Jesse** in my suite at Superbowl XL. There were some great conversations in the suite that day.

Tommy "Hitman" Hearns, me, and Barry Sanders. Two of Detroit's Greatest Sports legends. I played basketball, back in the day, with Tommy. He thought that he had game. It's a good thing he had boxing to fall back on.

My first mug shot. Taken after the very first arrest of my life, April 2008.

Coleman A. Young, Mom and me. From the day I met him as a youngster, I knew I wanted to be Mayor. He was a true warrior for the citizens of Detroit.

Me speaking in a judge's chambers in the United States District Court of the Eastern District. That same system has indicted me and forced me into the fight of my life.

Me and Former US Vice President Al Gore share a comedic moment.

Mom, Dad and me at my mother's first swearing in at the Michigan House of Representatives. The day that started it all! As I sat in awe, I knew that I wanted to be a member of that body.

Generation to Generation. My Grandfathers holding my twin sons, Jelani and Jalil. To this day, this remains one of the most poignant visuals that have stirred my soul.

Standing in my office in 2008.

Photo: Andre Smith

Me, Carlita and our newborns. We bought our first home and started on our journey.

A Redevelopment Plan. My administration redeveloped more old dilapidated structures than any Mayor in Detroit's history, ushering in unprecedented new development.

chapter 21

Storm Warning

W E WENT to church on a Sunday morning in early 2008. An elder approached me as we entered. I don't remember her name, but she looked me in the eye and said, "Son, you don't know me, but God put it on my heart that something big is about to happen to you. You be careful, young man."

I was caught off-guard, but I nodded and told her I would. The moment passed quickly, and we moved into the sanctuary for the service. But I had a hard time shaking the elder's words. I regained my focus just as Bishop Sheard rose from his seat to introduce Prophet Jeremy J. Gatlin, a guest pastor from out of state. God forgive me, I don't remember any part of Prophet Gatlin's message, but he did something at the end that shook me to my core. He ended his sermon and began the altar call, descended from the pulpit and stood directly in front of me. Touching me on the shoulder, he said to the congregation, "There is something very powerful about this man. I don't know you, my brother, but you are about to enter a very rough season in your life."

Some people smiled at first, amused that he didn't know I was the mayor. But their smiles disappeared when he said "rough season." Now, people were praying.

"You are going to have to endure a fight unlike any you've ever had," Prophet Gatlin said, "but God will never leave you." He told me to go to my office the next day and gather five people in whom I had absolute trust, and pray to strengthen each other for the fight. I heeded his instruction and called Anthony Adams, Triette Reeves, Kandia Milton, Jonathan Quarles and Christine to my office for prayer the next morning. I told them about what happened at church, and the six of us prayed. Triette, an ordained minister and member of my staff, led us. She'd been like the Bible's Nathan to my David, always telling me the clear truth when I needed to hear it. After the prayer, she turned, hugged me, and asked if I'd remembered my promise to God.

"What promise?" I said. She said that she didn't know, but I sure should. After a moment, I did! I just hadn't lived up to it. At day's end, I called Carlita, asking if she and the boys would like to go out to eat. We went to a Chili's restaurant. Our meal was pleasant, but I was troubled. I couldn't stop thinking about the past two days.

Carlita noticed my restlessness. "What's wrong?" she asked. I was pained, looking at her. "Let's talk when we get home," she said.

"Okay," I said.

Why didn't I have my wife in my office for that prayer? Why wasn't she the very first person that I told? I grew more nervous as we drove home. It was time for me to take responsibility for my actions. I had to tell Carlita the truth.

The boys went to shower and get ready for bed when we got home, and Carlita and I went straight to the bedroom. She took a seat in a silver reading chair that sat in front of our bed, and I kneeled beside her. She looked at me with fear and confusion in her eyes, and said, "Baby, what is it?"

After a long pause, I told her about the text messages. I also told her I'd learned earlier that *The Detroit Free Press* would soon publish a story revealing them to the public.

She paused for what seemed like an eternity, and then said, "I hate you."

She didn't shout her words. She sharpened them. It would have been better had she attacked me. And then, she crumbled. And the world stopped. The house felt big, empty and cold. Carlita was hurt beyond articulation. Humiliated. Betrayed. By me. God, I wish she would have kept talking, but she was visibly shattered. I felt worthless. The woman I'd sworn to honor and cherish sat before me, insulted. Her pain dazed me. Nothing was worth this. Not the affair, not the job, not Detroit. I wanted to scoop her up and run away, but that wasn't possible.

The story broke on January 24, 2008, and even though I'd known it was coming and had made my staff aware, I still couldn't believe that two million people were reading the same headline:

"MAYOR KILPATRICK, CHIEF OF STAFF LIED UNDER OATH, TEXT MESSAGES SHOW"

It was the leading story, a detailed, sordid expose' that described the nature of my texts with Christine. It cursorily mentioned exchanges about City business, but dove deep about my lying on the witness stand, and the texts' proof of that fact.

I stared at the headline, aghast. Mortified. The story read as if I'd simply incriminated myself, with no explanation of Stefani's actions. But worse, Carlita was going to see it all. I'd told her about the affair, but she didn't have to read any quotes. She cried even more when I did, and would not stop for two days. I saw more anguish, more soul-stirring hurt in her than I'd ever seen. I wouldn't wish that kind of pain on my worst enemy.

I released a statement explaining that the affair occurred during a difficult time in our marriage, and asked for the public's understanding. Then I went into seclusion for a week. Not to hide, but to gather myself, and be alone with my wife. I also chose to sit down during that week and explain to Jelani and Jalil, who were twelve by then, what I'd done. I hope no father ever has to go through something like that. It was agonizing.

I asked them to take a ride with me in the car. We pulled away from the Manoogian Mansion and drove slowly up Jefferson Avenue toward the serenity of Belle Isle, the unique island park that connects to the city's mainland by bridge. The silence was awkward. I asked how they were doing, and, like typical twelve-year-olds, said, "Alright," before returning to silence and peering out the window. The Detroit River seemed as still and deep as that moment.

I found a quiet place to park, turned to my boys, and asked if they knew what was going on. They said they didn't understand the whole thing, but they'd heard some terrible things about me. I asked what they'd heard, and both turned away with looks of sadness and confusion. I took a deep breath and began to speak. I apologized to my sons for the pain and embarrassment they had to endure because of me. I then got out of the car and moved to the back seat, putting my arms around each of them.

"I really messed up," I said. I told them that I'd been lying to their mother, and that I'd cheated on her. Jalil then broke his silence by asking if I'd done something with "Auntie Chris."

Damn! Auntie Chris, I thought. I was utterly disgusted with myself. I was my sons' hero, and I'd disgraced myself, and their name. I hated myself. I explained that I got caught in a horrible lie, and now the press had exposed it, only they were sensational-izing their reporting. I told them that Carlita and I were talking and working things out. Jelani asked if we would be getting di-vorced.

"No!" I said, emphatically, although I wasn't really sure about anything at that point. I pulled them closer and tried to be as honest as possible.

"Fellas," I said, "I know you both thought of me as a hero, and that I never messed up. But guys, I am human, and I still mess up. Although I am an adult, I still make bad choices. And I feel so bad that my choices have now hurt you. I feel like crap! And I would understand if you both don't like me much right now."

They looked at me, and then at each other—they have that twin telepathy thing going—before speaking. "Dad," Jalil said, "we are upset, but we forgive you. But you need to be real nice to Mama."

Jelani followed. "Because there is no way we are letting you all get a divorce. So you better fix it." I gave them my word. We gave each other big hugs, and then went home.

I then had to accept Christine's resignation, which wasn't easy either. It was time to change things, but it was hard. Resignation from her post also meant her resignation from my life. My mother had warned me about this. She said I would lose a lot of friends. I just never thought that Christine would be one of them. But we set that exact course, and brought more than twenty years of friendship to an abrupt and tragic end. What a painful lesson to learn.

Carlita and I appeared on television a week after the story broke, exhausted and in turmoil, as we went live from our home church. It felt like we were holding on to the last threads of our sanity, and our relationship. We were shells of ourselves.

I spoke from the heart, knowing that my apology to the citizens of Detroit would be heavily scrutinized.

> *Good evening, Detroit. I want to start tonight by saying I'm sorry. To all of you who have believed in what we've been doing here since 2002, to all of you who have believed in me and my leadership, to all of you who have stuck with me through very difficult times, to all of you who've prayed for me, I'm sorry.*

I'd embarrassed the people of Detroit. I wanted them to know that I realized that, and that I was determined to make it right. I apologized to Carlita, but almost broke down when I looked her in the eye. I try to reserve my emotions for private moments, but it was impossible to make eye contact with her without seeing the pain she was feeling.

Carlita impressed me by speaking on her own behalf during the telecast. She said that she was hurt, that we weren't perfect, and that she was angry, hurt and disappointed, but without a doubt, she loved me. She then asked the citizens of Detroit to remain committed to me. I couldn't stop thinking about how incredible a woman she was.

The last request I made was for people to leave my family alone. I asked the news cameras not to follow them around, to allow them their privacy. That would not happen.

News coverage of City affairs shifted to *my* affairs. My political career was mortally wounded, and my detractors moved to hasten its death. The *Free Press* inaccurately reported that I approved the Whistleblower settlements as a knee-jerk reaction to prevent the text messages from being released. They kept inferring that I settled for more money in order to hide the messages. What they were really doing was going into overdrive to cover their own asses—protect Judge Callahan, the *Free Press*, and Michael Stefani—and distract people from their complicity in reporting illegally obtained documents. They ran editorials on the front page of the paper instead of the normal Op/Ed page; and they partnered with local news affiliates to have editorial writers conduct live interviews, regularly using key phrases like "alleged" and "secret" to describe the nature of the agreement. I must say, it was masterful, so much so that it rendered nearly every community leader who'd supported me silent. Fear of media retribution rose. The press also told people I knew and respected, like Wendell Anthony, Sharon McPhail and the Council of Baptist Pastors, that they shouldn't help me because I'd spoken negatively about them.

I tried to explain the nature of the agreement to seal the texts, but the *Free Press* had a much bigger platform, and had filed suit to obtain the rest of the messages, which hadn't been released. They also called for my resignation. It was a lopsided fight; a Mayor's administration vs. the Internet, blogs, television cameras, YouTube, smartphones, talk show hosts, and editorials. Several people tried to broker conversations with the press on my behalf. Bob Berg, the PR legend who'd aided me years before, even tried in vain. I couldn't temper the voracious editorial campaign.

Wayne County Prosecutor Kym Worthy soon entered the fray, and brought with her an intense personal disdain for me and my family. While the press wanted me out, Worthy wanted me imprisoned. Sharon had warned me about her intent. For the first time in Michigan legal history, criminal charges were levied against someone for an infraction committed in a civil case. Though it was unprecedented, it wasn't impossible. She and the press executed the most coordinated effort since the Super Bowl. Soon, reporting about the affair morphed into widespread stories about mine being a corrupt administration. New stories were pounded out, weaving threads between the party rumor, the texts and the inquiries about how various funds were managed. No evidence of wrongdoing appeared in the now 140,000 text messages that were published, but it made for good news, and better TV.

The strain this caused Carlita and me was palpable. But as the months passed, we began to do a better job of working through it together. I thank God to this day for my wife's sense of defiance. We'd decided months earlier that our family was worth fighting for. We'd already embarked on the healing process, and that including dealing with my philandering, and our mutual expulsion of one another from our lives. The public crisis galvanized us, and Carlita decided that if there was going to be a fight, she was going to wage war with me, spiritually and physically. I was so happy because I really needed her. The months between January and October 2008 became a firestorm of nasty headlines and editorials, court hearings, heinous violations of my family's personal space and legal run-ins of historic proportions.

chapter 22

Selfish Ambition

If you keep on biting and devouring each other, take care that you are not the cause of destruction of one another.

~GALATIANS 5:15

THE MESSAGE to the Galatians is thought to have been written between 53 and 57 A.D., but it was also highly appropriate for the people of Detroit, circa 2008. The city was hot, literally and figuratively. The Wayne County prosecutor did indeed charge me with multiple felonies, all stemming from my lying under oath about the affair, and it seemed like half of every newscast and newspaper were all about me. It was an absolute circus. How the newshounds found new stories to write is beyond me.

To help restore some order and attempt to assuage the storm developing around me, I hired Judy Smith, a crisis communications specialist. Judy worked on huge cases, and she had a talented team, but she was no match for the Detroit press. Their assault was highly organized, and Judy admitted to me that its personal nature and voracity was new territory for her. She put up a good fight, though, and I appreciated her.

It wasn't long before business leaders joined the chorus of hoofbeats. Pandering to cameras and microphones, Tony Early,

CEO of DTE Energy, Detroit's leading energy company, became the first to give his on-air opinion. His words, as I recall, had to do with "not believing that I sat there and lied like that." When asked if he thought I should step down, he said I should.

I believe there's a difference between corporate leaders who built their companies, and those who were promoted into executive management positions. The builders were tough self-thinkers, while the managers tended to be little more than corporate politicians. Tony Early was the latter. I thought we had a pretty good working relationship until he made his remarks without so much as a conversation with me. Instead, he scrambled for a position. Tony had formerly chaired the Detroit Renaissance Board, the City's Corporate Roundtable, and was a member of— *Cl-cloomp!*—the Comerica Bank Board. But the last conversation he and I had took place before I took that money out of his bank.

Tony's ability to throw a rock and hide his hand was emblematic of all the business community members who shifted against me. But he'd gotten a head start hating me years earlier. We had both served on the Host Committee, which traveled to five Super Bowls. We studied how the community prepared and carried out its strategy to host this huge event, attending meetings and events. We did everything we could to prepare ourselves to host Super Bowl XL when it came to Detroit.

Once, in Houston, after finishing a long day of meetings and heading back to our hotel, the rapper LL Cool J invited me to attend the Victoria's Secret Fashion Show and party, which he was hosting. We had met when he conducted business in Detroit and I took him to a boxing match at Joe Louis Arena. I accepted, excited to hang out with him, and at a good party, without a doubt. I probably gave someone fodder for another joke with that last sentence, but anyone familiar with Super Bowl Week festivities knows that dozens of parties take place. So I went, telling Roger Penske and Susan Sherer where I was headed, and promising to catch up to them in the morning. "Have fun," they both said. The next day, at breakfast, I gave Roger the typical description of the event, and we went about our business.

Days later, *Detroit News* reporter Daniel Howes wrote a story that ran the day we returned from Houston, saying that I was partying in Houston while my colleagues spent serious time working and attending meetings. Imagine my surprise. I never missed a meeting, nor was I even late! It's not my style. The story played up the "Hip-Hop Mayor" image, which was still maddeningly easy for people to believe. He even threw in a line about me partying with LL Cool J. I called Daniel Howes and asked him why he would write such a thing. Of course, I told him how wrong his information was. He apologized, and then said that he got his info from Tony Early.

The next day I gave a speech on business development and the Super Bowl progress at the Detroit Athletic Club, a Downtown Detroit club that caters to the city's business elite. Roger and Susan also spoke. Since we were all there, I showed Roger the *Detroit News* article. He got pissed, fast.

"Where did this information come from?" he asked. I told him what I knew, and he said, "We didn't need this. I'll put an end to it right away."

Tony appeared at that moment, walking toward us as if a movie director had timed his entrance. I fingered him as soon as I saw him. Yes, I snitched! And Roger went at him immediately. They were just far enough away that I couldn't hear the discussion, but it looked like Roger was verbally undressing him, standing inches from his nose, finger wagging in front of his face, which reddened rather quickly. Tony's palms pushed up in the air, and his shoulders lurched up. He was playing dumb, and it wasn't working. I eased closer, thoroughly enjoying it as Conrad Mallett, my former campaign director and current president of a Detroit area hospital, approached and watched with me. He seemed to get a kick out of it, too. The confrontation ended soon, and Roger headed back toward me, handing me the paper and saying, "We won't have any more problems like this." And we didn't. I glanced at Tony, who was busy picking his face off the ground.

When Tony later voiced his opinion about me stepping

down, I thought it would open the proverbial floodgates for voices of dissent. But it didn't. An attempted recall effort never got off the ground. And I was still holding my own in my daily activity until the day Doug Rothwell, CEO of the Detroit Renaissance, and Dave Bing, a retired Detroit Pistons player, businessman and current Detroit mayor, visited my office for a meeting.

Bing had been to my office a few weeks earlier with George Jackson, my chief development officer after Walt Watkins's retirement. He needed $5 million to help his residential development project, which was being built on the city's Riverfront. The City had already invested in the project through our Downtown Development Authority. Bing needed additional funding to gain leverage from his bank. George and the DDA supported the request for more money, and he wanted mine, which I gave to him. Bing's project has since failed, but it would have been the first of its kind for the Riverfront, and that meant momentum for Riverfront development. Doug Rothwell is a seasoned professional who worked with former Michigan Governor John Engler, and was recently appointed by newly elected Governor Rick Snyder.

I engaged the meeting as a friendly discussion. I worked with Doug in the State House, and enjoyed working with him as mayor. He was focused, organized and tough. He and Bing came to my office with pleasantries, asked how I was holding up, and even inquired about my family. I told them that I was well, all things considered, and that I was working and focused, myself. When Doug asked what message he should take back to the community, I gave it to him, and the rest of the conversation was light.

Imagine my surprise when, an hour later, breaking news on television announced that "business community representatives" had met with me and asked me to resign. I was aghast, because Dave was named as the source. I called his cell phone, and he lied to me, saying he was "shocked they would say that." I told him to call the station and get it right. I also called Doug, who agreed that the report was false and promised to send a statement to the news saying that "no part of our discussion was about the mayor resigning." Twenty minutes later, however, Dave was back on the news, saying that, although they hadn't specifically talked about that in the meeting, he believed that I should resign.

Dave is a longtime friend of Tony Early, and a member of the DTE Executive Board. A few months after this episode, he announced plans to run for mayor, after being drafted by Tony Early. Bing never mentioned that all of his businesses were in financial trouble at that time. Today, they are all either bankrupt or operated by others, the Riverfront development included.

Now the mayor, Dave brought several DTE "loaned executives" to run the City's demolition program. Of course, the press and business community celebrated the move, though it has produced poorer results than either my or Dennis Archer's administration. DTE also received a reported $150 million no-bid contract from Mayor Bing to manage the City's Public Lighting facility. Their move on me paid off, but not for the City.

It became apparent, not long after this, that the political folks also wanted a piece of me. People who came out against me were given primetime coverage. And Governor Jennifer Granholm, who was failing as head of the State thanks to a reputation for being unable to make a decision, seized a chance to prove that she was tough. She waited until the line of people calling for my head grew long enough, and then she took her cuts. That's leadership, in her typical style!

chapter 23
Threads

A S KIDS, we grew up watching cartoons. *The Looney Tunes* crew—Bugs Bunny, Elmer Fudd, Road Runner, all those characters—were some of the funniest on TV. Their crazy antics, Yosemite Sam's gun blowing up in his face, the Road Runner embarrassing Wile E. Coyote. We loved it.

I remember a bit where a 'toon would pull the thread on someone's garment, and it completely unraveled, leaving the person naked and embarrassed. The proverbial thread on my garment was pulled the day the text message story broke. By summer, I was naked, and the wind blew cold all around me. I longed for anonymity.

I *was* the news in Detroit. *The Detroit News* and *Detroit Free Press* had been operating in the red before the text story and subsequent scandal. They weren't alone. Newspapers around the country, like *The Boston Globe* and *The New York Times*, had either closed or attempted to sell. A generation of tech-savvy readers preferred the Internet over the newsstands. Now, the Detroit newspapers' newsstand sales increased from seven percent to more than twenty percent every time my face or name appeared on the front page. From a business standpoint, it was in their best interest to keep this story sexy as long as they could. They probably appreciate that I, through my troubles, still managed to honor my duty by saving their jobs. Three cheers for me.

Their news crews camped outside the Manoogian Mansion

for months. They knocked on my neighbors' doors, asking if they knew anything about a party, or any suspicious activity. None of them did. We became prisoners in our home, and it was hell on my family. One night, a news copter shone a light right through Jonas's bedroom window, then circled to the back of the house to pierce an illuminating light through that side. Multiple copters sometimes hovered. They would slowly circle, looking for any activity. The noise was deafening, so loud that it was impossible to hold conversation in the home without shouting. We'd retreat to the basement to escape. Though I had my press reps make several requests for the helicopters to cease, their requests were not granted.

I saw the worry and anxiety that gripped my wife after the release of the text messages change to a spirit of fierce protection, anger and courage. Our sons began to play games on the floor in the house so they couldn't be seen by the news cameras, which hovered like loud, metallic, blood-sucking mosquitoes. My sons were confused and scared, and that sickened and enraged me. They were behaving like a lynch mob. No man can stand to see his family feel so threatened.

Carlita and I vowed to survive it all. The press smelled awards in our blood, and we knew they just might get their wish. But we were no less galvanized. The rap artist T.I. articulated our feelings in his song "No Matter What," which I listened to often during this time. Our family would "conquer every obstacle, make the impossible possible; even when winning's illogical, losing's still far optional." Whether we liked it or not, it was us against the world. No one outside of our family, my administration and our immediate community was even trying to hear my perspective. No one cared about my family's sanctity, so we would care enough for the world.

So, the pundits talked about my arrogance. They called me stupid, a pimp, things I'd never in my wildest dreams imagined anyone would ever call me. Fine, I can take being called names. But call *me* names, not my family. Send *me* death threats, fine! But what measure of man would threaten my wife and children? A few of the threats were so racist and horrible that we gave them to the police chief, to the FBI, and the press. They did nothing. They were too busy investigating the phantom party, cashing in on the Kwame Kilpatrick sweepstakes. The press claimed I had brought it on myself. I was far more angry and upset than scared, and I had to fight back. We chose to do it through the State of the City address, which I had to deliver in March.

Detroit's Orchestra Hall filled to the rafters with people on March 11, mostly supporters. State of the City addresses are historically pedestrian affairs, but people expected me to say something about the charges being leveled against me. I didn't want the evening to be about me alone, so I used the speech as an opportunity to remind Detroiters about everything my administration had worked so hard to accomplish.

As Carlita sat with my family, I felt confident standing at the podium. We took pains to lay out every accomplishment that the press refused to acknowledge. We'd rehabbed seventy-five buildings in Downtown Detroit alone. We forced the Census Bureau to acknowledge that they had undercounted the city's population by 47,000 people. It was the first time Detroit had ever challenged a count and won. Those people were added back to our count. Detroit was paying $100 million less in salaries and wages than in the first year I took office, while putting mobile police stations on the street at the same time. We reminded them that Dr. Carl Taylor, the renowned Michigan State University sociologist, led a team that was developing a proposal for a City-based residential boarding academy for young people in need of more structured environments.

We weren't assholes who'd made no effort. The people were not going to be that easily duped without hearing about the hospitality and retail training programs that the Wayne County Community College District started soon after the successful sporting events the City hosted. It may have seemed like a small thing then, but now that President Obama is touting the importance of supporting community colleges across America, it seems to me like we were pretty prophetic. And people needed to know about it.

We had documented plans for the city: New police and fire stations. Remodeled neighborhood health centers. Improved the Lighting Department and Public Works. The people deserved to know about these things, and if I could help it, they would.

I was still pissed, though. After laying out our plan, while the audience was enthused and energized, in an emotive moment, I came off script and spoke briefly and strongly to my personal issues.

> *...I feel that I cannot leave this auditorium, with my wife and my sons sitting there, without addressing this issue. In the past thirty days, I've been called a 'nigger' more than any time in my entire life. In the past three days, I've received more death threats than I have in my entire administration. I've heard these words before, but I've never heard people say them about my wife and children. I have to say this because it's very personal to me. I don't believe that a Nielsen rating is worth the life of my children, or your children. This unethical, illegal, lynch mob mentality has to stop! And it's seriously time. We've never been here before. And I don't care if they cut the TV off. We've never been in a situation like this before, where you can say anything, do anything, have no facts, no research, no nothing, and you can launch a hate-driven, bigoted assault on a family! I humbly ask members of Council, I humbly ask the business community, I humbly ask the religious community, I humbly ask the brothers and sisters of the City of Detroit. I humbly ask that we say 'no more,' together. I love this city with every part of my being. And I will continue to stay focused on building the next Detroit. God bless you. Detroit, I love you.*

My heart weighed so heavily that I trembled while speaking. I said it the way I needed to say it, on live radio and television, for anyone listening to see and hear. And sadly, in a talk that lasted an hour, it was the only thing the press heard, and they skewed and spun the meaning behind my words. Every headline that ran the next day said that I threw a temper tantrum, and used the "N-word." The TV, radio and print media pounded me for two weeks about that alone. The night after the speech, a cross-section of African-American media personalities pounded me in print and on TV, including an African-American writer, one of the few at the daily papers, and the NBC affiliate's most seasoned black anchorwoman, Carmen Harlan. None of them said anything in the press about the aggressive attitude and pursuits of the media, or even the death threats to my family. Even the NAACP President, Wendell Anthony, issued negative comments about the speech because of my use of the "N-word."

It was becoming painfully clear that my side of this story might never see the light of day. Whether I liked it or not, I had a fight on my hands.

chapter 24
Trouble

B Y THE summer of 2008, I all but officially ceased to be a mayor, and became a tabloid sensation. I tried my best to focus on work, but it was difficult. My travel had been restricted, making it very difficult to conduct City affairs. At several points, "Kwame Kilpatrick" was among the most Googled names on the Internet, even more than Britney Spears, whose infamous head-shaving episode and related psychosis was among the biggest entertainment news at the time. My story turned up on the home page of the BBC World Service's web site. Watchdog reporters followed me on business trips. And news cameras still followed my young sons to school.

The press had no interest in anything we were doing at that time. Detroit was in the discussion as an international player, but this story was killing that image. My head swirled trying to keep things together. It was an amazing story, but I didn't have the time to think about documenting it all. So I was intrigued when Khary Turner approached me at a family wedding and opened a discussion.

"What you're going through is historic," he said. "Are you writing this down?"

I wasn't. "I need help," I said. I'd thought about it on more than one occasion, and I knew that at some point, I'd have to tell my story. But where, between stress and not knowing whom I could trust, did I even have the time to write? Khary had the same thoughts, and he agreed that my insight into City affairs and the developing scandals, would never be properly published in the press. If I ever wanted a chance to tell my story, uninterrupted, I would have to do it on my own.

"You want to work on something?" I asked, and he said yes. It would be another month before we'd begin, though, because another wave of trouble that would completely rob me of time and focus was on the way.

——*Flash Sideways* (Hoofbeats)——

I should have responded at the first hint of any attempt to bring me down. I should have vigorously defended myself against the first articles that subtly suggested any air of impropriety. Any news story. Any editorial. I didn't take action because I felt the lack of evidence of wrongdoing on my part was protection enough. I felt that people would eventually see how ridiculous it was. But the furor never subsided and, when an exotic dancer was killed in a drive-by shooting between two known drug dealers on the City's West Side, the entire story took on a very sinister tone. No disrespect to the deceased or her family, but I had lived in Detroit my entire life up to that point, and never saw or heard of anything "mysterious" about two people shooting at each other's cars, and a passenger being killed in the process.

Once I was linked to a party, and now, God forbid, a murder. And people seemed to believe anything. Parties, strippers, you name it. Before I knew it, the court of public opinion began to convict me more with each passing day. I now know that my detractors also declared a silent war against me, and the press became a viable tool that they used to carry out their offensive strategy. I had no idea how low they would sink, but, as it's said, war is hell. And I was being introduced to it.

Losing the Whistleblower lawsuit only exacerbated the deterioration of my public image. By then, we'd gotten so far behind the eight ball internally that every move in my defense was tantamount to jumping a bucking horse from behind and trying to ride it. Rumors persistently added embers to the smoldering resentment, distrust and suspicion surrounding me. The movement became formulaic. Organized noise, plus deafening silence, gave the rants of detractors, area racists, bloggers and talk shows increased validity. People lost their connections to the facts. The truth became relative. Groupthink became so prevalent and coordinated that even those who weren't part of it got caught up in it. And it wasn't without precedent. "King Kwame," recast as an arrogant dictator, stood poised for a coup.

Governor Granholm actually decided to hold a hearing to consider what should become of me—whether or not I should be removed from office—and held a meeting in downtown Detroit with Council members and business leaders to discuss the matter. Sharon was made privy to it and attended. What she heard, and shared with me, was harrowing. Granholm, she said, presented four of the felonies I was charged with to the group, and suggested that I should plead guilty to those.

Sharon said she challenged her by asking if she was interested in hearing my defense. She knew Granholm couldn't remove me unless I was failing to do my job, and that wasn't the case. In fact, she couldn't force me to plea to anything. According to Michigan statutes, a governor can legally remove a mayor only when he or she fails to fulfill the duties of his office. As much trouble as I was in, I was doing my job. But Sharon heard hoofbeats in that meeting. They were mounting an offensive. Against me.

Granholm had company beyond those in that room trying to oust me. The Detroit City Council was also hot on my trail. They were led by their President, Ken Cockrel, Jr. Ken is one of those guys your grandmother would look at and say, "Bless his heart." But he finally saw his chance to be mayor, because the Detroit City Charter has a provision that, in the event a sitting mayor is unable to fulfill his or her duties because of death, resignation, recall or incapacitation, the City Council President automatically will be appointed until the next scheduled election.

Ken, the son of the late, legendary Detroit attorney of the same name, could never win a mayoral election by running for it. The people had no confidence in him to lead on that level. He even lost to Dave Bing in the special election that would follow my departure from office. But he leaned on that Charter provision, and did whatever he could to get rid of me. For the first—and last—time, he had a way to be a shoe-in for mayor. With that, the governor, the City Council and the Wayne County prosecutor came at me simultaneously.

The governor and the City Council decided to hold their own separate hearings, while the prosecutor plodded in pursuit of her case. It was a circus. Grounds or no grounds, with twelve felonies for a first-time, non-violent offender or not, everyone grandstanded.

Sharon represented me as counsel to the mayor in the governor's kangaroo court proceeding. Granholm spent about $200,000 of the State taxpayers' money to build a makeshift courtroom in the State of Michigan's Detroit offices. She would sit as judge, jury and executioner.

During the proceeding, Sharon did get Stefani to admit that he hadn't notified City attorneys about the subpoena he used to obtain the text messages, but the admission was suppressed publicly. Of course! Publicizing it would have damaged the validity of everyone's claims against me, and it would have exposed the newspapers. Stefani would later perjure himself under oath in front of the Attorney Grievance Commission, and admit to all of his nefarious activities. The press would laud him as a hero. They needed to. It was in their legal interest to do so. And the Grievance Commission gave him a slap on the wrist, telling him to behave in the future. It would be justice for all Kilpatrick haters.

At least Sharon pulled no punches. She also went at the governor, based on the bias she displayed in the clandestine meeting, but Granholm denied everything. She left office with abysmal approval ratings at her term's end, leaving the State in more than a $1 billion deficit, and seeing hundreds of thousands of jobs and residents flee from the State of Michigan. She was totally ineffective in moving policy through the State legislature. But hey, she did put on a heck of a show when it came to me.

I look back on this period and realize how many of my detractors' transgressions were selectively overlooked, and I wonder. While I would never excuse myself from what I did do wrong, I can see in hindsight why such a groundswell of negative sentiment rose up against me so quickly and decisively. It was easy as printing and broadcasting every controversial 'Kwame' issue, while giving moderate coverage to their steps, at best.

Some will read this and argue that I should be expected to pull the 'conspiracy' card as some vain attempt to salvage my dignity. I can see the newspapers' online comment section lighting up with couch potatoes' rants now. And my response to them is simple. You're right. Coleman Young used to say, "Just because you're paranoid don't mean it ain't true."

When I perjured myself, I gave my enemies a lane. And they turned that lane into a highway. My intent upon entering office was to empower Detroiters, and my actions heading into my second term suggested that we had the ability to do it. And that threatened too many peoples' bottom lines. Their bottom lines for me, then, became simple. Get rid of me. And they're not finished.

The sheriff's deputy's timing couldn't have been more menacingly perfect. I was at Ayanna's house in late July 2008, attempting to escape the glare of the spotlight. I was strained, stressed and struggling with my own psychological state. My family has always been my sanctuary, and even though I hadn't gotten the chance to spend the time with Ayanna that I did while we were growing up, she and the rest of my family were always a phone call or a drive away. News cameras could be camped outside the house all night, and I couldn't care less, as long as I was with friends and family.

Sheriff's deputies showed up at Ayanna's doorstep, claiming they were there to serve a subpoena to Bobby Ferguson, our longtime family friend who is, unfortunately, battling the same legal web that I am dealing with today. Why the hell they came to my sister's house looking for Bobby, who lives on the other side of town and was easy to find, is very easy to figure out. It was a setup. They knew I was there, and I reacted as soon as I heard the officer at the door. I lunged past my relatives and confronted the officer, touching his shoulder, which, I imagine, startled him. He took a step backward, and appeared startled to be suddenly berated by the Mayor of Detroit. It was a dumb thing to do, but I was past my limit. By the next day, more headlines were in the paper, with the officer saying I had assaulted him, and I was charged with assault. Just like that, I caught a criminal case.

What was happening? The world caved in on me. I began to have to use decoy vehicles when going to work. Worst of all, the court restricted me from leaving the county without prior 24-hour notice from the pre-trial bond department.

My grandfather, James Bernard Kilpatrick, loved the phrase "all is well." He said it all day, every day. That was my personal theme on the morning of August 7, 2008. I'd been mandated to appear in court nine times since being charged. Usually, a defendant's attorneys represent their client for simple procedural motions, but my being a mayor/media attraction changed all that, and Judge Ronald Giles ordered me to show up for every little thing that had to be discussed.

The backdrop of this session, however, was serious. I'd gone to Canada on business without notifying the court. Big mistake! Windsor, Ontario, the city that sits on the other side of the Detroit River, is closer to my office than the City's West Side, but it didn't matter. It was another country.

I did it because the long-term lease on the Detroit-Windsor tunnel that the two cities had been working on, the one that would yield $75 million for Detroit, was in danger of falling apart. We had been working on it for more than a year and were right at the finish line. And like most deals, something went awry. I thought it was very important that I be there. And in my usual style, I rushed to the meeting, which was just a hundred feet or so into Windsor's border. I interceded, and we got the deal back on track.

And I must say that I was wrong. I violated the provisions of my bond.

So, I had to answer for my error. Before heading to the courthouse, I read a passage from a book of daily inspirational spiritual writings called *God Calling*, by A.J. Russell. My mother had given it to me months earlier. The book offers spiritual passages for every day of the year, written as if God dictated them. Each day has a different message and, on more than one occasion, the submissions spoke to me exactly where I was on each given day. But this day was special, because I knew I was facing a tough situation.

The title of the August 7 passage? "All is Well." Needless to say, it resonated within me.

> *Oh, Lord, bless us and keep us, we beseech Thee.*
> *My keeping power is never at fault, but only your*
> *realization of it. Not whether I can provide a shelter*
> *from the storm, but your failure to be sure of the security*
> *of that shelter.*
> *Every fear, every doubt, is a crime against My love.*
> *Oh, children, trust. Practice patience daily, many times*
> *a day, saying, "All is well." Say it until you believe it.*
> *Know it.*

I read it several times. I believed it. With each review, I actually began to feel the tension ease all over my body. I started to feel really good. When I arrived at the 36th District Court, several people stood in the hallway with smiles, hugs, and well wishes for me. The press corps was there, as usual. About five cameras were in the courtroom, all set to broadcast live what should have been a routine hearing. Nothing was out of the ordinary. Not for me. Interestingly, an elderly woman looked me right in the eye as I made my way to the courtroom, gave me big hug and said, "All is well." Wow! There it was again! Something about this moment began to feel ordained.

The session should have been simple. We were there to waive our right to a preliminary examination and then a conduct a hearing on my bond provisions. The Prosecutor, Kym Worthy, wanted to restrict my travel to the State of Michigan. She and her cohorts were always biting at me about something.

The first issue was the waiver of the preliminary exam. The arguments were going just fine, at first. The prosecution and defense teams had an agreement, and both had stated it for the record. The judge was moving the proceeding in what seemed to be a normal direction. I remained patient, thinking, "Let's see how this turns out." I stood, verbally waived my right to a preliminary examination, and sat back down. It was a very simple action. And then, something far less simple happened.

Attorneys for the *Detroit Free Press* and *The Detroit News*, from the back of the courtroom, stood and demanded to be heard. They were not parties to this case, and were not representing anyone involved. They had no standing, but this was the fourth time that they had been allowed by this Judge, Ron Giles, to interject in the proceedings. Giles was a new judge. He'd only been seated for a few months, after several unsuccessful bids for election to the post. He was nervous as hell, and shaking like Don Knotts. He'd started off strong in the case, but the newspapers focused on him soon after, suggesting that I was a close associate of his wife, Joyce, who was a senior executive at DTE Energy. I knew her, but we were far from "close" or "associated." The day after the papers suggested that, he chummed up to the prosecutors, laughing at phantom jokes. I waived the preliminary exam just to get out of his courtroom, and closer to some semblance of fairness.

I'd been told that none of the lawyers or judges around town had ever seen anything like the proceedings in this case before, but this had become somewhat "normal" in my case. Still, Giles allowed them to put their appearances on the record and make arguments for the sealed (they were still calling them "secret") text messages to become public. They made a full argument, after acknowledging that they truly didn't have a standing in the case! Judge Giles also asked them several questions and wouldn't allow my attorneys to object or interject anything. As a matter of fact, he asked my lawyers to be quiet! I was now, in a State proceeding, being prosecuted by not only the Wayne County prosecutor's office, but by the Detroit newspapers' attorneys. Unprecedented! But this is normal. For me.

It had also become normal for the prosecution to fail to keep its word on any agreement brokered throughout the entire process. Giles never once held those attorneys accountable to orderly court procedure. And maybe I shouldn't have expected him to. Alas, late former Detroit Mayor Coleman Young once said, "You don't grow balls. You either have them or you don't." Let's just say a swift knee to Judge Giles' groin may piss him off, but I don't think it would hurt.

The bond hearing began, and the prosecution brought their formal motion to revoke all my travel outside the State of Michigan. No one seemed to care about the significance of City business. My reason for going to Canada was hardly acknowledged, much less considered. Instead, the prosecutor began to verbally batter me in an almost surprising manner.

She called me a criminal. She called me arrogant. She said I disrespected the law and the legal process. She said I *needed to be taught a lesson.* My attorney, Jim Thomas, stood and gave a rebuttal, if I can call it that. He knew that I was technically in the wrong, but he couldn't figure out how to argue. Jim's an excellent attorney, but I knew at that very moment that he was tired. The media scrutiny and pressure was gradually overwhelming him. The courtroom rumbled with a low noise when the judge asked whether Jim knew that I had gone to Windsor. I'd called him from Windsor as soon as my mistake dawned on me. Jim mumbled, stuttered and half-answered. I couldn't tell if he said he knew or not. But I was perplexed. I had told him the truth.

I understand attorney/client privilege, but this was a critical moment. He needed to stand up! Heck, at least ask to approach the bench and talk to the judge! He didn't, though, and I realized that I was alone on the legal front. Not only would there be no fairness, but it was going to be impossible for me to get justice.

The judge then stopped the proceedings and asked all of the

attorneys to gather in his chambers. After about fifteen minutes, they all emerged from the room together. The look on my attorney's face reminded me of the first time that I saw *The Exorcist*. Pure fear! He was so scared and nervous that I wanted to slap him and tell him to pull himself together. No need, because he leaned over and told me that I was going to jail.

Jail!? Wow! At that moment I knew that I had to speak for myself. I was drained, and had no address prepared, but I refused to go quietly. So I asked to speak.

> First of all, Judge, let me say that I apologize. This is not at all a front to you, or this court. I don't believe that there's ever been a person who's ever been through this process that respects it more than I do.
>
> I've been living in an incredible state of pressure and scrutiny for seven months. And I know Your Honor has, as well. And I want to thank you for serving, for what you've done in this court.
>
> Last week was a tremendous wake-up call for me in two respects. One, you said as the Mayor of this city, as a lawyer and member of the Bar, I should not have put myself in that position. Whatever the facts were you said about what happened—which, of course, we disagree with—you were right, Your Honor. I remain in agreement with you on that.
>
> What I've been doing, to the best of my ability, when I wake up in the morning, is trying to make sure that the importance of this court and these proceedings are intact. I've always been on time. I've always listened to my attorneys in everything that we're doing. I hear Your Honor's ruling. But I've also been trying to be a good Mayor, at the same time, even with incredible odds, and incredible scrutiny.
>
> In the city of Detroit we have been working on, for 18 months, Judge, a deal between two countries, Canada and the United States, a provincial

government of Ontario, and the State of Michigan;
two cities, Windsor and Detroit; and in all of the
records and agencies, Coast Guard, Homeland
Security, and those same agencies on the other
side of the water. Because of the politics that were
involved at City Council on our side, there was a
rush vote, which got the Windsor City Council
and Windsor Mayor, and the lawyers that had been
working on this deal for eighteen months, in a flux.
That is the last part of a $300 million deficit that
the City has been carrying since before me, Your
Honor. If I don't close that deficit, 2,000 jobs are
gonna be lost in the city of Detroit. There's no way
I can have recreation programs. There's no way I
can cut grass, fix streets. I have to lay off about 700
police officers, and about 251 firefighters.

Facing that reality, what I've been doing for
six months is digging in, and trying to get that deal
done. I don't believe that that's more important than
this court proceeding. I don't believe that I would
ever disrespect these proceedings at all.

I respect this process, more than I've ever respected any process in my life. And I'm sorry. I did
violate the conditions of the bond, because I got a
phone call that the Windsor City Council—everything
was going off the rail—they were gonna back off the
deal. This was a very, very serious issue that stopped
me from shutting down the Recreation Department.

It's been presented that I went over for a
couple of hours. The office that I went to, it's about
fifty to 100 feet from the tunnel. I ran in. I made a
presentation. And I ran back. And we got the deal
back on track. We're now moving forward to close
the deficit.

What I've been trying to do, Your Honor,
throughout this process, is not lay anybody off. I

know there's a gentleman that came and sat in your courtroom, Your Honor. That gentleman sits outside of my house. They have helicopters fly around my house. And so, I do understand the pressure that you're going through. I'm on the news every single day. And I think 99.9 percent of the time, when people see me, Your Honor, it's cool, and collected and calm. I have respect for this court. And I have respect for you. But I don't believe that there's a person who can sit in this type of scrutiny, this type of pressure, these type of issues where I have to deal, personally, with my wife and children, in my office, to keep the chief of police and the fire commissioner and all the requisite forty-seven agencies working at optimum levels, and have to come here and deal with this issue in court, without having respect for this institution.

My life has been revolutionarily transformed! And it's transforming in an eye of these media people that don't know me at all. Your Honor, I'm asking for your forgiveness. It will never happen again. I've said that. My lawyers said that at the bond hearing last time.

I can give you the cut plan, and show you what we have to do on September 2, if this doesn't go through. September 3, I have to shut down Recreation. I have to fire firefighters. I have to fire the police officers, lay off police officers. And, at that particular moment, to get that deal on track, all that was in my mind is, 'We can't let the city go right now.'

We have bond rating meetings out in New York in October. And I promised certain things for the last two years. I've met each one of those promises. Every single promise that I made to the bondholders I kept. This is the last one. Every deal

I said I would close—economic development—I've
closed. Every labor agreement and changes I've gotten. I have a focus on this process, Your Honor. And
I don't disrespect you, or this court, at all. And I'm
asking for another chance.

I apologize to the citizens, as well. But, mostly,
to you. It was never a front to you. I respect you,
and the job that you have to do, and the position
that you're in.

I'd placed my heart in my hand. I spoke as honestly and
sincerely as I could. Judge Giles recessed for about ten minutes.
During that time, my lawyers told me how well I did. Supporters
in the courtroom were in tears. It was a very touching moment
for everyone but Giles.

Giles' response was that I shouldn't do anything without
making arrangements. He said I should have included him and
the court in those arrangements. Though he understood the
pressure I professed to be under, he had to adhere to the system
(now he had to adhere). As he talked, I clasped my hands together, pressing two fingers from each against my mouth. I listened
as he took away the drug screening mandate that had been placed
on me by another judge at my original bond hearing. He called
it meaningless. He then opined that it mattered to him how the
court is perceived.

"I have a responsibility to treat every defendant the same,"
he said. If "John Six-Pack" went to Canada, he said he would send
him to jail. Therefore, he had to treat me like "John Six-Pack."

"The court is revoking your bond," Giles said. "The court
is gonna order that all travel be suspended, and two, that you be
remanded to the Wayne County Jail for processing."

The press went crazy. Some slapped high fives. It would be
determined the next day that this was a gross abuse of judicial discretion and a violation of Michigan law but, for now, I was about
to be locked up!

But all is well, I kept thinking. All is well.

I rushed to call my wife, using a cell phone that I borrowed. I talked to her and my sons. They all cried for a moment, and then Jelani took over. He stepped up. His presence of mind, sensibility and spirit still give me a sense of awe today. He grew a lot that day, and I'm eternally thankful to God for what He did for my family at that moment.

I was escorted downstairs, in my three-piece suit, placed in handcuffs, put into a paddy wagon and taken from the courthouse to the Wayne County Jail. Central Booking. I was fingerprinted, had mug shots taken, and then had to remove all of my clothing to put on the inmate uniform. It was a green outfit with "WAYNE COUNTY INMATE" inscribed across the shirt and pants. I was then cuffed again and escorted by three deputies to my cell. All along the long walk to my cell, other inmates shouted out how much they loved me. One said that God was working through me. It actually felt good. As I turned the final corner before I arrived at the place I would be kept for the next twenty-seven hours, a final loud outburst came from the corridor behind me.

"Hey, Kwame!" the voice said. "Just know that all is well!" A calm and comforting feeling came over me. I had no tension, no anxiety, no fear and no anger! I walked into my cell, turned around for the handcuffs to be taken off, and asked the deputy the time. "12:43 p.m." he responded. And then he slammed the door.

You know that slam that you always hear in the movies? That's exactly how it sounds, except it's much louder. I sat down on the hard mattress, looked around my tiny cell and began to think.

My first thought: "I am locked up." My next thought: "All is well."

chapter 25
Days of Reckoning

J AIL WAS macabre. And peaceful. It was jail, bottom line. But for
one night, I was away from the hype. And then, I was released.

I felt something headed my way after that night, but I wasn't
sure what something was. The world around me reeked of over-
reaction. I felt like an example in the making, the subject of an
operative. I loved representing Detroit, but some hated the fact
that I existed. Detroit drives Michigan's economy, and I never
hesitated to stand on that awareness while administering on the
City's behalf. Yet there are Michigan counties far removed from
Detroit's urbane atmosphere whose residents know nothing
about the city, live very differently, and assess the city based on its
negative image. They don't respect Detroit or recognize its value
to the State of Michigan. So who would like a mayor who forced
them to see us? I could see why a chorus of naysayers wouldn't
mind seeing me gone. And I see how my mistakes gave them just
enough rope to hang me. The witness stand lie was the rope,
and it led to a snowball of stress and scrutiny that formed in me
a tornado of anger and exasperation. By the time those sheriff's
deputies made it to my sister's house, the tornado had consumed
me. And now, they had me.

I thought about this heavily during that night in jail, and
about how divisive a topic I'd become. I can think of no better
example of this than when Senator Barack Obama visited Detroit
just days after accepting the Democratic nomination for U.S.

President. Obama had once been a supporter, but sent word suggesting that I not attend a rally that would take place at Hart Plaza, literally across the street from my office. He even released a statement that echoed the wind in Detroit, declaring that I should resign from office. Not only had I become that much of a distraction, but the Republicans had a commercial ready to air as soon as I showed up on any stage with the man who would become the forty-forth and first African-American President of the United States.

I was floored and insulted, at first. Some felt that Senator Obama was selling out. The more I thought about it, however, the more I felt that he made a wise decision. I know Barack. He's a good man, and a cool guy. But he's also very smart, and he had to remain America's candidate. Appearing with me in public would be a statement against all the people who opposed me, and many of them supported him. His opportunity was too big to gamble. I gracefully accepted his request, and stayed home. Heavy on my heart, though, was the feeling of true loneliness.

The prosecutor had me where she wanted me. Worthy wanted to put me in jail for up to fifteen years. She intended to drum up enough charges to come after me as if I were a violent, multiple offender. I even heard rumors that she murmured her disgust for me and flatly stated her intent to destroy me. Worthy's attorneys, while conferencing with mine, acknowledged her dastardly ways and, as we progressively learned more about her intent to destroy, it became clear to me that I could not fight this devil with carnal weapons. I was officially fighting a losing battle. Carlita knew it, too. We talked and prayed together like never before, and we remained open. My family needed to plan for a healthy emergence from this situation, even if it aged us. We were wise to prepare ourselves spiritually because, after considering all things, and then consulting with my lawyers, the best recourse was the one we didn't like.

I reported to court in early September, with Carlita at my side. My attorneys had met with Worthy's team of prosecutors and worked out an agreement. Wearing a bronze sport coat and navy blue slacks, I stood before Judge David Groner, who requested my plea.

> *"I lied under oath," I said, "with the intent to mislead the court and jury and to impede and obstruct the fair administration of justice."*

For the record, I lied when I made that statement, as well. The real reason I lied under oath was because I didn't want my wife to know I cheated. But be clear. There was absolutely no justice to obstruct in the Whistleblower suit. The case was manufactured. I was just cornered. Immediately following those words, I agreed to do the following, under the terms of my agreement:

- resign from my post as mayor of the City of Detroit, with an announcement to be made that day;
- serve five years probation and 120 days in the Wayne County Jail,
- pay a restitution of $1 million, $20,000 of which was to be submitted on the day of my sentencing,
- forfeit my State pension against my restitution,
- surrender my license to practice law, and
- seek no public office for five years.

The plea hearing was broadcast live on network television and streamed across the Internet. Many people told me afterward that I appeared happy... light. I also heard, of course, that some people felt I didn't take the hearing seriously. Well, after going through a daily hell for the nine previous months, it did feel pretty good to lay down that burden. I suppose some believe a man's visage should appear beaten when he's sentenced. I was simply relieved. My wife and I sang songs, laughed and exchanged humorous quips with each other on the way to the court that day. We felt free for the first time in nearly a year. Our yoke was being lifted, so please, excuse me if my smile offended you. But that day, in court, I was getting my praise on.

The fight I couldn't win appeared to be over. Say what you want about the law, but public opinion sways courtroom decisions.

The negative press had swayed public opinion, and my historically bad relationship with the press swayed the tone of their coverage.

My goal now was to start working to fix everything. My life and marriage still needed repair that could only happen away from the spotlight. My family was emotionally damaged, and the family name was beginning to symbolize something negative to many people. My mother, father and sister were wracked with pain, which permeated my entire family.

Christine, meanwhile, had also been charged with obstruction of justice, and was a fixture in the news herself, although far less than I was. We hadn't been in contact, outside of hearsay from mutual friends and acquaintances. Later, she would also plea, and be sentenced to ninety days in jail and $150,000 restitution. I shuddered every time I thought about my role in her plight.

I delivered a televised address to the city later that day. I spoke honestly, placing our accomplishments on the record. I was and am still proud of what we did for the city. We progressed. We changed the way the city operated. But it was over, and Ken Cockrel would now become mayor in my stead. I wished him the best, and asked that the citizens wrap their arms around him and support him. And I meant it. He would need it.

One of the parts of my address that garnered the most news commentary was a critique I made of Gov. Jennifer Granholm. I think the governor and her advisors truly believed that her record of doing absolutely nothing for the State through her first six years would be forgiven or forgotten if she aggressively went after me. She'd spent her tenure going with the political flow, and remained consistent when my troubles arose.

I ended my speech by saying, "Detroit, you have set me up... for a comeback." As I expected, that statement was attacked, called arrogant, and teased. All of the critics missed the mark. I was in no way talking about coming back as mayor, or even as a politician. I had completely divorced myself from that. I was happy to finish my political career, and was ready for the next part of my life. I was talking about coming back a better, wiser and more dynamic man. And, again, I meant it.

I was given six weeks to get my affairs in order at home. We packed up and moved out of the Manoogian mansion. That was another media spectacle. Carlita commandeered that effort while I prepared to vacate my post. It's probably cliché to describe every news attraction as some sort of media frenzy at this point, because just about everything we did became a headline. But I'd never been more relieved to get out of a house in my life.

I was a husband and father again. For a moment, there were fewer headlines and gossip. The news cameras, the tether strapped to my ankle for the entire summer (yes, I was a mayor on a tether)! were gone. I became plain ol' Kwam, and it felt great. It was an incredibly important time for me and Carlita. We started dressing our wounds. It wasn't easy, at all. Time together was also time to face our issues. We'd become different people, and we had to get reacquainted. We were committed, but there sleepless nights along the way.

The night before my sentence was to begin was one of the roughest for Carlita and the boys, which made it hard for me. All of them were wracked with anticipation now that the moment was upon us. Sleep eluded us as completely as serenity. So, the next morning, we spent our time together quietly, just being in each other's presence. I'd spoken with my mother the night before, but she wasn't up to seeing her son sentenced and sent to jail. Besides, I wanted her to distance herself from my situation. She had enough to worry about with her own political career, and my detractors were already trying to ruin her just because she was my mother.

Another packed courtroom. Another live broadcast. Another meeting with my attorneys in a nearby conference room. Another nervous, confused appearance by my legal team. They'd been beaten up pretty good over the past six months, and the sentencing hearing hit them a few more times. Still, they just never seemed to be prepared for these things (or at least it appeared that way to me).

The prosecutor, my lawyers said, made changes to the final sentencing agreement we'd ratified six weeks earlier. It turned out the prosecutor and Judge Groner worked together and added a few requirements to my guidelines, and wanted me to agree to them on the spot. The judge offered me a choice to concur or withdraw my plea and go to trial. This, mind you, was after I'd already completed every other tenet of the previous agreement except serving my time and paying restitution. I was out of office. My law license was gone. *Now* I could withdraw my plea?

My lawyers shoved the new requirements at me and advised me to sign them. The new conditions called for the immediate surrender to the City of the funds in my campaign account, as well as other organizational funds. I held no affiliation or fiduciary responsibility with many of the funds noted in the new document. I was also called to give up any tax refunds that I or my wife, who was in no way involved in this saga, generated.

As for the law license, the judge arranged for the director of the State Bar of Michigan to come to the courtroom and assist in the public revocation. This was a new twist. I'd agreed, in the deal that was previously ratified, to surrender my license specifically for the "period of my probation." The prosecution changed its position on sentencing day, demanding permanent rescinding. The judge, of course, agreed, and I was promptly presented with the voluntary revocation document, but not before the judge reiterated his offer to withdraw and go to trial.

My attorneys again advised me to sign everything. They were scared, and completely outmatched. I took their advice, but I still believe my entire sentencing was illegal and a complete abuse of judicial discretion and authority. I'm determined to find out one day. The proceedings lasted for hours. It was one of the longest sentencing hearings in the court's history.

Groner rehashed the details of every charge. It made little sense, given that I'd already pled guilty and was there to begin my sentence. But he did his best to make it good TV, reading his lines for his big scene. After exhausting the proceedings, he adjourned the session, and I was led toward a rear exit. I wasn't allowed to kiss Carlita, but I reassured her that I loved her and would be in touch soon, and headed to my temporary home.

chapter 26
Surroundings

A TUNNEL SNAKES underground beneath a downtown Detroit Street, connecting the Wayne County Circuit Court to the Andrew Baird County Jail. Footsteps tend to echo in that corridor hauntingly, like recurring thoughts, or reminders. It's long, cold and damp, with yellow cement block walls. The floor is grey concrete. It's a gloomy, clandestine walkway reserved for law enforcers, and those people the law convicts. I now took this walk, under one of the very roads that I administered for six years, as its most infamous political prisoner.

A phalanx of Sheriff's deputies, all very professional, escorted me, while turning their faces to avoid eye contact. Still, I could tell what they were feeling. Some couldn't hide their excitement, others their discontent. A few were sad.

Prisoner Processing was surrounded by a number of holding cells filled with new inmates. I heard a chorus of the same profane and supportive chants from inmates that I'd heard months earlier, when Giles jailed me.

We got love for you, Big Dawg!

Away from the cameras and lights for the first time in ages, I quietly exchanged my navy suit for a green prison uniform, handed my dress shoes to a deputy, and accepted a pair of slippers. I was assigned a number, which would replace my name for the next four months.

Kwame Malik Kilpatrick, former mayor of the City of

Detroit, was now Inmate No. 2008-34589. I began a long, slow walk to my cell, entered unit 14J-4 on the second floor, and quickly surveyed my surroundings. The cell boasted the warmth of a military brig. The walls were made of the same neutral block. The stainless steel toilet and sink sat adjacent to an open shower stall. The convenience was fantastic—I could crap, shower and shave in a single step. There was a pay phone with a six-inch cord connected to it from which I could make fifteen-minute collect calls to an approved list of friends and family. I imagine the short cord protected certain inmates from harming themselves. For a 6'4" man with no suicidal tendencies, it was just plain uncomfortable.

I walked to the far wall and peered through a tall, slim, filmy window. I could see the courthouse across the street. Because I was the mayor, I was placed in isolation. Ironic, the designation, given that the people of the city had always demonstrated a familial affection for me. Even the deputies showed it at times. One of them, a man whose name I don't remember, but whose sullen expression I'll never forget, mentioned how much he hated having to do his job the moment I arrived. I wondered if I'd have more peace of mind in General Population. No matter. I was a high-profile prisoner, which made Gen Pop impossible.

Aside from one other inmate on my cell block who was slated for transfer, I was alone. That concerned me. Budget concerns had prompted the Department of Corrections to grant early releases all non-violent offenders a few weeks earlier, so not only would there be no prisoners on my block, but half the jail would be empty by Christmas. I was a non-violent offender, but there would be no early release for me. Suddenly bereft in a sea of thought, I anticipated the solitude, and also felt a sense of peace.

That's right. A peace—I'd have to call it that—settled over me. It was a passing feeling, brought on more by the absence of public chaos and silence, than anything born of my spirit. This was my first encounter with stillness in twelve years. I hadn't been alone since running for my first office in 1996, and was accustomed to organized chaos. Accompaniment. Obligation.

Paranoia. What a stifling existence. I could keep my game face locked, and think through situations. My thought process is one of my biggest weapons, and it helped me keep my composure. But that didn't mean it was good for me. Being alone, even in a jail cell, brought relief for the moment.

Surely, this odd but strangely comforting feeling of peace wouldn't last. Carlita and the boys would certainly enter my thoughts. I would have to console my mother, father and sister to assure them that I was doing well. I was going to worry about them. People would soon visit. The press would come looking for jailhouse interviews. Whatever. But at that moment, I just stood at that window, its film like a metaphor for everything that once challenged my sense of clarity, managing nothing but the moment.

It had been a long day. It was amazing that they managed to sentence and process me, given that gaudy courtroom show, just in time for chow. And what an eclectic menu it was! Italian link sausage with spaghetti sauce, with a side of tater tots, buttered peas, Texas toast and an orange. I would learn within days that this was as good as the food got. I have diverticulitis, a condition that requires a strict diet. I shouldn't and usually don't eat beef, pork or any high-cholesterol foods. A diet without high amounts of protein and fiber will trigger a chemical reaction that will cause my colon to flare and burst. I could die.

This was serious. After withstanding years of scrutiny, inaccurate reporting and an eroded constituency, jail food, of all things, was my biggest threat. Three days passed before I received any water to drink. The usual beverages were artificial fruit drinks, high in sugar. Snacks were assorted Little Debbie products and Better Made potato chips. All meals were consistently saturated, fatty and devoid of green vegetables. When a guard delivered my dinner, I didn't recognize the meat on the tray.

"What's that?" I asked.

"I don't know," she said.

"You don't *know?*" I said. "Well, I'm not eating that."

Reality sank into my head as I realized I had little choice

in deciding what I would be able to put in my body. Until my scheduled release in February 2009, I would have about as much freedom as a babe in a crib. I'd be on lockdown in my cell for twenty-three hours a day. I'd be awakened at 5 a.m., told when to eat breakfast, when to go for recreation, when to eat dinner, and when to go to sleep. That little bit of peace faded as I stretched out on my mattress, another cement-filled luxury model, and fell asleep. I guess the stress of the past eight months finally put me down and, instead of drifting, I plummeted into a deep slumber. I slept for three days, only to awaken for an occasional visit from a staff nurse, doctor or psychiatrist, family and friends; mealtime, or a deputy making rounds.

During that first week, a psychiatrist came to the cell every day. He feared I was losing my grip on sanity. Varied levels of insanity were normal for people in isolation, he'd later tell me. His concern was that I'd fall susceptible to strange thoughts, or vertigo. I shared his concern because I was accustomed to activity. I appreciated stillness, but my capacity to dwell there was about to be profoundly tested.

A panic button in the cell would alert the deputy in the Master Control station if the conditions he warned about took root. The psychiatrist mentioned this on several visits, and I would tell him I was fine, and go back to sleep. I was totally listless. Completely drained. Hell, that hard, horrible, *far* too short mattress felt like a Westin Dream Bed for the first few days. I woke up several times completely unaware of where I was.

Revelation

Sensation. Realization. Caging. *Caging.*

One week in, I crashed into reality. Anger and hatred gripped me as fear and the outside world teased me. It was November 4, 2008—Election Day. During my first two weeks, I'd been let out of my cell four times for one-hour recreation periods, taken to a very small gymnasium, and locked in. I could do whatever I pleased for one hour.

I wasn't allowed any reading materials for the first six days, no form of mental stimulation whatsoever. I was simply placed in a cell. A few Sheriff's deputies were reprimanded once for bringing me a book and a magazine from the jail library. They were told not to bring me anything. Both deputies told me that no one had ever been treated this way.

The nurses at the jail were truly a godsend. They were professional, and did outstanding work. They were also tough and caring, and fought for fair treatment of all inmates. On the sixth day of my stay, one of the nurses took the radio from her office and put it in my cell. And her boss backed her on the move when administrative authorities resisted. Whew! I had a radio! After six days of solitary confinement with absolutely nothing, a radio was like a little slice of heaven!

The nurses, a couple of deputies and some community members banded together on my behalf at that point, and spoke with Sheriff Warren Evans about how I was being treated. Warren Evans would later run for mayor and lose to Dave Bing, only to be later appointed chief of Detroit Police by Mayor Bing. Evans was dubiously talented. He never saw a TV camera or newspaper reporter that he didn't like, and would be forced to resign his post as chief after using City resources to produce a pilot for a reality show about himself. He was also romantically involved with another officer, one he'd supervised, and it all blew up in a mini-text message scandal that slightly mirrored my own. He could capitulate to any political or media whim that would grant positioning. That said, even after declaring on TV that I would not be getting any special treatment and would be handled like any other inmate, he turned up the bad treatment a notch. Why? I believe he pandered to the press. Only after receiving calls from people who mattered to his upcoming mayoral bid was I taken off of 'Hannibal Lector' status and given a television to watch. Nine days had passed. A commanding officer brought it to my cell at 6 p.m. on Election Night.

I saw the long lines of Detroiters at polling sites as soon as I turned it on. Throughout the state of Michigan and the entire country, the scenes reminded me of the historic election of Nelson

Mandela to South Africa's presidency. The voting lines were much shorter, of course, but the energy was similar. In Detroit, in Jackson, Miss., in Brooklyn, the atmosphere was amazing. It was a theater of hope, faith, love and transformation! From my small cell, my spirit momentarily soared above my present circumstances, beyond the past months. It was a special feeling.

Hours into the viewing, I felt tears roll down my cheek in steady streams. I hadn't cried like that in years. As a student of history, I remembered triumphant spirits of the past. Nat Turner. Denmark Vesci. Booker T. Washington. Carter G. Woodson. Marcus Garvey. Medgar Evers. Malcolm X. Martin Luther King, Jr. The four little girls killed in the Birmingham, Alabama, bombing. The Mississippi freedom fighters. I felt. I saw. Tears. Joy. Jubilation. So many people, so many races. I cried forcefully, and screamed, "Victory!" from my cell. And as I stood with my fists raised to the ceiling, I caught a reflection in the stainless steel sink and toilet in my cell. I saw the big door that locked me away from the movement, and I hated Sorrow for laughing so sinisterly as he barreled and tackled me. Freedom, for me, was immaterial.

Oh, the emotional abyss I fell into. For the first time in my life, I felt like a complete and utter failure. I was removed from a monumental moment in American history, one in which I'd played a significant role, and sent to a dungeon like a miscreant. A criminal. I couldn't share it with my wife and children. I was an absent father, an adulterer, a liar, a creep. In that moment, I didn't feel I deserved much beyond the nothingness into which I had been tossed. I grew enraged at myself, but I shouted blame toward everyone and everything else, including God. I threw wild, violent punches at demons. I thrashed and gnashed my teeth as election coverage became a haunting, taunting score in the background. The scenes looped. The jubilation mocked me. My rage grew and my thoughts turned evil.

Blind with rage and wet with tears, I fell to the floor. Lord knows if the guards were within earshot. I lay on the floor screaming, cursing and crying. And then, I turned toward God. God had it coming, and I cursed filthily, profanely. I challenged Him with my exasperated taunts.

I plunged to the bottom of my life as if I had fallen from its final slope. I lost all sense of respect, protocol and honor. It was my most honest moment ever—I was robbed of diplomacy on American history's biggest political night. How poetic. Detroit's biggest political figure, prostrate on a jail cell floor as Barack Obama wins the presidency.

My demons, those bastards, rubbed fear, rage and doubt across my back like jesters, self-pity and deceit a funky lotion. And I dared call out God in the midst of this spiritual chasm.

"What the hell do You want me to do now!?" I screamed. "I'm tired of this shit! You got me beat down! If You want to kill me, just kill me! I really don't give a damn!

"You're allowing these people to do this to me because I was messing around on my wife? What about all the good shit I did? I worked my ass off for these people! I damn near killed *myself* in this job! And now, I have to suffer. My children have to suffer. That's some bullshit, God!"

I then turned my enmity toward President-Elect Barack Obama, the man with whom I'd been very cordial. We'd developed a mutual respect over the years. He attended a fundraiser for my mayoral campaign, which was held in Chicago, and even spoke a few words about me. I returned the gesture in Detroit, when we held a fundraiser for his U.S. Senate campaign.

Unbeknownst to most, he and I talked after he issued the statement about me before visiting Detroit during his campaign. We had a very good conversation. He was sincere and wished me well. And I told him I was so very proud of him, and wished him and his family well. That night in my cell, however, I hated him a little, asking God, "Why? Why him, and not me?" I never wanted to be president. I had never been a jealous man. I just wanted answers. I was in a free fall, and anyone who wasn't helping at that moment was my enemy. And then...

Surrender. Not my voice, but it was in my head. It spoke through the struggle. It was strange, and it poked a bit of peace through my agony. It was poignant and sudden. It grabbed me and arrested my demons, and dried my back. Enough, it commanded.

The cell was dark, and I was still sorrowful, but I couldn't talk. I was still prostrate on the floor, vulnerable to this new presence. A fear like nothing I'd ever felt washed over me. I trembled. I was too afraid to even lift my eyes and gaze around the room, so I closed them and pressed my face against the floor. I was a child afraid of a boogieman, all 6'4" and 300 pounds of me. The monster was in the room with me.

So I prayed and pleaded in a case of turnabout so typical of the biblical stories I'd grown up reading. I asked for His help. I prayed and apologized with the same emphasis and aggression I'd used to blame and criticize Him. I told God that I would do whatever He wanted me to do. I asked Him to save my life!

Accept. Yes.

If my circumstance wasn't going to kill me, it would prepare me. I prayed for hours, conversing with God, reconciling and meditating. And then, I lifted myself from the floor, turned back toward the TV, and refocused on the Election Night coverage. I saw a park in Downtown Chicago. President-Elect Obama prepared to address the excited and anxious crowd. I felt proud now, watching him walk to the podium as a sea of humanity rolled around him like waves. And I felt his victory. And I felt prepared. My bags were packed, my journey apparent, a fresh wind in my lungs. Settle, Kwame. *Settle, for a surge will come. This is a cusp. It may seem long-lasting, but it is fleeting, a moment. Peace be still.*

I knew the voice. It wasn't my own, but it was mine. And it was permanent.

I felt proud—of God, and yes, of my new President.

By the time my first visitors arrived the next day, I'd begun to make sense of my emotions. I was a mere few weeks into my sentence and focusing on my myriad feelings, and then on the stories behind them, gave me a great sense of clarity. So I embraced them, and began to discuss this with them – with my mother and Ayanna, as they arrived. Certainly with Carlita when she called, because it helped our healing. If I was going to emerge from this a better man, it would be on God's terms, not the court's, and not my own. It was time to come out of my dry place. Truth and admission needed a place in my spirit, and I was ready to admit some things.

chapter 27

Reconciliation

To the people of Detroit and the world, I let you down. You supported me. You were excited about my vision for the City. You felt progress. But my personal issues impeded my judgment. I cheated on my wife. I lied about it while on the witness stand. Of that, I am clearly guilty.

Know that I have also been accused of things for which I am not guilty, but my enemies are artists, and they paint vivid images. Unfortunately, you have been bombarded with these accusations with no counterpoints. If I am you, I probably think there is so much news, so much rumor and commentary, that something must be true. To that, I suggest that you consider a few things. Newspapers are not 'truth' papers. They sell headlines. Judges are elected, and they have agendas of their own. Lawyers can be opportunists. And politicians often build careers on the backs of people they destroy. Feel how you will about me, but think critically. The wisdom of entire communities depends on it.

DETROIT IS a great city, but we are a depressed people. We won't progress until we learn to truly love each other. I believe our collective depression—our frustration with the lack of adequate City services, historic racism and national respect—causes us to fight ourselves. We are the only major city in the country that does not benefit from a productive regional relationship. As far as Detroiters are concerned, the suburbs are the enemy next door, and they feel the same way about us. That alone is a recipe for disaster.

I thought a lot about what I did to contribute to the City's misery, and what I didn't do. It's important to me that people know how deeply personal these thoughts were. It's impossible not to dwell on every little thing when you're alone in a cell for twenty-three hours a day. It's even harder when things dawn on you, and you have to face yourself, alone. I fought through states of despair in those months. To an extent, the Parable of the Wheat and Tares applied to me. I was responsible for charting growth for the City and for my family. It's similar to the seeds that God wanted to be well tended, but was offended when they were planted on unstable ground. By cheating on my wife, however, I believe I offended God. And then, by the way I handled things when the information went public, I embarrassed the people who admired me. I hurt my family. For that, I became deeply sorrowful, and I longed to apologize—first to my wife, and then to the people of Detroit.

Gaining perspective between making amends and pinpointing a political railroading made my cell feel a bit bigger. Spiritually, I was freeing myself. I was physically locked down, but I began to understand what I'd heard from men who'd been incarcerated before me, that a sound mind and spirit can open your world in ways that physical freedom cannot. I was a long way from Nirvana, and I would have given a leg to get out of that cell, but jail strengthens the psyche. Strong minds get tougher in prison. Weak ones rot. I resolved to use this time as personal training.

Occasional assistance came in the form of key conversations and visits. My wife and sons were like respirators. Talking to them always made my day. Carlita had taken the boys to our house in Tallahassee, where they were finally able to enroll in new schools and make new friends, benefiting from living in an environment that knew little and could care less about Kwame Kilpatrick and the City of Detroit.

My visitation list included about ten people, whom I'm thankful to say came to see me every week. My parents, sister, grandfather, uncles, aunts and cousins soldiered through one of the harshest winters on record to help keep my spirits up. When prisoners talk about the importance of the letters they receive, the calls and the visits, that is real. I received hundreds of letters and cards from supporters throughout the community, along with my family's visits. It sustained me when my cell, which did not have heat or insulation, dropped to near-freezing temperatures. The newspapers reported that I received preferential treatment. That's laughable. I could run my finger through the frost on the window and couldn't ask for enough sheets to keep warm. I celebrated my first Christmas away from my family. On December 26, my phone cut off while I was talking to Carlita. I was told that the power failed, but learned later that my cell was the only unit in the building where it happened. It wouldn't cut back on for three days. I was taking showers and shitting in full view of deputies, every day. Had I allowed my ego to wage a bigger battle, these conditions may have driven me crazy. So, yes, it helps to know that people are rooting for you on the outside. I don't know how I would have fared without the support.

Nothing lifted my spirits more than seeing their faces. But a few key visits came close. Minister Farrakhan made a highly publicized visit. And I received counsel from Bishop T.D. Jakes soon afterward. His Christian perspective almost mirrored Min. Farrakhan's ministering.

"Everything you need is in your house," Bishop Jakes would tell me. He was referring to our bodies, our temples, which house our spirits. By trusting God, that small voice inside me, I receive all the answers I need. And then, there was my home with Carlita. Everything we needed to survive our storms, we already had. We had the ability to make godly decisions, to exercise godly discernment, access godly resources and make godly transformations. It doesn't come from outside, but from within. It was not the last time Bishop Jakes would counsel us.

Both men told me that it was time for me to die, not physically, but in that phase of my existence. New life required space. Minister Farrakhan likened my incarceration to birth. The birth canal, he said, is the closest that a baby comes to experiencing death, because its struggle through the canal challenges its instinct to survive. On the other side of the canal, however, is a new realm. They both agreed that I was being reborn.

Bishop Jakes wrote to me, quoting Jesus's teaching that those who try to save their immature lives will ultimately lose them. But in faith, in Christ, he wrote, they are reborn. As he wrote, I imagined how incredible it might have been to have these two great men in the same room.

I accepted God's will. I resolved to be led by it, to be reborn, renewed and rededicated. Some people may never accept me, but they have their own issues. They may always mock me. But people mocked and crucified Jesus, so who am I to avoid a similar path? My directive, and my inspiration, was clear. I had to trust God.

My release date arrived on February 3, 2009, ninety-nine days into my sentence. Maybe it was foolish to think this, but I truly looked forward to quietly leaving the jail, kissing my family, packing my things and leaving Detroit. That was all I wanted. Carlita and I had decided months earlier to make Dallas our new home. Detroit needed to be free of me, and I needed to get out of the city's way. I also wanted the people of Detroit to heal. The City couldn't move forward as long as I was in town, because I couldn't be invisible. The best thing for me to do was disappear, get a job elsewhere, pay my restitution and stay away. Whatever my legacy in Detroit would be, let it be, or let my future work make amends for whatever happened while I was in office.

What wishful thinking that was. My release was an event.

Physically, I was a spectacle. I never cut my hair while in jail, so I'd grown a full afro and beard. I also lost about thirty-eight pounds because of the quality of prison food, and my reluctance to eat it. So yeah, if the press wanted a spectacle, they were about to get one. Sheriff Evans caved under the pressure to publicly release me, resolving to have me walk out through the front door just after midnight so news crews could carry it live. My family had fresh clothes delivered to me, and Minister Rasul

Muhammad, a friend and spiritual leader who'd stood by me throughout my trials, sent the Fruit of Islam (FOI), the Nation of Islam's security, to escort me. The FOI are highly disciplined, exceptionally well-trained men. I was thankful for their presence more than anything because, when my paperwork was processed and I walked through the lobby, I could see a phalanx of news cameras and reporters outside the main entrance. I could also see my friend DeDan Milton, Khary, my cousin Ajene Evans and my brother-in-law Daniel Ferguson, standing on the perimeter of the news crews. My directions from the FOI were simple. Walk out, go limp, and let them guide me as they saw fit.

Once the deputies pushed the crowd back, we moved. As soon as I stepped out the door, the cameras and reporters rushed toward me. It was madness, and they were violent! They pushed us, so one of FOI guards grabbed me and yanked my now-285-pound frame as if I were 100 pounds lighter. As they pulled me toward a waiting SUV, the army of newshounds advanced in a virtual stampede. Two cameramen fought for position, and one of them hit DeDan in the eye with his camera. DeDan's eye was already swollen by the time we got out of there. As I was literally tossed into the SUV, a reporter grabbed the door, preventing us from closing it. One of the FOI—they were all as big as houses —warned the reporter to step back, and he did. We sped off as quickly as we could, and Daniel, DeDan, Khary and Ajene followed.

Fortunately, we anticipated being followed, and decided not to go straight home. We drove around for a while, and then stopped to get some real food to eat. It was like heaven, eating real food. About an hour later, we went to my mother's house, where my family waited. The news crews were there by the time we arrived, and we had to fight through more trucks and microphones just to get into our driveway.

The news carried it all live, and reported that we were the aggressive ones, even though the reporters outnumbered us significantly. The media was so out of touch with the heart of the city that they couldn't even describe the FOI accurately. They described them as something closer to henchmen. It was so indicative of the mainstream press's ongoing effort to undermine and rewrite Detroit's history.

Whatever. That night, it didn't matter. I was out of jail and, though I wasn't with Carlita and the boys, who had stayed in Dallas to avoid the frenzy, I was home.

chapter 28
Revelation 2: *Clarity*

─────────── *Flashback* (and forward) ───────────

WHEN I GOT up from the cold hard floor that night in the Wayne County Jail, I was a changed man. I knew it. I could feel it. I turned the TV off and looked around for one of the three-inch pencils the jail provided. I then began to think, away from despair and guilt, and toward more positive moments—events and encounters that had truly blessed me.

I thought about a time just after the text message scandal broke. Carlita and I were at home in Tallahassee. We still had our house, and went there to get away from things and collect ourselves. A program featuring Bishop T.D. Jakes aired on TV one day. He was preaching a sermon called "Potholes."

Carlita and I were drained at that point, and we were both struggling to find something that could help us, individually and as a couple, and we were familiar with the Bishop. He and I both participated in the funeral for Mother Rosa Parks, the matriarch of the Civil Rights Movement. I'd also heard him preach, and he was excellent. I suppose a crying soul has a way of honing your focus, because he seemed to be speaking directly to us. As I sat next to the woman I'd completely disrespected and desperately wanted to win back, I was riveted. The sermon's content was buoyed by the spirit the man conveyed.

Bishop Jakes affected Carlita and I so much that we ordered

the sermon online and requested next-day delivery. How ironic it was that we heard another of his sermons before the package even arrived. Another day, our painter, Warren, was listening to Bishop Jakes while he worked, but had mixed the sermons with instrumental hip-hop music. Carlita asked him about it, and he said he mixed the tapes so his children could bob their heads while absorbing positive messages.

Warren told us about other preachers whose sermons he'd mixed to music, I asked him to make some for us. He brought several of them over to the house the next day. They had uplifting titles, like "God Never Meant for You to Lose," "Famine to Favor," and "From Disgrace to Grace." And they flowed over beats like Common's "I Used to Love H.E.R." or Jay-Z's "Encore."

We targeted the messages that seemed to especially fit us, and they helped us slowly repair our foundation. We absorbed the messages, prayed together and tried to remain open and obedient. That period was such a Godsend that in April, after an opportunity arose for me to take a business trip to Dallas, Bishop Jakes's home, I asked Carlita to accompany me. We called ahead and scheduled a meeting with the Bishop and his wife, First Lady Serita. We had no idea what we would discuss with them, but the urge to be in the presence of people whose closeness to God touched us just seemed right.

We met for lunch after I finished my business, and immediately thanked Bishop Jakes for his guidance and teaching. We opened up a little to them, but spared them the details of our recent past. It didn't matter that we were guarded. Bishop Jakes is a master counselor. He does it even when you don't know it's happening. By telling us about his and his wife's past situations, about being assaulted by the press, experiencing fear and emotional fatigue, he smoothly canvassed everything we were going through. They were both patient, calm, loving and funny. They made us so comfortable that we stayed an extra day to attend services at the Bishop's church, the Potter's House.

In the meantime, we spent quality time together, walking

around Dallas's shops, enclaves and talking about the weather. We noticed the peace there, and it felt wonderful. A few people recognized me, but they weren't angry or vitriolic. We realized how foreign this feeling of anonymity had become. What a sad and hopeful adumbration our hometown had become for us.

Dallas felt like home. We had no family there, and had never visited before. But it felt like we tried on suits that fit perfectly. No tailoring required. But, it didn't help that we kept encountering old acquaintances who'd moved there. We bumped into old friends from FAMU walking through the mall, and Carlita's old hairdresser, Melissa. Even at church the next day, we met NFL Hall-of-Famers Deion Sanders, Michael Irvin and Emmit Smith, all of whom encouraged me.

"If you leave Detroit," Deion said, "Dallas is the place to be."

The service was awesome. We cried at several points throughout the service, and headed for the airport directly afterward, feeling sad about having to leave. We knew we belonged there. We returned to Detroit with newfound hope. The future, even if it had to be delayed, was bright and real. Our marriage, we also learned, was solid at its core. We built it using old-school materials such as values, ethics and beliefs, and they all withstood the elements.

Each subsequent visit to Dallas was better than the last. After each trip, Carlita would return to Tallahassee, and I'd go back to Detroit to work and weather. My rose-colored Detroit glasses were removed. It was no longer the city I knew growing up. I loved Detroit, but the particular spirit that once articulated my affection seemed dead. I yearned for the flavor of the past, the people's *can do* spirit. The fight. Where was the love? And what was up with the sense of depression and hopelessness that replaced it? Certainly, some would pin the blame on me. And yes, I felt like an outcast myself. A pariah. I was an easy target, though, because the *work* we were doing was defying the economy's downward spiral. No, Kwame Kilpatrick was not the illness. The illness were the times. An era of fatigue had dawned on Detroit. Our freedom fighters were mute. Our children lacked guidance. Our mojo was gone.

In that cell, I counted my blessings. I'd gained a great deal of understanding. A meeting and conversation with Reverend Jesse Jackson, just before I was jailed, came to mind. Reverend Jackson and I have had numerous conversations over the years. His sincerity and concern gave me pause. Honestly, I don't know how he found me. I was trying hard to keep away from anyone outside of my family and attorneys. He was in town for a speech, and I knew he was looking for me. To be quite honest, though, I was deeply embarrassed and fatigued. It's easy to shut yourself away from everyone when you feel like a failure.

So I planned to hide until he left town. Reverend Jackson, though, is a hawk. He's accustomed to people hiding from him when he's in their city. But he knows how to find them, so I shouldn't have been surprised when my office phone rang and, thinking it was my father, I answered to hear Reverend Jackson's legendary baritone. He'd been in my position years earlier when an infidelity scandal threatened his family. He spoke to me from inside my situation. I'm glad he found me. He told me to put everything down and cleave to my wife. Forget politics, the media and my image. Forget trying to save myself.

"You already messed up," he told me. "So now, make it right with God. God gave you a partner for life. Go, apologize and renew your life with her." In clarity, I remembered it all, and my pencil began to flow across the pages of the small notepad with words and names.

New words and phrases began to gnaw at me. And I found one key phrase that I'd heard as a young adult, before I assumed my post. I leaned up, looked at the ceiling, and said, "All men cheat."

My father said that to me in 1985. My hero and best friend who had taught me everything, including that statement. When he and my mother divorced, he assured me and Ayanna that we'd never be separated from him. And he made good on that promise, showing up and driving me to every achievement. But I rebelled in 1985, a few days after my father and his new wife, Bettye, moved into their new home. I learned that he had cheated on my mother, more than once. One of the affairs was with Bettye. I stood as my Dad's best man when he and Bettye married, and now I felt we had both disrespected my mother.

My father had some explaining to do. I was six feet tall, and about 220 pounds at the time. He still had six inches and thirty pounds on me, but it was time to man up. I got to the house and heard him talking to Bettye from the basement. When he spoke to me, I gave him a flippant response and abruptly asked, "Why did you cheat on my mother?"

He looked confused but oddly expectant of the question, almost ready to respond. He squared himself at me and said, "You won't understand."

"I *don't* understand," I said. "You're a sorry dude." That didn't sit well with him at all.

"Are you a man now?" he said, poised and ready to kick my ass. I was nervous, but stood my ground.

"Yes!" I retorted as, without hesitation, he punched me in the chest. Damn, it hurt! And immediately, I knew I wasn't quite a man, but I caught my breath, looked up from wherever I'd stumbled to and shot back at him, "I would never be a sorry dude and cheat on my wife."

"All men cheat!" His words seared my soul. We didn't speak for weeks. His words took root, and blossomed. Time and maturity would pass before the other words in that exchange—"… never be a sorry dude, and cheat on my wife"—applied to my own marriage.

Dad and I made up, but I considered the antagonism of it all from my prison cell, and could clearly discern the difference in my spirit between some of my good and bad decisions. I remembered the fear and guilt I felt while on the witness stand during the Whistleblower trial, and the exhilaration and joy I felt working on the Super Bowl. I bounced between similarly negative and positive charges when thinking about my personal life. Two phrases sparked a remarkable era of contradiction in my heart, my personality, my thoughts and, finally, my actions. Was I a hypocrite? No. I was discerning and deciding, choosing emancipation, finding me.

Pastors helped me. J. Drew Sheard. John H. Sheard. Robert Brumfeld. Claude Cline. Minister Rasul Muhammad, and an extraordinarily good brother name Victor Muhammad, who visited me every week at the County jail and guided me through numerous study materials on facing and overcoming difficulty.

Businessmen helped me. Pete Karmanos. Roger Penske. Jim Nicholson. Bob Johnson. I even remembered an encouraging conversation with former HUD Secretary Alphonso Jackson, in which he echoed the sentiment of those who implored me to focus on my family.

I stopped writing when a conversation I'd had with Minister Louis Farrakhan, before my incarceration, broached my thoughts. In August 2008, just ten days before my formal resignation as mayor, I was sitting in my eerily empty office, my mind cluttered, when the phone rang. It was my mother, telling me she'd just spoken with Minister Farrakhan at an event in Washington, D.C., and that he asked about me. He sent word that he was available if I wanted to speak with him. Mama being Mama, she suggested that I give him a call.

I was overwhelmed with stress and didn't want to speak to anyone. Guilt and abject loneliness made me very unreceptive. I sat at my desk weighing the phone call for several minutes before finally picking up the receiver and dialing. A Brother answered the line after a few short rings. After telling him who I was, he greeted me with the Muslim words of peace, *"As Salaam Alaikum."*

"Wa alaikum salaam," I formally responded. The Brother exhorted me to stay strong, and then put Minister Farrakhan on the phone.

"Hello, dear Brother," were the first words he spoke. His sense of humility and peace shone through his attributes. I immediately responded to his composed energy. We spent several minutes discussing my concerns, including my facing jail time, and then he said three words that foreshadowed the voice I heard in that cell a few months later.

"Surrender, dear Brother," he said. "You have been stressed, angry, vengeful and hurting. Surrender it all to God, and allow His will to be done. And that may mean that you must go to jail. But jail won't be the end. It will be the beginning, the beginning of your purification process. God wants to use you, Brother. And he wants you to surrender all to Him, so He can use you for His glory."

It was the first time I seriously considered the prospect of jail, and hearing the word "surrender" in the same breath, well, took my breath away. I was no longer in control. Not one bit. Minister Farrakhan added one more jewel to our conversation, offering for the first time his thoughts on my wife and our marriage.

"Many people believe that they get married on their wedding day," he said. "But actually, the couple simply gives notice to God, their families and the greater community of their intent to marry. The actual marriage takes years of trial, difficulty, suffering, success, failure, good times, bad times, laughter and tears. Only then are the two truly united as one."

I thanked him, hung up and headed straight home, feeling very grateful. His visit to the Wayne County Jail would be one of my more humbling days. His perspective had nothing to do with politics or social issues. We talked, man-to-man, spirit-to-spirit, and I thought deeply about my life, my marriage and my purpose. It was time to stop hanging on to the past and move triumphantly toward the future.

I told Carlita about my conversation with Minister Farrakhan, and shared that he also wanted to speak with her. She called him later, and they talked. I then told her that I was ready to surrender and move forward. I just wanted us to speak with our sons first.

We called Jelani and Jalil, then twelve, to our bedroom for yet another "talk." They were my big boys, so I wanted to talk to them first. They were also tiring of the attention and stress, but they'd remained strong and loving. Even today, miraculously, all three of my sons want to move back to Detroit and help lift the city from its current state. They still feel a connection to their hometown. Children's ability to love unconditionally amazes me.

I had a choice, I told them, to continue fighting the charges, or accept a plea deal and serve 120 days in jail. What did they think about it?

"If you don't win after fighting the charges," Jelani asked, "how much time would you get?" I told him I could receive up to five years in prison.

"So, your choice is either to do 120 days now," Jalil said, "or maybe five years later?"

"No," I said, and explained that my choice was for us to decide as a family what we wanted to do—continue to fight as mayor and First Family, or move forward into whatever God had in store for us.

Jelani and Jalil looked at each other. After a few seconds, Jelani rose to his feet, and assumed a spokesperson's role. What he said inspires me to this day.

"Dad, Jalil and I want to move forward. We love Detroit, but it's time for all of us to go. We are tired of seeing our mother unhappy and crying all the time. And we want to come back to-gether as a family." He looked at his brother, and then continued. "Dad, I can handle being the leader of this house for 120 days, but I can't do it for five years. I got Mama. And I got my brothers. We will stand strong, Dad. We love you."

My oldest son broke me down in a way that I didn't know was possible. I didn't even know he had it in him to put all of that together. I looked at Carlita, and she was sobbing quietly, filled with strength and pride. Jelani walked around the bed and hugged his mother tightly, whispering to her, "I got you, Mom," while Jalil came over and embraced me.

"I love you, Dad," he said, "and I always will."

It was settled. We chose the purification process, assured that our team was united. My wife gained new strength that day, and my sons taught their father a lesson in true love and strength. I reflected on all of this from my cell, and felt called back to my purpose. I continued to write, created a study schedule, an exercise plan, and made a list of goals for myself. I eschewed self-pity, arrogance and selfishness. I then asked God to walk with me through the entire journey. I knew an arduous process was to come, but I was determined to finish. Turn off the overhead light. Go to sleep. Rest.

chapter 29

Ghosts

MY INTENT was to leave jail on February 3, and be in Dallas, reunited with my wife and sons, by February 4. I landed in Texas at dusk, and news cameras met me exiting the airport. Dallas's news crews wanted to chronicle the family's move to Dallas, especially my arrival. But these reporters and cameramen kept a respectful distance from me until I actually reunited with my family.

As Carlita's truck pulled through the gate of a parking lot, all I could see were her headlights. I could also see Jonas's silhouette as he jumped up and down with excitement. Man, I was so excited that I dropped my bags and starting walking quickly toward the vehicle. Jonas, Jelani and Jalil hopped out of the truck and ran toward me, shouting my name. They'd all gotten noticeably taller in the months since I'd last seen them. Jonas leapt into my arms, and Jelani and Jalil ran behind him. When Carlita walked toward me, smiling, it took everything in me not to break down. This was all I wanted, a moment to embrace my family, to tell them I loved them, to hear them and see their faces. And they were beautiful.

We all stood there for what seemed like an eternity, just gazing at each other. Jonas had a million things to tell me about, and he wasted no time getting started. I loved it! Finally, the reporters approached. I braced myself for a battery of questions, but they kept them light, allowing me camera time to express my love for my family, along with my regret and hope for the City of Detroit. It was brief. I thanked them, and we all piled into the car and drove home.

The court gave me a few days to spend with Carlita and the boys, but I was scheduled to return to Detroit at the beginning of the next week. I had to secure employment and have my restitution agreement approved before I could move to Dallas permanently. So, we made the most of our time during that long weekend. My friend DeDan traveled with me in case I needed assistance with my daily activity. I got a chance to see our temporary home, which Carlita had moved into and decorated in a matter of days. I also got to visit the boys' school, take in the sunshine, greet my new neighbors and envision life in this new environment. It didn't take much for me to imagine a happier life in this place.

Alas, it was too short a trip. I returned to Detroit to honor the court's orders. My restitution was already set at $1 million, and thirty percent of the gross receipts from my income would go toward it. Income, according to the terms of the agreement, was any money given to me as the result of rendered labor. That definition would become critical in the months to come.

Setting my restitution at $1 million was completely arbitrary. The prosecutor, and seemingly the press, decided on a set of "facts," which mandated that I should pay back that money because the officers in the Whistleblower case won. The underlying sentiment was that my lie lost that case for the City, even though the suit was not about the affair. The restitution was a measure for me to pay something back, although there was no direct loss that warranted compensatory action. It was unjust, and probably illegal. But I agreed to it, because I wanted the City's citizens and my family to move forward. I actually gave the prosecutor and judge a foothold—a kind of insurance, in case I slipped, tripped or even relaxed a little.

My departure process should have been fairly simple: meet with Probation, establish my employment, hop a flight and get out of town. But Judge David Groner apparently saw the situation differently, and I spent thirty days languishing in Detroit after being released from jail. First, he wanted confirmation not just of my job, but my start date. Check. Pete Karmanos hired me to work for Covisint, a subsidiary of Compuware. I was going into sales, pitching a large healthcare software package to large companies, municipalities and corporations. My salary was $180,000 plus commission. The job offered me the potential to make far more than my City salary, which meant I could bust my tail, pay my restitution to the City early, and keep it moving. All of this information was immediately forwarded to the court from my new employer. He then demanded that we forward information confirming the interview process, detailing how I got the job, and including who was present for it.

Check. Groner got everything he wanted and, a few days after, I returned to Dallas. But Judge Groner still wasn't satisfied. He wanted to see a documented start date before signing the release that allowed me to transfer my probation to Texas. I wanted that, because the transfer would take my situation out of the hands of Detroit's judicial system. I'd be free to work, raise my family quietly and pay my debt. I believe Groner didn't want that to happen, because having no responsibility to me would rob him of camera time. So, in an unprecedented decision, he ordered that I pay thirty percent of the price of a two-year Cadillac Escalade lease, and thirty percent of lease payments for the house we rented in Southlake, Texas. He demanded this in lump sum payments, which meant I had to pay more than $15,000 in a one-time recompense.

One of my attorneys told me that Judge Groner was upset because I was "trying to get away from him." So he stalled, making my attorneys wait for hours before he returned calls, and then leaving for a Jewish holiday, going on vacation and forcing me to wait over long weekends.

I literally lived like a college freshman during that waiting period, staying at my mother's house while she worked in Washington, D.C.—I ate cereal and found ways to keep myself busy. It was much more serious than I'm making it sound, because my new employer was waiting patiently for me to get out of town and get to work. My wife was also going nuts wondering whether the court was stalling until it found a reason to keep me in Detroit permanently. Groner had already opened his door wide for the prosecutor, while keeping it cracked for my attorneys, and the appearance of a mutually beneficial rapport between him and Worthy didn't help me ease Carlita's fears. Actually, it was much more than an appearance. Prosecutor Worthy's chief assistant—the number-two guy in the Prosecutor's Office—is Judge Groner's brother-in-law. So I couldn't blame Carlita for being nervous. It felt like they wanted to make my life miserable.

To make the most of my days, I spent time with my nephews, Ayanna's sons. I went to their games. I reconnected with old friends and attended some Detroit Public School league basketball games. It was hard to enjoy myself, though, because news cameras even followed me to these places. Along the way, I communicated constantly with my lawyers, waiting for a breakthrough in the process. And I kept my bags packed at all times.

I must say that the respect I got on the street was nothing like the tone that the newspapers set. I couldn't believe the difference, and was so heartened by the love that people on the street showed me. Khary and I continued our work on the book, having conversations on the record as often as we could. But that pace was consistently choppy, since my legal and work affairs always got in the way of consistent interviewing. I asked him to spend one Saturday morning riding around town with me so he could see it for himself. I'd told him that people's response on the street was *nothing* like the news reports. He was surprised, to say the least.

We rode around town on a day when I knew people would be off work and out in the street. We went to eat, and the owner of the restaurant where we dined refused to let us pay for our meal. Parking lot attendants thanked me for my service, and bristled about me being railroaded.

The most riveting moment we experienced happened when we stopped by my nephews' basketball game. While sitting in the bleachers, a nine-year-old boy (I know, because I asked him) named Thomas approached me.

"Aren't you Mr. Kwame Kilpatrick?" he asked.

"Yeah, Brother, I am," I replied, "and this is Mr. Turner. What's your name?"

"I'm Thomas," he said. "When did you get out of jail?"

"A few weeks ago. You heard about that, huh?"

"Yes. My mama thought you did a good job."

"Did she?" I said, feeling really grateful. "Do *you* think I did a good job?"

He shook his head up and down, and then pointed to his left, where his family sat. "That's my mama, right there."

I waved to his family, and then turned back to the young boy, just as he asked, "Are you okay?"

"Yes!" I said, impressed at how personable he was.

"Okay. It was nice to meet you." Wisdom, as the Bible says, truly does come from the mouths of babes.

"Man, that was tripped out," Khary said.

The blur began upon my return to Dallas. On one hand, I was excited about my new life. Carlita, the boys and I missed our family in Detroit, but we settled nicely into Dallas life.

At Southlake, we got involved with the congregation at The Potter's House. As Carlita and I desired, this became our new church home. The Potter's House was the perfect place for Carlita and me to reset our relationship. We both hungered for a closer walk with God. And our sons, seeing the two of us regularly discussing God, and God's purpose for our lives, began adding conversations about faith to their rhetoric. Nothing was more fun than when the family would pile in the truck and sing to the music of artists like Israel, Karen Clarke-Sheard or Tye Tribbett, and just ride. Of course, we'd throw a little Michael Jackson and Frankie Beverly in the mix, too. Bottom line, life was good.

My job required weekly travel. I was responsible for a region that included the Eastern Seaboard, and some West Coast and

Southern territories. My job was simple—sell this massive health software system to cities, and incorporate it into their healthcare structure. It put me in contact with power players, people who made decisions for entire populations. People like me.

My motivation to succeed in the job was manifold. I had restitution to pay, and I intended to pay it completely. Most restitution in the State of Michigan never gets paid in full. The Probation Department's goal is to keep ex-offenders honest while collecting as much as they can. Because of this motive, the department can be very lenient to those who remain in close contact. But not with me. I was too visible. Leniency would attract more media scrutiny, which would mean more public outrage. Knowing this, I planned to land two or three huge deals and use my bonus pay to settle the debt early. After that, I fully intended to get on with my life, and learn to live without Detroit.

Simple enough, except the Detroit judicial system had no intention of letting me go away so quietly. I was wrong to think that physically leaving Detroit would remove me from the city's collective consciousness. Although the sentiment I'd gotten from people in the street confirmed that most were desperately ready to move on and let me go, Detroit news crews soon showed up in my Dallas neighborhood. They photographed my home and ran stories on Detroit newscasts, saying that I was living extravagantly.

These weren't simply biased stories. They were inaccurate, grossly exaggerated and flat-out untrue. Their reports included line shots in front of stores where they said I spent money. They showed an Escalade, and suggested that I'd spent extravagantly on it, while arbitrarily leaving out the fact that I'd *already* paid restitution on it. They followed my wife and me to our sons' football games, through the grocery store and even to church. They picked their tabloids up right where they'd left them.

We tried to move through the days as casually as possible, but this was far from funny. I knew about the stories that were being written back in Detroit and, though I tried to avoid reading them for my own sanity, I was concerned. The editors were reckless, disregarding fact and journalistic integrity. My neighbors soon began telling us about reporters knocking on their doors, asking if they knew who was living among them, and if they knew they had a bad guy living in the neighborhood. But we had great neighbors who knew my story but never judged us. And I didn't hesitate to tell them upon meeting them, although they'd already heard about me and told us that what went on in Detroit was none of their business. We were welcomed in Dallas, as far as they were concerned. It felt great.

The few people in Dallas we knew who saw the stories on-line were appalled. Dallas news reporters called and apologized to my wife and me, and promised that they wouldn't "bother us." They were in genuine disbelief and expressed disdain toward Detroit's media outlets. In fact, one Dallas TV news producer came to my house and told me that he was not going to do any more "snake-like reporting for those Detroit assholes." He didn't bring a camera. He just wanted to be clear that "we don't do that type of crap in Dallas."

He shook my hand, wished me well and left. Considering what I'd experienced at the lens of Detroit's press corps, it was a remarkable moment. Two Dallas stations sent cards and candy to Carlita, offering words of encouragement and apologetic sentiments for what she'd endured.

I know it sounds like I'm angry with the media. I'm not. But who will tell you these stories if I don't? The press eagerly characterizes the worst Kwame Kilpatrick possible, but never dares to reveal the formula they used to create that guy. They suggested that my lifestyle was so flamboyant that I *had* to be spending money that should have gone toward restitution. The needling was invasive and biased, and based on a prejudicial premises.

Because restitution required thirty percent of my gross receipts, Compuware advanced me $20,000 a month for my first six months, and $10,000 a month for the next six. So my payments should have been $6,000 a month for the first half of the year, followed by an automatic drop to $3,000. The company did this to help my family transition, and also wrote a letter to Judge Groner, informing him of the reason and timeline. When I started paying $3,000 a month, the press ran stories saying that I was only paying half of what I owed. Not that I'd asked Groner to recognize the salary adjustment and the lower payment.

Worthy wanted to (and did) paint the perception that I was spending restitution money. She complained about money that was lent to me by four of the businessmen I discussed earlier. Peter Karmanos, Roger Penske, Dan Gilbert and Jim Nicholson, friends and staunch supporters of the city, lent me $240,000 to further help me get re-established. While I did set up a comfortable lifestyle for myself, my wife and my sons, I never ducked a payment. I was simply paying my restitution from my earned income. I was also ahead of my payment schedule.

Once the Wayne County Circuit Court received word that I received these loans, however, the prosecutor hit the roof and accused me of hiding income. She was wrong. There's a clear separation between income and gifts and loans. Some people may say I was wrong or overly demonstrative in doing so, but I was not going to live hand-to-mouth. And that's exactly what the prosecutor wanted—an *appearance* of poverty and struggle.

Judge Groner will swear to his dying day that I was treated the same as any Michigan parolee, but the rules applied to me were manipulated. Thirty percent of gross wages, alone, was unheard of. Agreements were negotiated and ratified, and were clear. And wages are considered to be monies paid in response to a rendered service, i.e., work. Detroit media, Judge Groner and Kym Worthy wanted my family living in a two-bedroom apartment. They wanted to see me driving my big butt around Dallas in a Chevy Aveo, not a Cadillac Escalade. They wanted me to struggle. I think that would have satisfied my detractors, because it would have made them feel like I was struggling. Never mind that I'd just served four months in jail and languished for another thirty days, jeopardizing my initial job standing.

They hated that I was able to re-establish myself so quickly. In their minds, a portion of every penny that entered my bank account should have gone to the State of Michigan. We fundamentally disagreed on that point, but the restitution agreement should have made it clear. It didn't hurt, though, that disagreeing gave both the judge and the prosecutor a chance to yank me back into a courtroom. It granted both of them TV time heading into an election year, and it gave Worthy a chance to send her assistant prosecutors after me. All in the name of justice.

The press ran a series of stories investigating my finances and lifestyle. People close to me suggested that I should have just laid low for a while and kept my lifestyle quiet. And while that sounds like a good plan, everyone has a limit, and I already felt that I had been unjustly jailed. Now I had to *act poor*, just to please an establishment that hated me? *And* I had to hear people close to me vouch for a bent-back stance? No. I was appalled that the press even had access to my finances. Legally, my records should have been reviewed in a manner that was non-FOIA-ble, meaning they could not be accessed through a Freedom of Information Act request. I was entitled to *some* privacy. That didn't happen. They probed my personal spending and publicized expenditures that should have remained private.

The prosecutor then decided to subpoena Carlita's records. She wasn't a part of this process. So we had to hire an attorney in Texas to help stop that.

Judge Groner began ordering me back-and-forth to his courtroom. Every time he forced me to fly back to Detroit, I had to take time off work, away from the deals I was working on, away from the resources that would pay my restitution and allow me to go on with my life. Groner was pissed that I didn't report the loans I'd received, and the Detroit press corps consistently crafted stories that made it seem as if I were hiding money.

I flew back to Detroit for a series of hearings and took the stand to explain why I bought a motorcycle, why I paid for surgery for Carlita, why I leased another SUV, why I spent money on auto detailing, and all the flotsam and jetsam the court deemed significant. It was all framed as excess to attempt to showcase further evidence of my arrogance, and my flippant attitude toward the people of Detroit.

I was not hiding money. I was, however, deeply engaged in the process of reconnecting with my wife and sons. It was a very personal matter, and I approached it by giving them the life I felt they would have had had we not endured such rough personal times when I was mayor. I thank all the men and women who blessed me with their assistance, and I was not going to be angry with those who didn't share those blessings. What I hated, though, was seeing news cameras following my wife all over the Dallas/Forth Worth area. I hated them probing my sons' school administrators. The underlying message from the press to their readers and viewers was, *You need to hate him. Look how they're living, compared to how you're living.* Constantly framing me as a picture of arrogance and opulence gave people a lightning rod for their despair. But it made life potentially dangerous for me and my family. Because it was a storyline local to Detroit, I was able to keep it away from Carlita. But otherwise, I refused to stop living my life.

The tone of the news was different between the two cities, as well. The news in Dallas, for example, does its share of investigative reporting, but they lift up their city daily. There's no political theater. The focal point is the business community and the people, not the members. I don't even know who their City Council members are. They also don't allow cameras in the courtroom, not in the State or City courts. The stories are reported on the news, but the sense of theater is absent. There's a healthy respect for privacy.

I saw firsthand how the mental and emotional capacity of Detroiters is regulated by the press. It's oppressive. Dallas ran a story in which a reporter said, "New resident Kwame Kilpatrick may be in some more hot water. We'll follow the story." And then, they went to the next story—not just *my* next story.

As I traveled with my employer, I observed this same press tone in other cities. I went to Washington, D.C., and Atlanta on business the week the restitution stories about me first ran. I'd also been to New York, Philadelphia and Los Angeles on business, and I took note of two things. One, people's source of information about me came from local news. Two, their decision, based on what they saw, was basic: this guy got caught up, and racism took him out. Many people, especially the more astute business and political folks I still had regular contact with, looked at it as if the City were falling apart since I'd left. They said things like, "You've gotta be glad you're not *in* that m----f----r any more."

I had always spoken positively about the city, but it was hard to disagree with the fact that things had gotten worse. Much worse. Detroit had tenaciously and aggressively managed to revert back to its 1980s image. I had to fight against that backdrop. Though the powers that be in Detroit put my story on simmer over the next year, the prosecutor, the court and the majority of metropolitan Detroit came to the conclusion that I was a crook. The people who believed I was being railroaded were quiet and felt disjointed. So, it seemed as if I had no supporters.

With news cameras on him, Judge Groner opined that the loans I received for my wife and children's benefit was income for which restitution should have been paid. This became the clarion call and the motivating factor in his endeavor to change the accounting structure surrounding the matter. He decided, therefore, that I violated my parole. He tacked on a few more judgments about money that my wife received while I was in the Wayne County Jail, long before my restitution.

Before finding me guilty of probation violation, however, the judge ordered me to pay the entire $240,000 loan amount within four months. I didn't have the money, and the court knew it because they had all of my financial information. Still, I struggled and came up with $40,000. Unfortunately, it wasn't good enough to satisfy the court.

Judge Groner's last words to me were, "Mr. Kilpatrick, I suggest you get your affairs in order."

I knew what that meant. And so, I did. I spent as much time with my family as I could. We laughed. We talked. We prayed. We accepted that the rules of normalcy no longer applied to me, but that God's will applies to everyone. If this were to be my lot, I would accept it.

On May 25, 2010, I was sentenced to one-and-a-half to five years in prison. The Probation Department recommended that, per guidelines, I be sentenced from zero to seventeen months. Judge Groner dismissed that recommendation. He said that compelling and substantial reasons warranted that he go outside the guidelines. He never stated for the record what these "guidelines" were. He simply sentenced me to a much lengthier sentence. Less than two hours later, I found myself in a Michigan Department of Corrections van, headed to the Reception and Guidance Center in Jackson, Michigan.

Damn. All I wanted to do was go home. But still, all was well.

We completed this book from behind the walls of the Federal Correctional Facility in Milan, Michigan. The prison is one hour from my hometown, which might as well be a galaxy away from my life. As this chapter of my life continues to evolve, I am preparing for yet the biggest battle of my life, which now includes federal charges. It's enough to make the head spin.

Prosecutors are working very hard to connect my friends to me. These are my friends, and I pray for them and wish their families the best. In the meantime, you now know my position, and my story. And I hope you find it within yourself to pray for me, my family and my beloved hometown, as we have for you.

chapter 30
Revelation 3: *The End... The New Beginning*

T HE BIBLE says that we are to "work out" our salvation, and yet God "works in us" to accomplish this. I knew God had not forgotten about me in this moment, but I had a whole lot of work to do. So, I spent the next several months working out! I read more than forty books. I scheduled at least one hour of Bible study daily, and at least another hour of general wisdom study. I sought truth from a spectacular array of materials, from East Indian meditation to African spirituality; from *The 21 Irrefutable Laws of Leadership*, by John Maxwell, to *The Power* and *The Secret*, by Rhonda Byrne. I sent off for a correspondence Bible and leadership development course, and completed those assignments. I also completed the Nation of Islam's *Overcoming Difficulty* workbook. I snuck in some fiction by James Patterson, Sydney Sheldon and a few urban classics. And lessons came from other fiction like *The Shack*, *The Traveler's Gift* and *The Alchemist*. But the authors who attracted me most were folks like Eckhart Tolle, Maxwell, and Bishop T.D. Jakes.

I worked out my body, too, four times a week. Why adopt such a regimen? I didn't want to be like the Children of Israel. They crossed the Red Sea to freedom after 400 years of bondage, finding themselves a mere three days' travel from the Promised Land. But because they were still bound by their thinking, they wandered around the same mountain for *forty years*. Imagine, mental slavery kept them from climbing a hill! As crazy as that is, I knew I had an enemy in my head, and I refused to be bound. The next time I walk out of any prison, I will be truly free.

Several interesting things happened after I moved to Milan. Umar Farouk Abdulmutallab, the infamous "Christmas Bomber" who tried to blow up a Northwest Airlines flight headed to Detroit on Christmas 2009, with a bomb hidden in his underwear, was the only other inmate in the hole when I arrived. But later, I had two good bunkmates in my cell, Nate Cox, a Detroiter, and Charles Fisher, who played important roles in my spiritual growth and maturity. Also, people started asking me for help or assistance in certain areas. I helped guys write letters, tutored them for GED tests, and even led Bible study. I was serving, for the first time in a long time, and it felt good to my soul.

A man I refer to as Mr. Oday approached me. He's spent forty years in State prison, and came to Milan to begin a five-year federal sentence. He didn't kill anyone. He's an example of the many people who are trapped in State and Federal prisons, mistreated, over-sentenced, and forgotten.

Mr. Oday is an incredible man. He reads and exercises daily, and keeps his cell immaculate. He is funny, articulate and smart, and has mastered several martial arts. He told me that one of his sons sent him an e-mail address, and asked him to communicate. This was big, because Mr. Oday hasn't had a visit since the 1970s, hasn't received a letter in years, and has never used a computer. Most of his family and friends are either dead, or have moved on. So I took him to the computer room and helped him establish an e-mail account. We then sent a query to his son and, a couple of days later, saw that his son accepted it. Mr. Oday was now free to send e-mail.

"What would you like to say?" I asked him, readying myself to type a message for him. And for the first time, I saw this rock of a man humbled in absolute fear. He paced the floor, walked in circles, and stop-started several times. I calmed him, and we wrote a simple message together and walked away. That was the easy part. Three days later, I approached him in front of his cell. "Did Charles write you back?" I asked.

"I haven't checked," he said. "I was waiting on you." I knew he was nervous, so I invited him to walk with me to the computer room. We opened his account, and Charles had indeed responded.

"Oh, man, there it is!" I said. It was a beautiful message about love, hope and relationship. I focused on Mr. Oday to keep from looking at the screen (it got a little personal after a moment), and saw tears stream down his face. I cried with him, because I'd never seen someone so happy.

"Thank you, Kwame," he said. We cried some more. Walking back to my cell, I felt stronger, more encouraged and more empowered. I felt like myself, like a servant of God. And that's when it hit me. That's who I am! A servant! I always have been! It's who I'm called to be! I hurried to my cell to think about all the labels I've been given—corrupt, criminal, thug, thief. I thought about the barrage of negative media about me, which continues to this day. Well, I am not who they say I am. But I realized who I'd become.

This may sound metaphoric, but look at the City's new man. She/Detroit constantly compares Bing to me. Detroit can't get me off her collective mind. Bing doesn't stimulate Detroit the way I did. He's older, slower, and devoid of spontaneity. But he's touted and I'm lambasted because they want the city to forget me. But she won't because, at her heart, she knows my intentions. I was supposed to be faithful to Carlita, but *Detroit* was the one I swore in my heart to honor. Foolish as that was, it was "the D" that I was unable to cheat on. That's why these accusations about me stealing from her are so ridiculous.

Metaphor considered, I was never committed to anything the way I was to Detroit. Accepting that Detroit stopped loving me was a jagged pill to swallow. When God showed up in the Wayne County Jail, He set my mind straight, and helped me move past the pain and realize who I am supposed to truly marry. Carlita weathered every storm, no matter how tremendous. Every year. Every episode. Every accusation. She endured. She stood. She protected our children. She forgave and believed in me. Carlita was awesome in rededication. Do you see why I say

God *showed* me my wife? How many men spend their lives taking their wives' strength for granted? Through Carlita, I learned what it means to be truly married. And that helped me let Detroit go. Detroit is my Egypt. Prison is my mountain. Freedom is my Promised Land.

I stumbled across this passage while reading *The Alchemist:* "If what one finds is made of pure matter, it will never spoil. And one can always come back. If what you had found was only a moment of light, like the explosion of a star, you would find nothing on your return." If I liken Detroit to a moment of light, I admit to loving the city, and I will always treasure what it taught me. But I will also say goodbye. At least, for now.

I lost my fear. I placed complete trust in God and emerged from my pondering, returned to the computer room, and sent my wife an e-mail—the birthday message that ends this book. My renewed commitment was to her, and only her, for the rest of my life. I left my past behind.

Some will not believe this. That's no longer my concern. I have surrendered… to God's will.

Columbus said that, "Truth is truth. If a thousand people believe something foolish, it is still foolish. Truth is never dependent upon consensus opinion. I have found that it is better to be alone and acting upon the truth in my heart than follow a gaggle of silly geese doomed to mediocrity." I agree.

I've been fortunate to have some amazing experiences. I have met with presidents, prime ministers and sheiks. I talked Monday Night Football with President Bill Clinton while riding on Air Force One. I walked on the road to Damascus in Israel, watched the sun set behind Table Mountain in South Africa, and strolled through the expansive corridors of The Louvre in Paris. I helped build Habitat for Humanity homes, and watched families cry after receiving their keys. I distributed water bottles and food to hurting people in Darfur, and felt the profound impact of hope while sitting in Nelson Mandela's Robben Island prison cell. I watched children dance in a Liberia, torn by civil war. I had lunch with Ellen Johnson Sirleaf, Liberia's, and the modern-day African continent's first woman head of State.

There were more experiences, and each blessed my soul abundantly. But nothing stirred me like the one I had in the computer room with Mr. Oday.

I don't know how all of this will end, or why I had to come this way. It's said that, in adversity, there are no problems to face, just choices to make. I choose to remain surrendered, to feed my soul faith, hope and love, even while I am doing time, because there is one thing I do know. Time will tell all. And all is well.

epilogue

by Carlita Kilpatrick

ANY WOMAN who has experienced the devastation of adultery can attest that the emotional road of recovery and forgiveness is long, arduous, painful, scary and lonely. This journey is one of highs and lows-a lot of lows. There are times when you seem to be finally coming out of the darkness only to be flooded all over again with anguish and self pity.

Each day you face a self-inflicted and constant emotional battle—"You need to leave his sorry ass!" "You love him and your faith will pull you through." "Even the Bible says that adultery is punishable by death." "But, Jesus saved the adulterous woman by convicting the crowd that was about to stone her." Some days my faith wins and others my fear does.

When fear has the upper hand, I believe that I and all that I hold to be true about love and marriage has been sent careening into a deep dark hole of nothingness, of which there seems no escape; each time recognizing that I've been in this hole before. Recently, I was struggling to free myself and was at a spot on my ascent where I could see daylight, when I was knocked back to its bottom; angry, ashamed and afraid that I would not be able to summon the strength to begin this slow, arduous and emotionally painful climb again.

In this hole you reside with loneliness, fear, anxiety, self-pity, rage, self-doubt, pain, bitterness and sorrow; each one knocking on the door of your heart as you helplessly let them in.

My first encounter with these familiar *frienemies* was the night of January 23, 2008. This was arguably the worst night of my life. I knew something was wrong. We had to inexplicably leave a restaurant where we were having dinner as a family. Kwame had spent most of the short time we dined there in the car on the phone. He gathered us up and said we needed to go. He then called his father and asked him could we drop the boys off at his house for a while. It was at this point I knew. My inner voice screaming at me, "You dummy! I told you!" But, that part of me that believes in "happily ever after," however, was holding out hope that something else was wrong.

It wasn't.

Upstairs in our bedroom as I was seated in my silver reading arm-chair, arms clasped, bracing myself for whatever horrific news was about to be disclosed, my husband proceeded to tell me that he had been engaged in an affair with Christine Beatty several years earlier, but it had ended before his re-election in 2005. He also cautioned me that this "old news" was soon to hit the headlines.

My first reaction, interestingly and surprisingly, was relief. I had a fleeting moment of edification. I wasn't crazy after all. My intuition had been right. My unyielding need to rid her from my life had merely been a form of subconscious self-preservation. How fleeting that moment was! It was promptly replaced and compounded with rage, hurt, hate, shame and a plethora of other emotions that I don't even know how to describe. I was shaking uncontrollably, but my voice was eerily low and calm, "You bastard! You bastard! How could you? How could you make me think I was insecure and wrong about my discernment toward her? How could you dishonor us like that? You selfish bastard."

As he tried to plead his case about what state of mind he had been in at the time; how much pressure he was under in his position; how he didn't feel like he could come to me, I began to cry- or, more precisely, wail. The pain in my gut was so profound I thought I might actually pass out. I began to hyperventilate. I couldn't breathe. I couldn't stand. He tried to console me, but I didn't want him to touch me.

"Bastard!" I felt that if I had really expressed the intensity of my emotions, I would have found any object that I could swing and tried to beat him to death or at least until I felt better, which ever came first. I made a conscious choice in the middle of this emotional collapse to hold on to my civility. I would allow neither him nor her to determine or decide how I would respond to their despicable behavior. I chose to wrap all of my rage in tears. I curled up into a ball on the floor by the window, looking for relief from the heavens and cried. And I cried. And I cried. And then, I prayed.

So, here I am in this hole again; a recurring tenant. For the better part of three years my healing and reconciliation have been a struggle. But, this visit is strangely different. This time my closest *frienemy* is rage instead of pain. My first visit I was enveloped by so much pain, I honestly didn't think I could make it through. Depression became my companion and loneliness became my mate.

This time I am pissed. I'm pissed and I'm scared. Confused. Shaken. Likewise, I'm stronger. I'm pissed, but I'm wiser. I'm girded with the Word. So although the initial impact of this fall is brutal, I now stand up, brush the dirt from my skinned knees and look to the heavens, not for relief, but this time for resolve, knowing that I can and I will climb out and stay out of this pit.

The emotional battles that I have had to endure over the past few years I wouldn't wish on my worst enemy. My reflection at times has been unrecognizable. The physical and mental toll has been high. But, by God's abounding grace and endless mercy, I am still here. I'm not the same woman I was three years ago. I'm wounded, but I'm better. Now I would be delinquent if I lead you to believe that I've finished my transformation and I no longer harbor any emotional issues. On the contrary, I am still on my journey of forgiveness, I struggle with depression and I fight everyday to stay optimistic about my life and the future of my family. Some days I win. Some days I don't.

To say these last few years have been the worst of my life would be simple and without any real investigation or insight, but life is full of contradictions. While my family and I have had to endure some incomprehensible as well as reprehensible situations we have also grown immensely. We have had to cleave to one another thus deepening our love, respect and admiration for each other. I marvel at the maturity and resiliency my sons have shown throughout this time. There were times when they were my examples, getting me through stagnant or backsliding moments. My relationships with my sister-in-law and mother-in-law have grown tremendously. My mom and dad tell me how proud they are of me (No matter how old you are having your parents utter these words just make you feel great!). Our new home, Dallas, Texas, has received us with open arms, welcoming us without judgment and making the transition easy. I have been blessed to be surrounded and supported by a wonderful group of sister-friends, the Nobus, as well as positive, gifted and giving women who pour into me unselfishly. I have a church home that loves and supports me and my family, and we are pastored by a Bishop and First Lady who wield the Word as a mighty sword giving us the strength to continue.

As the great author Charles Dickens laments, "It was the best of times; it was the worst of times..."

Perspective is what determines what kind of time it is. A different perspective can broaden your view of your situation. A different perspective can offer solutions when you think there are none. A different perspective can turn a problem into an opportunity. A different perspective can turn your life around.

That is what I hope Kwame's story offers, a different perspective!

While I am apprehensive about the release of such personal, intimate details about our lives, my husband's betrayal, and the subsequent sequence of events that bring us to this moment, I am hopeful this book releases me from the humiliation and shame of his transgression. I hope this book releases me from Christine and the resentment that I still harbor not just for the affair, but for the unmitigated gall of encroaching upon my family. I hope this book can propel me into the kind of forgiveness of which the Bible speaks. I hope this book makes me take a long, hard look at myself-the good, the bad and the ugly- so that I can be transformed and renewed into a better wife, mother daughter and friend. I am hopeful that this book can release me and Kwame from the past. It's self-defeating to be held captive by something that you can no longer change. I hope this book can release me and my husband from our old selves and transform us into new creatures who honor the vows we spoke nearly sixteen years ago and make our marriage an example of a union ordained by God.

I am not totally prepared for what this book may bring. But, even in the face of this uncertainty is the more powerful need for clarification and purification. There exists an intrinsic need to tell the other side of the story-not in defense of or out of an egoistic necessity, but because there are some real truths that need to be told and a different perspective that needs to be offered.

It is my prayer that this different perspective offers healing.

~CARLITA E. KILPATRICK

Kwame's Letter to Carlita on Her 40th Birthday

From: 44678039
To: Carlita Kilpatrick
Subject: Mama's Birthday Letter
Date: 8/3/2010   12:10:36 PM

I was so nervous on that warm April afternoon back in 1990, but I tried to be cool. You were so beautiful, smart, intriguing and, yes, very intimidating! "Certainly, she's just a girl," I told myself. Yet I sensed that you were unlike any other. Even then, I was sure that you had been truly touched by the hand of the Living God.

    I wanted desperately to know you. To talk to

you. To somehow make you a part of me. And the day finally came, the long-awaited moment in which I had the courage, the nerve, and the audacity to tell you how I felt. Sure, I had spoken to you in class, but I wanted to connect with you on a deeper, more spiritual level. I was completely overwhelmed!

Looking back on those moments, my spirit knew that this seemingly simple act of engaging you was the inauguration of my future. The wife and mother of my children. I felt the danger of being rejected and swallowed alive, but I soldiered on with dogged determination, guts and pure adrenaline. I stepped smoothly to you with a slight pimp in my walk and a serious gangsta lean. I softly and casually stood by your side. I steadied my mind to deliver, with insatiable eloquence, the opening line that would spark the flame of our eternal bond. You gracefully turned to me and said, "Hello." And I looked into your eyes and said...

..."Um, um, um, uh, uh... what you about to do?" Damn, I blew it! Panic flowed through my mind. She must be thinking that I am ignorant, a fool, a buster, a complete idiot. How could I sound so stupid? My mind was racing.

In typical Carlita form, you calmly replied that you were heading to the library. Though I had never been to the library, and I couldn't remember the last time I actually studied, I said, "Me, too! Can I go with you?" You said yes, and that was it. I had climbed my own Mt. Everest. No one, not even you, saw my anguish, sweat, nerves, shortness of breath or my conquering spirit, but I had achieved a major goal. I got her fine self now.

Baby, we went to that library more than twenty years ago. Of course, we didn't get any studying done, but we began to emotionally and spiritually connect immediately. We laughed. We laughed a lot! As a matter of fact, we laughed so much that we were threatened with removal from the premises several times, and ultimately got kicked out. I fell head over heels in love with you that day. And after a few short months, I couldn't imagine a universe where I could love you any more than I did on the campus of Florida A&M University. But my love for you has grown, exponentially!

I want you to know, on your fortieth birthday, that I can't thank God enough for how He has manifested His love for me through you, in so many ways.

Marriage is a process, one that takes courage, selflessness, failure, success, loss, victory, ups, downs, good times, bad times and many other life experiences before a couple is truly united as one in marriage.

Your love, which can only be explained through faith, and the awesome power of God inspires me to be who God made me to be. You helped me understand this, as it says in 1 Corinthians 13, **"Love never gives up, never loses faith, is always hopeful and endures through every circumstance."**

I have to admit that there have been times I was a little nervous when you were in the kitchen making grits. ☺ But faith, hope and a lot of prayer got me through, as well as my occasional and sudden needs to leave the house until I was certain the grits had substantially cooled. But I digress!

Thank you so much for being my much better half, and answering God's call to be my wife, and Jelani, Jalil and Jonas's Mom! Happy birthday, Carlita Ebony Kilpatrick. **Celebrate, and enjoy being forty and fine!**

about the author

Photo: Joshua Band

KWAME KILPATRICK, former Mayor of the City of Detroit, started his political career at the age of twenty-five after teaching in the Detroit Public School system for nearly four years.

He was the youngest and first African-American to be elected Leader to the Michigan House of Representatives. At thirty-one years old he was elected as the mayor of Detroit and served in that office for nearly seven years. Kwame Kilpatrick graduated from Florida A&M University earning a B.S. in Political Science. He also earned his Juris Doctor (law degree) from Michigan State University College of Law. Today, Kilpatrick is an author, educator and public speaker. He resides in Dallas, Texas with his wife of sixteen years, Carlita Kilpatrick, and their three sons, Jelani, Jalil and Jonas. He enjoys reading, writing, golfing and spending time with family.

July of 2011 and the release of *SURRENDERED* marks the beginning of a new life for Kilpatrick.